Crossing Over

A JOURNEY FROM THE RIVER TO THE SEA

Deena Ragless

Ark House Press
arkhousepress.com

© 2024 Deena Ragless

All rights reserved. Apart from any fair dealing for the purpose of study, research, criticism, or review, as permitted under the Copyright Act, no part may be reproduced by any process without written permission.

Unless otherwise stated, all Scriptures are taken from the ESV (Holy Bible. Copyright© 1996, 2004, 2007, 2013 by Tyndale House Foundation. Used by permission of Tyndale House Publishers Inc., Carol Stream, Illinois 60188. All rights reserved.)

Some names and identifying details have been changed to protect the privacy of individuals.

Cataloguing in Publication Data:
Title: Crossing Over
ISBN: 978-1-7637394-3-7 (pbk)
Subjects: BIO026000   BIOGRAPHY & AUTOBIOGRAPHY / Memoirs; HIS019000 HISTORY / Middle East / Israel & Palestine; POL035010   POLITICAL SCIENCE / Human Rights;

Design by initiateagency.com

CONTENTS

ABOUT THE AUTHOR vii
ACKNOWLEDGEMENTS ix
INTRODUCTION xi

CHAPTER 1. ABOUT ME 1
    MIXED CULTURE 6
    MOVING NORTH 8
    EMBRACING CHRISTIANITY 10
    STUDY TRIP TO PALESTINE 13
    DISCOVERING MY TRUE HERITAGE 21
    FAMILY LINK TO THE PAST 27
    FURTHER ACADEMIC STUDY 30

CHAPTER 2. TWO COVENANTS 31
    FIRST COVENANT 32
    SECOND COVENANT 45

CHAPTER 3. DEAKIN UNIVERSITY 49
    THE OTHER 49
    COLONIALISM 52

ANCIENT ISRAEL AND COLONIALISM 54
AL NAKBA 56

CHAPTER 4.   PALESTINE AND PALESTINIANS 63

A PLACE CALLED PALESTINE 64
PALESTINIANS 66

CHAPTER 5.   PALESTINE AND JEWISH ISRAELIS 72

EVANGELICAL CHRISTIAN VIEW OF JEWISH ISRAELIS
AND PALESTINIANS IN PALESTINE 73
PUBLIC'S VIEW OF JEWISH ISRAELIS AND PALESTINIANS
IN PALESTINE 77
CONNECTION BETWEEN CHRISTIAN & JEWISH ZIONISM
IN MODERN HISTORY 78
JEWISH HISTORY IN PALESTINE FROM MID-1800s TO 14
MAY 1948 80

CHAPTER 6.   BEYOND OCCUPATION 85

STATE OF ISRAEL 87
WEST BANK 90
THE GAZA STRIP 106
WHO IS HAMAS? 107
LIFE FOR PALESTINIANS IN GAZA 113

CHAPTER 7.   REFUSING TO GIVE IN 123

TERRORISM 124
RESISTANCE 132
ISRAELI DEFENCE FORCES 146
JEWISH SETTLERS 152

CHAPTER 8. FEATHERING THEIR OWN NEST 154

THE UNITED STATES AND THE MIDDLE EAST 155
THE WORLD CAN ONLY WATCH 159

CHAPTER 9. 7 OCTOBER 2023 162

ISRAEL'S RESPONSE 165
GENOCIDE 166
KIDNAPPINGS, IMPRISONMENT, AND TORTURE OF PALESTINIANS 175
MAINSTREAM MEDIA 177
AUSTRALIAN NATIONAL RACISM 183
WORLD PROTESTS 187
UNIVERSITY STUDENT PROTESTS 189
THE WEST BANK 190
INTERNATIONAL COURT OF JUSTICE 191
WILL ISRAEL ACHIEVE ITS GOAL? 193
ISRAELI OCCUPATION IS ILLEGAL 198

CHAPTER 10. FINAL THOUGHTS 199

THE BIBLE, THE STATE OF ISRAEL, AND CHRISTIAN ZIONISM 199
ISRAELI GOVERNANCE 201
OPERATION SWORDS OF IRON 204
THE PALESTINIAN COMMUNITY IN AUSTRALIA 205
AS A PALESTINIAN CHRISTIAN 206
FUTURE HOPE 210

RECOMMENDED SOURCES 213
BIBLIOGRAPHY 215
NOTES 269

ABOUT THE AUTHOR

Deena Ragless is Palestinian and Irish and lives in Australia. She is passionate about her Palestinian family and heritage. She wants to encourage everyone to know the truth about what is happening on a tiny patch of land in the Middle East. She has a Bachelor of Ministry after studying under the Australian College of Theology at Malyon College in Brisbane, Australia. At Deakin University in Victoria, she studied for a Bachelor of International Studies with majors in Middle East and International Relations.

Deena lives in Brisbane, Australia, with her husband. She has one married son who lives in Brisbane and another who lives and works in South Korea.

ACKNOWLEDGEMENTS

I am so thankful to the people who have helped make this book possible, whether they realise it or not.

This journey may not have even started if it had not been for Miko Peled's book, The General's Son. The writing from Anna Baltzer provided me with my first initial look at how Palestinians live their daily lives. Writings from Salim Munayer, Stephen Sizer and Timothy P Weber opened my eyes to Zionism and Christian Zionism. The writings of John Lyons let me see how the Israeli government is courting government leaders, politicians, journalists, and anyone in influential positions. Munther Isaac enlightened me on the sad journey of Palestinian Christians, who are invisible to many within the international community. Through the writings of Nur Masalha and Mazin B. Qumsiyeh, I have learned much about the area known as historical Palestine, which is an actual place.

To my lecturers Sally Totman and Mat Hardy. You both opened my eyes to the rich history of the Middle East, teaching me things that I never knew before and things that I will never forget.

I am incredibly thankful to Stephen Sizer, Helen Rainger, and Melinda Narguet, who encouraged me to continue writing after reading my initial introduction and first chapter.

Improving and editing this evolving manuscript was a monumental task. I thank Melinda Narguet, and Helen Rainger for taking the time to help with this process, even though you were both extremely busy. Thank you, Nasser Mashni and Omar Ashour, for answering specific questions when I was working on different sections of the book. Without all of you, this book would not be a reality.

Lastly, I want to thank my family. My mum Yvonne, my husband Peter, sons Danny and Aiden, and daughter Shell. Mum, thank you for your love and ongoing encouragement, personal stories you have shared throughout my life, and for obtaining information from extended family members to include in this book. Peter, your ongoing love and support remain constant. You always encourage me in my ventures and patiently let me spend many hours in my den writing the manuscript for this book. Danny and Aiden, as adults you have much love and care for others. Because of that, I am sure wherever you walk in the world, you will both succeed. Shell, when you joined our family, you brought added vibrancy and fun, thank you. Therefore, I dedicate this book to Yvonne, Peter, Danny, Aiden and Shell.

Deena Ragless.

INTRODUCTION

Australia has not always been my home, but it is the only place I can clearly remember, having arrived in Melbourne, Australia, on 22 December 1969 after a four-week journey on a ship. I also turned five years old while on our trip. My parents and I were known as 'Ten Pound Poms'. Yes, I was born in Leeds, England, but I was not a regular Pom. Dad was born and raised in Hartlepool, England, to Irish parents. Mum was born and raised in Amman, Jordan, to Palestinian Arab parents who were both born and raised in Nazareth, Palestine. My maternal grandparents married in 1929 and moved to Amman in the same year. Mum left home when she was nineteen, following in both of her sisters' footsteps and headed to England. When I was 2-3 years of age, my mum began teaching me the Arabic language. Unfortunately, the lessons only lasted briefly as my dad felt left out since he could not understand Arabic. Many years later, I am still trying to learn the language. One day, I might succeed.

Even though I am an Irish and Palestinian Arab woman living in Australia, my short social media bio says it all, "My heart is proudly Palestinian."

...

Hearing of another war beginning with Russia invading Ukraine on 20 February 2022, I opened my computer to do some searching and try to find out why it was happening. I am not usually too curious, but I had time, so why not just look it up? It did not take too long for me to discover that it could continue an internal crisis that started in November 2013 after President Victor Yanukovych rejected an invitation for Ukraine to integrate further with the European Union. It seems like his citizens were unhappy with the government's decision, so they held a protest. Unfortunately, the government did not like its citizens protesting, so they used violence against their people to stop them. Russia backed Yanukovych, while the United States and Europe supported the protestors. After that unfortunate move, the Ukraine government collapsed, which forced Yanukovych to flee. Russia then used the situation to invade and annex Crimea.[1]

Nobody knew why Russian President Vladimir Putin invaded Ukraine on that February day. Some speculated that he might intend to rebuild the old soviet bloc, maybe to stop Ukraine, as they intended to join the North Atlantic Treaty Organisation, or even to prevent the potential Westernisation of Ukraine, which may influence citizens of other surrounding nations to do the same. Whatever the reason, some Western governments, including the United States, United Kingdom, countries within the European Union, and Australia, were unhappy about the invasion. It did not take too long for the governments of some nation-states to place sanctions on Russia, aiming to convince Putin to pull out of Ukraine and go home.

During my research, I also found that various media organisations had targeted Western governments, particularly the United States.[2] They accused them of hypocrisy for placing sanctions on Russia and being willing to investigate Russian war crimes but refusing to do the same with Israel. They considered it as despicable, the ongoing treatment of the Palestinian Arabs residing in East Jerusalem, the West Bank and the Gaza Strip, which

INTRODUCTION

had, at that time, been ongoing for 74 years. Millions of people have suffered and are continuing to suffer. It is unlikely that this group's suffering will end shortly. I also found that not only governments had been targeted, but also social media had been scrutinised as to why they do not block hate speech against Russia, but they block hate speech against Israel.[3]

...

Many people encounter potentially debilitating changes and challenges in their lives through no fault of their own. The war between Ukraine and Russia, or any war for that matter, does not pick sides. It affects all people concerned, including the attackers, defenders, and everyone else who is in the middle, such as women and children, older adults, and others suffering disorders or mental health issues.

Thinking beyond wars, younger children struggle with their parents' divorce, as they no longer feel secure because they perceive everything around them as broken. What is worse is that they must also endure the constant shuffling between their parents' homes until their country's laws allow them at a certain age to choose which parent they want to live with or until they come of age. Considering further, adults can often encounter significant change and find it hard to leave their long-term jobs and adapt to retirement, especially if they do not have any interests outside of their work. Lacking interests outside of work can be especially true of men, whose sense of worth often comes from being attached to "being a good provider, being useful, being independent, and being an achiever."[4]

Some people may suffer the unexpected loss of a partner whom they have spent many years with, whether it is from a sudden event such as a heart attack or an accident of some type. Loss may also happen from one suffering from a debilitating sickness that could have lasted for years.

Even recent years have brought many changes and challenges with the onset of the SARS-CoV-2 virus, which has brought death, loss of employment, bankruptcy to many who run small or self-employed businesses, and economic breakdown of some nation-states globally.

People may not encounter potentially debilitating changes and challenges, such as some of those mentioned above. They may face challenges to their current belief system or ideology. These challenges may cause some people to begin to view aspects of the world differently. It is as if a pair of glasses was being worn for the first time, causing a blurred vision to become clearer. For others, their view of world events might be clearer. Still, they may need clarity, much like a lens prescription tweak, to make that person's long-distance view its clearest. What confronted me in my situation resonated deeply, challenging and changing parts of my belief system, so now I see one aspect of the world differently.

As with anyone who shares a journey of any kind, as much as they try, it is virtually impossible to share it from an unbiased perspective. Our environment, upbringing, culture, economic and societal status help shape who we are, how we think and what we believe.

Through the following pages, it may appear I care more about Palestinian Christians than Muslims, but that is not true. Yes, I identify more with those of the Christian faith because of my familiarity with it, having become a Christian in 1983, and I still hold to the core belief today. However, from May 2022, especially since October 2023, I have come to know more people who practice the Muslim faith and find they are indeed those who care for and embrace others without showing partiality.

As I share about the emotive issue of Palestine and Israel, I will cover various themes and topics and start providing initial answers to a broad cross-section of questions that some people reading this may have or might just be curious about, whether spoken or otherwise.

INTRODUCTION

The sources I have used are many and varied, including journal articles, information from government agencies, the United Nations, including the various organisations and departments that come under the United Nations umbrella, Non-Government Organisations, media articles not behind a pay wall, and other information from the internet. I also own approximately 85 books in paper and digital format, which I continued to purchase as needed while undertaking this project. The authors of the information are varied, including historians, clergy, university lecturers, political analysts, humanitarians, activists and journalists. Some are Palestinian, some are Jewish Israelis, while others are neither.

I acknowledge that the British promised the European Jews land at the end of World War I and the land officially became the State of Israel in 1948. However, I will use the name Palestine when referring to the whole of the land that currently encompasses the State of Israel, the Golan Heights, the West Bank and the Gaza Strip. I use the name Palestine because, throughout my life, I have predominantly heard that land called Palestine by my mum and by members of my extended family. Calling it Palestine is natural and is what I am used to. I will also use the names of the different areas when referring to them separately and use Gaza when referring to the Gaza Strip. I will be using the term Occupied Territories when I refer to East Jerusalem, the West Bank and Gaza concurrently because that is their current state under Israeli government rule.

In May 2024, I attended a function and learned from Professor Mazin Qumsiyeh that the Middle East should be more accurately called West Asia.[5] It was named Middle East because of its proximity to Britain as a colonial power. Although I now call the region West Asia, I will use the term Middle East due to its familiarity with most people.

Because of its historical value, according to historian Nur Masalha, the term 'Palestine' refers to the area commonly called Palestine from 1300 BC until the State of Israel became an official entity in 1948.[6] Therefore, I will use the term historical Palestine to refer to the whole territory before 1948. It was from then that the name on maps began changing to Israel, and now it is virtually impossible to find any map that still calls the area Palestine. The people living in historical Palestine were known as "Arab Muslims, Arab Christians and Arab Jews."[7] When referring to Palestinians and Jews who have Israeli citizenship and live in the State of Israel, I will refer to them as Palestinian Israelis and Jewish Israelis.

Because I find it valuable and necessary, I will be using the Christian Bible because portions of it underpin the belief that all of Palestine belongs only to the State of Israel. The Bible contains the Old Testament and the New Testament. This division does not render the Old Testament as no longer having relevancy, to be done away with and ignored. Instead, for this writing, the Old Testament is critical as portions from the Old Testament are regularly used to justify what is happening between Jewish Israelis and all Palestinians in Palestine.

Since not everyone has easy access to the Bible, I will include some of its content to provide a background and plausible reasons for the current Palestinian situation. It has been ongoing in Palestine for the past one hundred and twenty years. The Bible mentions two sequential covenants. It is the first one that can provide some insight.

After expanding a little about myself in Chapter 1: About Me so that you know more about who I am, the subsequent chapters will cover various topics and themes. In Chapter 2: Two Covenants, I will examine the reason why the covenants, or what we would call legal contracts, were necessary. While considering the whole issue of the land belonging to Israel, I was questioning what I had already learned and believed, so I revisited the content of the covenant, which was relevant for me in clarifying, changing, and then solidifying my current beliefs. The first covenant, recorded in the

INTRODUCTION

Old Testament and initially made with Abram, then passed through to the children of Israel. The promise of land is the primary emphasis of the first covenant. Having the promise realised is based on the recipient's obedience, making it conditional. The ownership of the land of historical Palestine always hinged on the recipient's obedience.

I will then look at the second covenant in the New Testament, which brings a significant change, where the primary emphasis is no longer on Israel's adherence to a set of rules and regulations or even on owning a patch of land. It centres on the coming of the Messiah, Jesus Christ. This second covenant provides information about Jesus' birth, life, death and resurrection, and how His arrival was essential for all, including Jews and non-Jews (Gentiles), throughout the world.

Chapter 3: Deakin University deals with my studies and their relevancy in providing information regarding the colonisation of many indigenous populations over the years, including Palestinians in historic Palestine and today, especially since the Al Nakba in 1948 and Al Naksa in 1967 with the ongoing occupation.

Over the years, I have heard many say that Palestine as a state did not exist because it did not have a legitimate government. Also, that as a people, Palestinians do not exist, and that Yasser Arafat only invented the name to birth some fake nationalism. I found it necessary to find some answers. I have discovered a rich history rarely promoted outside of the Middle East. One must purposely engage in one's own informal or formal study, which I have undertaken, and continue to study informally to learn its history. I will share what I have learned about this group of people in Chapter 4: Palestine and Palestinians.

Since I covered a little about the Palestinians, I wanted to know what the thoughts of the general public were about the Jewish Israelis. In Chapter 5: Palestine and Jewish Israelis, I look at sections of the Evangelical Church and their emphatic support of Israel. It is more than feeling sympathy for the Jewish nation because of their suffering throughout World War II or for their desire for a piece of land of their own. Instead, their theology hinges on the Jewish people returning to that specific parcel of land. I then looked internationally at how the public views both Israelis and Palestinians since the surveys I found compare the two people groups. Also, with the promise to Abraham and the belief that Jewish people need a Jewish homeland, I thought it was necessary to provide information about historic Palestine from the late 1800s to 1948, when part of it-78%- became a State for the Jewish people.

From there, I change direction and consider the current occupation of the Palestinian people. In Chapter 6: Beyond Occupation, readers, especially those who do not know what is happening in Palestine, will get a good overview of suffering in the daily lives of the Palestinian people. I look separately at three areas. I look at the State of Israel, where I consider the effects on the Palestinians of the 'State Basic Law'. When looking at the West Bank, which is under military law, I cover various topics, which are by no means exhaustive and include land confiscations and settlements, house demolitions and villages razed, the separation wall, checkpoints, restricting movement, night raids and administrative detention. I will also look at the city of Jenin. Lastly, in this chapter, I look at Gaza, which is also a military law but is also under an almost complete blockade. I consider what occurred during the Great March of Return, an event held in Gaza in 2018-2019.

In Chapter 7: Refusing to Give In, I address the phenomenon where because of the attacks against the United States on 11 September 2001, the word 'terrorism' appears to be labelled against individuals or groups who have perpetrated any form of violence towards others. This includes minority groups who resist being dominated by others. I consider what

INTRODUCTION

terrorism is. I also look at resistance, which usually comes in two forms: armed and non-armed. I find when governments, in particular, talk about what is happening in Palestine, the conversation quickly moves to the topic of Hamas. Therefore, I found it necessary to consider Hamas through the lenses of terrorism and resistance. Since there are two major opposing parties in this occupation, I will also look at some of the actions of the Israeli Defence Forces over the years, especially since they call themselves 'the most moral army in the world'. Lastly, in this chapter, I look at the Jewish settlers. After all, housing or settlements, as they are commonly known, are being built for them, particularly throughout the West Bank and in East Jerusalem. I look at how the Israeli settlers are exacerbating what is happening in Palestine.

Some may refer to Hamas as the 'elephant in the room'. I believe the United States is the elephant that somehow must be removed. In Chapter 8: Feathering Their Own Nest, I share the insights I gained, especially from one lecture I listened to in 2017 that I will always remember while studying at Deakin University. This lecture opened my eyes to what I saw as being the plausible reason that the Palestinian people are still under occupation today.

I have added Chapter 9: 7 October 2023, as I needed to speak up about what happened on that date and what has been happening since then. I have included a brief overview of the first four and a half months of the Israeli Defence Force Operation Swords of Iron, from 8 October 2023 to just before the 'Flour Massacre' at the end of February 2024. I consider the topics of genocide, media, and Australian racism. I also look at what has been happening within the broader international community, including the actions of global citizens, students and the international judiciary.

In the West Bank, since 8 October 2023, there have been an increase in the number of vicious attacks undertaken on Palestinians by soldiers and Jewish settlers, with a dramatic increase in the number of those killed. Villages have also been razed to the ground, and hundreds more Palestinians are being jailed without a reason under administrative detention. What is happening in Gaza could continue for many months, so this chapter is unfinished.

Up until the end of June 2024, which was nearly nine months into the operation, the Israeli Defence Forces were still bombing Gaza. A report released on 5 July 2024 by the Lancet suggests that 186,000 Palestinians could be killed as a result of the current genocide in Gaza.[8]

Most of the information in this chapter now describes a reality that has become much worse for Palestinians than the picture painted in previous chapters. What is happening now is far worse than I could have envisaged.

In Chapter 10: Final Thoughts, I have summarised the previous chapters and revealed my thoughts about how I feel as a Christian and Palestinian. Lastly, I have reiterated my hope that Palestinians' dream of justice and freedom will become a reality.

I am sharing my story for several reasons. First, as a Christian, I want to encourage other Christians to consider their currently held theological belief system and ideology, especially as it relates to Palestine and Israel. Second, during my university studies, I became aware that few of my peers understood what has occurred and is currently occurring in Palestine. So, there is a chance that significant numbers of people in society do not understand what is happening in Palestine either. Often, the little people did know was media biased according to the media source they engaged with. Lastly, I am sharing my story so that somehow my story will reach and encourage you, my fellow Palestinians. Maybe you are Muslim or Christian, have another belief or no belief, and are living in Palestine. Know that *ant la tansaa,* you are not forgotten.

INTRODUCTION

Ultimately, I aim to reach those who want to learn what is happening in a tiny area of the world. Yes, anyone can start an internet search or go to the library, borrow some books, and start reading. Most books on this topic focus on one area. With this primer, I present an overview of what has happened and is happening, hoping that you will become enlightened about the injustice occurring in one part of the world to the people I belong to. I hope that you will no longer shrug your shoulders or give it a cursory glance but instead engage yourself further and tell others what you are learning.

1

ABOUT ME

A letter decided where we were to live in Australia. My mum wrote to two of my aunts at the same time. One aunt was an older sister of my dad, who lived in Speers Point, New South Wales, and the other aunt was one of my mum's sisters who left England for Australia a couple of years before we planned to go. She lived in Woori Yallock, Victoria. The aunt who replied first would determine where we would initially live. With my aunt in Victoria replying first, we boarded an immigration ship at Southampton, England, and disembarked in Melbourne, Victoria, after four weeks at sea. We lived with my aunt, uncle and three cousins for approximately three months before securing a place to rent in Mt Evelyn, roughly a 40-minute drive away.

Moving to Mt Evelyn, my mum gained employment in the local Riteway supermarket. For my dad, though, as many migrants experience, Australia does not always recognise overseas qualifications. Although he was a qualified driving instructor in England and was trained in various positions in the Royal Air Force, he had to settle for whatever work he could find. He obtained a position working in the control centre at the David Mitchel Cave Hill lime quarry in Lilydale. The major downside of the work at the quarry was the rolling weekly shift work of day, night, and afternoon shifts. While Dad was on the night shift and sleeping through the day, Mum and I had to be careful not to disturb his sleep. While he was at work at night, sometimes my mum and I would sit up all night watching movies on free-to-air television, long before Netflix, Stan, Prime, or Binge became available, which was always fun. My parents stayed in their respective jobs until, as a family, we left Victoria over ten years later.

Growing up, my life did not differ from most others. Apart from my aunt, I did not know anyone else who came from the Middle East. Although I am half Palestinian and half Irish, I look more Irish than Palestinian, having a fair complexion. Six of the nine first-cousin girls in the family look Middle Eastern. I am one of the three that does not. Because of that, I sometimes felt envious of the six. Due to my fair complexion, I have not had to endure any racist comments being hurled my way, which seems to be more prolific towards those who naturally have a darker olive skin toning, especially in a post-September 11, 2001 era.

A funny incident happened recently. I attended an event to raise funds for an organisation to unite families living in Gaza with their families here in Brisbane. While a group of us were eating shawarma, we talked about the Arabic language and the methods different people use to learn it. Upon mentioning that I was learning Arabic, one of the women gave me a strange look, followed by the question, "Why are you learning Arabic?" She understood after I explained that I am of mixed nationality, Irish and Palestinian.

Over the years, while living in Victoria, we spent many weekends at my aunt and uncle's place. We cousins, spent many happy hours occupying ourselves. From climbing a tall pine tree as high as we could in their front yard, perched amongst its branches, we could see a long way across the rooftops to the rolling hills in the distance.

ABOUT ME

We kept busy entertaining ourselves by riding bicycles, creating plays, playing dress-ups, and doing whatever else our creative brains could come up with in their hall. It used to be the local community hall during a different era, as it boasted a stage and a large area for the audience to gather. We also played billiards on a pool table and spent many hours in their pool, especially during the hot summers.

The worst part about the summers in the early years of living in Australia was having to contend with mosquito bites. I remember one time we counted thirty-two bites on my body. They were so itchy; no creams or sprays helped relieve the itch. Thankfully, my reaction to mosquito bites decreased as I became older, and they are minimal now.

Our family also forged friendships from within our suburb. Some were work colleagues of my mum. We also became close to one family who lived near the house we rented for two years after leaving my aunt and uncle's place. Even though we were unrelated, I grew up calling the parents aunty and uncle rather than mister and missus, and I continued to do so until their respective deaths.

Their youngest daughter and I were similar in age. If we were not at my aunt and uncle's place on weekends, we would spend many weekends in their round above-ground pool, especially in the summer. During those years, pool fencing was not legally required like it is now. We also indulged in eating mangoes, which their family always had plenty of.

As it was the 1970s, we also spent hours listening to the music of the latest bands recorded on cassettes, including ABBA, Sherbert, KISS, AC/DC and Bay City Rollers. Once my parents bought our first home, we would play at a nearby creek or ride our bikes on the streets and in the bush near our house. Years later, some of these connections remain.

I began my schooling at a government state school but my parents were not happy that the same readers were being sent home with me daily, even though I could read them fluently. They moved me to a Seventh-Day Adventist School for my primary education in the Melbourne suburb of Croydon. I ended up there because while growing up in Jordan, my mum and some of her siblings attended a Seventh-Day Adventist School, which was established and run by the British, so it seemed appropriate for me to be sent to the same.

The Seventh-Day Adventist School was small, with four classrooms and a small office. Grades 1 to 4 were in one room, and grades 5 to 7 were in another. There was an art room; the last was the teacher's staff room. I enjoyed arriving at school early to do some painting. The painting I enjoyed doing the most during those early mornings was splatting different paint colours onto A4 paper and then folding the paper in half and pressing gently. Opening it revealed a colourful pattern, which was then left to dry. Unfortunately, I could not produce anything special enough to frame and keep from my years there.

My nickname in my later years of primary school was 'Smelly'. It was not until years later that I realised that because both of my parents smoked cigarettes, my school uniforms would have been impregnated with the odour of cigarettes. Being a Seventh-Day Adventist School, none of the teachers or parents of the other students smoked, so the smell would have been pungent to them.

Shortly after I began attending primary school in Croydon, I was getting myself to school. Leaving home at 7:15 a.m., I would walk for 15 minutes, catch a public bus to the nearest train station, ride a train to two suburbs away, and finish by walking thirty minutes to school. After school in the afternoons, I would do the reverse and arrive home by 4:45 p.m.

I enjoyed riding on the trains. Three types of trains were being used in Victoria in the early 1970s. The most modern was the silver Hitachi trains, where we could easily prop the doors open with our feet as we sat on the

ABOUT ME

floor. The blue Harris trains had doors that did not have to be propped open to stay open. The oldest trains were the Tait trains, also affectionately called the red rattlers. Each row of seats had a door, and the interior was ornately fitted. Keeping the train doors open was great during the hot summers.

During the last year of primary school, another student joined me on the walk and train journey from school. While waiting at the far end of the platform for a train, we would ensure that we were out of view of the train staff in the station office. Ensuring nobody was watching, we would quickly jump off the platform onto the track area, place ballast rock on the track, and climb back onto the platform. We enjoyed seeing the rocks crushed to dust as the train ran over them. We never placed large pieces on the track that would cause an issue, but we were still naughty doing what we did. As Lilydale Station ended the train line, we would catch different buses to continue our separate journeys home.

I especially enjoyed the bus trips from Lilydale Station to Mt Evelyn. As a regular passenger, I found the Invicta bus drivers to be amiable. Once I was old enough, I would help the bus driver by selling bus tickets to the other passengers as they boarded the bus. I enjoyed helping because I could sit up front or lean against the Invicta bus dashboard and talk to the driver as we travelled.

As I aged, I would get off the bus near the supermarket where my mum was working. I would busy myself by restocking the supermarket shelves or helping at the checkout counter by packing the customers' groceries into paper bags, which were free back then. Paper bags were used before the creation of plastic bags. Some communities are reverting to using paper or biodegradable bags to help save the environment, which is polluted with plastic waste. Mum and I would walk home together or ride her Honda scooter home. I loved being with my mum and would spend lots of time with her.

CROSSING OVER

After completing primary school, I attended Lilydale State High School until the end of Year 11. Since we were not church members, the school fees would have been significantly higher if I had attended Seventh-Day Adventist High School.

MIXED CULTURE

I found it exciting growing up and belonging to a mixed-race family because it did have its benefits, including a variety of food served at mealtime. We ate typical English meat and vegetables or exotic Middle Eastern foods. These included Cousa Mahshi, which is Lebanese, or regular zucchini cored and stuffed with minced meat, often lamb, rice, and spices, and cooked in a big saucepan with tomato sauce. When I was old enough, I began helping Mum by coring the zucchinis with a unique tool. While learning, I would always make holes in the sides of the zucchinis. Wari Diwali is stuffed vine leaves using fresh grapevine leaves, usually picked from my aunt's grapevine. Eating the grapes was nice, but having fresh and tender vine leaves rolled up and stuffed with the similar mix that went into the zucchinis would make our taste buds dance at mealtime.

Malfoof was similar, but cabbage leaves were used rather than vine leaves, and the mixture was placed inside. These were placed in a big pot, with lamb shanks on the bottom and cabbage rolls layered on top with some water and seasoned with spices. Sfeeha was another delicious meal we would indulge in. A basic bread dough was prepared. Balls of dough were flattened either with a rolling pin or by your hands and covered with a mixture containing lamb mince, onion, pine nuts, cinnamon, salt and pepper, and yoghurt spread over the top. They were then placed on a tray and baked in the oven. They were so delicious to eat while still hot out of the oven. It was also still delicious over the days that followed. Eating these

ABOUT ME

delectable mini pizzas, as we sometimes affectionately call them, was done by themselves or with other dishes.

The table was only ever complete with tabbouli, which was burghul, cracked wheat, chopped parsley, finely diced tomatoes and cucumber, salt and pepper, in various quantities, and all gently mixed. Yoghurt with diced cucumber, hummus, a mix of crushed sesame called tahini, garlic, lemon juice and chickpeas. My mum would make baklava, a sweet made of layers of filo pastry, a mixture of crushed nuts, spices, and honey syrup poured over, for a special treat. Getting together at my aunt and uncle's place was extra special as there was always more than the usual Middle Eastern foods to enjoy. My mum and aunt were great cooks, and they loved to cook. Hospitality is significant in women's lives in and from the Middle East. It is the same for my mum. We affectionately call her home "Tayta Yvonne's home of health and happiness."

Traditionally, within the Middle East, after Ramadan or Lent and before Easter, Ma'amoul was always made and eaten as a nice treat to end the fasting period. Small amounts of a semolina pastry were made into a ball and flattened out in the palm of your hand so that a hollow was formed. A mixture of crushed nuts and spices or a date would be placed on the pastry while it was still in your hand. It was then sealed up and gently pressed into a wooden patterned mould to emboss a pattern onto the pastry. It was then removed and then baked in the oven on trays. Afterwards, they were sprinkled with a fine coating of sifted icing sugar. Having these yearly became a lovely family tradition.

Along with the food, another aspect of Middle Eastern culture I have always loved is music. It is vibrant and encourages joy, even though I could not understand the language. I have always found it interesting that some songs sound mournful and unhappy, yet the lyrics are the opposite.

Regarding the Arabic language, I am finding it challenging to learn, and I am still trying to master it. There are different forms of Arabic, including

Modern Standard Arabic, which is predominantly used in formal environments, and numerous other dialects, depending on where you live, that people speak daily. The type of Arabic spoken by my mother and her family was called Levantine Arabic, which uses words and phrases from Lebanon, Palestine, Egypt and Jordan.

MOVING NORTH

With our family wanting a fresh start, my dad made a large trailer from a caravan chassis to which he had welded a steel frame around the sides. During the 1981 summer school holidays, we loaded all our earthly belongings and towed them behind our Holden Kingswood to Atherton in Far North Queensland. On the way, we had two incidents. Because we wanted to avoid as many main roads as possible, we unknowingly found ourselves driving on dirt roads, which were only sometimes indicated on maps. Travelling along one of these dirt roads, a tyre from the car suddenly rolled into the distance. In the country, where it could be hours before one sees another vehicle, people always stop to help others. Thankfully, we did not have to wait long before a truck driver stopped and helped change the tyre.

Stopping overnight at Miles in Queensland, Sammy, our cat, had had enough of the trip. He ran off after our letting him out of his box that was on the trailer. The following morning, we called and looked for him but could not find him anywhere, he had disappeared. Over the years, we have wondered what happened to him. At Sarina, near Mackay, we stopped at a camping ground to use the toilets. When flushing the toilets, there were quite a few green frogs in the toilet bowl. They gave us a bit of a fright, but it was also quite funny. Our trip took a couple of weeks to reach our destination.

ABOUT ME

I undertook Year 12 at Atherton State High School on the Atherton Tablelands. Being there only for my senior year, I did not have time to forge more than superficial friendships. Since we lost Sammy during our trip, we also got another cat. Its breed was Tonkinese, a mixture of Siamese and Burmese with a beautiful nature. He was a grey, so we named him Smokey. We would play hide and seek, and he would wait for me in my bedroom doorway when he wanted to go to bed. I would climb into bed with Smokey joining me between the sheets. Once he was asleep, I would sneak out of bed. He was fearless, jumping from high up in a tree onto the house roof or into our arms. Although we rented a house on a large block, unfortunately, one day, Smokey ran onto the road and was hit and killed by a car.

During my year living in Atherton, my mum told me one day, "We never had you christened as a baby so that you can choose for yourself what you want to believe when you grow up." I appreciated my mum's words at the time, knowing that I could choose for myself what beliefs I wanted to hold and follow once I left home, which I did within a year when I was 18.

My High School Certificate results were sufficient and allowed me to study further. I moved to Rockhampton in February 1983 to study at the Capricornia Institute of Advanced Education, which today is Central Queensland University. I was unable to complete a business degree for which I had enrolled. In hindsight, if I had known then what I know now, I would have undertaken studies that could have been applied within the humanitarian sector and headed to the Middle East.

While I was in Rockhampton, I considered my spiritual state.

EMBRACING CHRISTIANITY

Growing up, I went to Sunday school occasionally when a neighbour invited me. I also attended one Adanac CYC camp with one of my cousins, but that was all.[9] I was not involved in any other religious activity.

Shortly after arriving in Rockhampton, some religious teachings I had received during my days at the Seventh-Day Adventist primary school began to resurface, invading my daily thoughts, especially learning and having a genuine sense of knowing that I had to become a Christian to go to heaven when I die. This meant that I needed to understand that I had become separated from God because of Adam's sin in the Garden of Eden, which is passed down generationally to all peoples of the world. I had to believe that God wanted to restore His relationship with humankind through the birth, death on the cross, resurrection, and ascension of Jesus Christ. If I genuinely believed all of this and wanted to live a life in such a way that honours God, then I would become a part of God's family and go to heaven when I die. I learned that this does not mean that I must go door to door inviting people to join my religion or travel to other countries to be a missionary, as if I must 'earn the right' to go to heaven.

While a child in primary school, I refrained from responding to the teaching I received because I feared how my dad would react. However, having left home, I was living my own life. Shortly after, I embraced what I had learned six years earlier. I was living at the residential college attached to the Capricornia Institute of Advanced Education, and two weeks later, I walked across the highway and started attending a local church under the Australian Christian Churches umbrella.

As a new Christian, attending church meetings regularly was a new experience I was happy to adopt. It did not take me long to become part of the

ABOUT ME

community because we did so many activities together. Along with work and school, there was no room for involvement in other outside activities.

Within a few months, I undertook a full immersion water baptism, similar to what is recorded in the New Testament. It was undertaken inside the church building in a small pool built into the stage.

Along with most church members, I attend two services on a Sunday. In the morning, we would sing songs unto God and then listen to a preached sermon. The sermons were usually general teachings about a theme from within the Bible based on what the children of Israel went through or a specific focus on how to live a better life based on how Jesus lived. Once a fortnight, we partook in communion during the morning service. The evening services followed the same structure as the morning, but the sermon centred around the life and work of Jesus on the cross. Inviting people who would not know about Jesus was encouraged. I did not know anyone outside of the church community, so I never asked anybody.

I also attended a mid-week youth Bible study. These often followed the theme shared during the Sunday morning sermon or covered topics that general youth faced as we learned how to successfully live and be active and worthwhile contributors to society.

I became an assistant leader for the Royal Rangers outdoor youth program on Friday evenings. It runs much like Scouts and Girl Guides. One learns skills to be able to live and survive in the outdoors. For those who enjoyed roughing it, there were opportunities for the girls to apply what they learned by undertaking overnight camping trips. Since I have never enjoyed camping, I did not enjoy these times. I tried to resign, but the Senior Pastor would not allow me to. I suspected it was because there was nobody else to take my position.

Every Friday evening, as leaders, we also reinforced that these impressionable girls should live as believers and followers of Jesus. This was usually done by facilitating a lesson and discussion based on a Bible passage.

On Saturday nights, I enjoyed being involved in the youth group. It was either a night of fun activities, such as games nights, movie nights, car rallies, a myriad of other possibilities, or a regular meeting where we sang songs and the Youth Pastor shared a passage from the Bible that could be applied to individual lives.

After youth group, a group of us would always end up at the local petrol (gas) station and enjoy some fast food. It was always fun, and I am sure the owners were happy about the extra business they received.

As I approached twenty, I began attending women's meetings, held semi-regularly and often run like mini conferences. Special speakers came in and shared Friday evening and Saturday. The speaker was frequently invited to speak at both Sunday services.

A yearly highlight was attending the annual family camp. I enjoyed going away for a few days. We slept in dormitory-style buildings. For married couples, there were usually a few cabins available. These camps were held over Easter, giving people a few days to be away and refresh physically and spiritually.

Again, there were meetings held every day where a guest speaker shared. Usually, these speakers were well-known pastors and evangelists from within the movement, who usually had larger churches and often preached globally. In the afternoon, planned sports activities were available, and everyone could join. I avoided getting involved as I was not sporty, and the activities were quite competitive.

Overall, I found that the teaching within the church community encompasses living a good life and honouring God. Because of particular teachings, we looked to world events and also ensured we were ready for a secret rapture that could snatch away believers in Jesus into heaven at any time. We also looked at Israel because we were taught that the more land that belonged to Israel, the closer it would be to when Jesus would return. I spent many years in Christian churches in Rockhampton and Brisbane, where this was taught.

Looking back on those years, living in that community was more like living in a cocoon, as every part of one's life revolved around it. Unfortunately, I observed that if someone moved away from the community for any reason, whether work, marriage or for any other reason, contacts from within that community were usually lost, which made me conclude that relationships forged in those places were only superficial, with no lasting benefit.

Back in 1983, I did not know then that there would come a time when I would no longer accept some teachings, such as the secret rapture, and that the amount of Palestine that Israel owns would help determine when Jesus would return. In hindsight, my journey was relatively easy. I only sometimes entirely accepted what was taught because I saw biblical passages that I believed contradicted what I heard being preached.

I left Rockhampton for Brisbane in 1987 after getting engaged and was married in June 1988. My husband Peter and I are still married, and we currently have two sons and a daughter-in-law.

STUDY TRIP TO PALESTINE

Although I undertook a year part-time Bible certificate course in 1989, I had wanted to do some in-depth Biblical study for several years. As our two sons were 19 and 17, I took the opportunity from February 2010 to October 2015 to study a Bachelor of Ministry through the Australian College of Theology's Malyon College in Brisbane. I studied part-time as I knew my academic limits, plus it had been 27 years since I had attempted that level of academic study.

The highlight of my time at college was going to Palestine on a study trip. I was excited to be able to go. While preparing for the trip, I spoke to a friend who had been there a few times to get some idea of what to expect and what I would see while there, as I had no idea. I cannot remember much of what she said, but some things stood out. She said that when you look out from the old city of Jerusalem, you can distinctly see the different areas where the Jews and the Arabs live. The Jewish areas are clean, and the Arab areas are dirty, with rubbish lying everywhere. This revealed, in her mind at least, that the Arabs do not care how they live. If there is one thing I have come to understand, Arabs are meticulous about everything being clean.

I have found out since that following the 1967 war, when neighbourhoods and towns of East Jerusalem were annexed to Israel, roughly 400,000 Palestinians became a part of those areas.[10] Unfortunately, most Palestinians do not vote in local elections, which would give them local representation and municipal services, including rubbish collection. If they vote in these elections, others could see that they are possibly 'normalising' the current political situation.[11]

She also mentioned that often, the authorities cut off the electricity in the West Bank because the Palestinian Authority does not pay their electricity bills. It was a reasonable manoeuvre and response to unpaid bills, which would happen in any country. I found out since that trip that if the Palestinian Authority does not pay their electricity bill, it is mainly due to a dispute between them and the Israeli authority. However, it is becoming more apparent that the Israeli government often cuts the electricity to the Palestinians so that they grow weary. Beyond that, the primary aim of the Israeli government is to control the land and then annex large portions of land.[12]

ABOUT ME

Lastly, she said that some Arabs serve in the Israeli Defence Force, with Druze units being happy to serve.[13] My friend also said that the other units respect them. At the time of our conversation, I thought it was good that some Arabs wanted to help protect Israel from any potential enemy, either from within Palestine or from the surrounding Arab countries. After all, the land belongs to Israel, so I thought at the time.

I wanted to know more about the Druze units. They began during the 1948 war when elders of the Druze community signed a pact of allegiance with the Jewish state. While the Druze expected to be made first-class citizens, they were confined to special units in the army.[14] I also discovered that the Druze's willingness to serve comes from their desire not to live as a separate group but to integrate within the dominant group in the country in which they are living. Doing so has also helped them not be persecuted or killed over the centuries.[15]

There were approximately 65 of us going on the study tour to Palestine. Our group, which included two male lecturers and two female staff members, gathered at Malyon College. We were all excited. From there, we boarded coaches and travelled together to the Brisbane airport.

Leaving Brisbane, we headed to Singapore. Once we landed at the Singapore airport, there were quite a few hours to wait for the next flight, so we did some exploring. From there, we headed to the Middle East, our first stop being Amman, in Jordan. While we were approaching the inbound runway, I unexpectedly became very emotional and teary. It was the first time in my 47 years that I had the opportunity to be there in the place where my mum was born and raised, even if I was only going to spend two hours at the airport. I sensed that it was more than that. I felt such an affinity with Jordan and beyond to the greater Middle East, as if I belonged there. It was not long before we were bound for Tel Aviv on a short thirty-minute plane trip. Arriving in Tel Aviv was an anticlimax as nothing could surpass what I experienced while we were landing in Jordan.

As a student of the Bible, my time in Palestine was exciting and educational as we could correlate places with what was written in the Bible. We visited important places associated with Jesus, such as Bethlehem and Nazareth, the Mount of Olives, the Garden Tomb, the Garden of Gethsemane, and the Holy Sepulchre Church. Being in Nazareth was extremely special, as it was where my maternal grandparents were born and raised.

We stayed overnight in the Galilee area and visited places where Jesus ministered to the people, such as the Mount of Beatitudes, Bethsaida, and Capernaum. I have come to understand that Jesus lived in Capernaum after being forced out of his hometown of Nazareth, having been nearly pushed off a cliff. One could consider Him to be an internally displaced refugee.

We even ventured onto the Sea of Galilee in a boat. It was so peaceful on the water. These were all beautiful experiences.

Being in the north of the State of Israel, we headed to the Golan Heights, which was part of Syria until it came under Israeli military occupation in 1981. From there, we could see into Lebanon. Looking very carefully, we saw a Palestinian flag in the distance. Since we were close to the border of Lebanon, further up the hill from where we were, there was a military tower. For our own safety, we were warned by our tour guides to not take any photos of the military area. It is hard to believe that Lebanon used to be called the 'playground of the rich'. Now, it is a country that is currently in decline and has a struggling economy.

Visiting Be'er Sheva was significant to the British Empire. We saw the open plain where the ANZACS battled to defeat the Ottomans near the end of World War 1.

ABOUT ME

We also visited Ein Gedi, a place of general biblical significance. This included the field where David battled Goliath, viewing the area where David hid from King Saul and Jericho.

Visiting Jericho provided a short but memorable time for me. After we had visited the site of the old city of Jericho, which was a lot smaller than I expected it to be, we had a couple of hours free to wander the local market and have some lunch at the cafe about 200m from the entrance to the old city. After indulging in lunch, I returned to the old city entrance gates and conversed with some older local Palestinian men. I had an instant rapport with them when I mentioned that my mother was born and raised in Amman, Jordan. It would have been easy to stay talking to them for much longer, but I could not. They told me to come back to visit them with my family. I would love to visit again, especially since my eyes have been opened to what is the actual state of the Palestinian people within Palestine.

Travelling by coach for two to three hours to Qumran was worthwhile. It was incredible to see the caves in the nearby distance, where the Dead Sea Scrolls were found. These papyrus scrolls contain parts of every book of the Old Testament except for the Book of Esther. They also include hymns, prayers, commentaries, and the earliest versions of the Ten Commandments.[16] The scrolls are being preserved and displayed in The Shrine of the Book, a dedicated museum in the State of Israel.

The day we visited the West Bank cities of Hebron and Bethlehem was very different. We had to change into bulletproof buses with Palestinian drivers and tour guides because, due to Israeli regulations, all Israeli citizens are not permitted to enter the West Bank. Conversely, all Palestinians wanting to travel outside of the West Bank are forbidden without permits.[17]

Changing into bulletproof buses gave us the first clue that we would be venturing into a potentially volatile area, which was a little scary, although exciting. Boarding the bus, I greeted the guide with *"Marhaba."* Hello. His eyes momentarily lit up. A little later, he asked me if I could translate for him. I replied, *"La ana arif alarabiya shway."* No, I only know a little Arabic.

In Bethlehem, we went to the Church of the Nativity, which is said to be built over the place where Jesus was born. Not knowing anything about Christian orthodoxy, I found the decoration, ornaments, and icons excessive. Today, I still have trouble with those same things. To me, even the purported spot of Jesus' birth was decorated excessively, which took away from what would have been the reality of His actual place of birth. Consequently, I did not linger but took a photo and moved on.

While studying at Malyon College, I did a unit called Theology for Everyday Life, which at times I found uninteresting as it involved encouraging us to utilise tools that are often found within orthodoxy, such as candles, icons, ornaments and pictures to help enhance our Christian experience. Attending a solidarity event of Indigenous people of Australia and Palestine in May 2024, I was challenged by a comment made that inferred that those from within Christian orthodoxy tend to have a deeper spiritual relationship with God than those outside that form of Christian expression. The person's religious belief was not Christian, so I considered his observation. In time, I may revisit the lecture notes from the unit.

We also drove past Bethlehem Bible College and spent some time in their gift shop. I did not find anything to buy because many items sold were associated with orthodoxy, which did not interest me. Also, I did not need anything. The bus drivers dropped us off at the shop's entrance and picked us up after a set time. We were not permitted to leave the shop and wander around the city, which seemed strange.

The itinerary was tight. It would have been nice if we had more time to talk with the local Palestinians. I reflected years later that Palestinian tour

ABOUT ME

drivers and guides have strict guidelines to follow to keep their jobs. Also, it is more than likely that the Israeli authorities do not like tourists talking to the local Palestinians for fear that the truth of their situation will get out to the rest of the world, as suggested by Australian journalist John Lyons.[18]

Apart from being the place of Jesus' birth, Bethlehem was also where they buried other people mentioned in the Bible and Old Testament, including Rachel. It was also where the home of Naomi and her family stood and where Ruth gleaned in the fields, met, and married Boaz. Today, the site is under the control of Palestinian Muslims.

On 17 October 2023, I looked again through the photos I had taken during that trip and found one picture I had taken in Bethlehem that caught my attention, especially upon viewing it again. A mosaic sign on a wall displayed the distance between Bethlehem and Jerusalem. High above the mosaic was a small billboard with half of the message cut off in the picture, but there were enough of the letters showing to make out the message "Pray for the Freedom of Palestine." I did not see the billboard while on the trip. If only I had, and if only I understood what it meant while I was there.

Based on the limited area we drove through, Hebron seemed very run down, and there were restrictions on where one could or could not go. Shuhada Street was one such place. I did not know what had happened on Shuhada Street, but I later learned that in 1994, a Jewish Settler attacked and killed 29 Palestinians in a mosque not far from Shuhada Street.[19] Although the perpetrator was a Jewish Settler who killed Palestinians, the Israeli Defence Forces punished the Palestinians by welding shut all the Shuhada Street entrances to their businesses and homes, rather than Jewish settlers' homes. Some Palestinians who still have homes on the street must enter via a rear door, which often means climbing over roofs and going through other properties.[20] Since 2000, Shuhada Street has been closed to Palestinians, with them not even being allowed to enter the street on foot.[21]

Fully armed military personnel were present at the entrances to Bethlehem and Hebron, and security barriers and border checks were in place.

I found it interesting that Bethlehem and Hebron are significant to Judaism, Christianity, and Islam. Our tour guide informed us that Hebron is the place of the Cave of Machpelah. This is where Abraham, Isaac, Jacob, Sarah, Rebecca, and Leah are all buried. Herod the Great originally erected a wall enclosing the area and, later, a roof.[22] Even though a mosque now stands on the site, people can visit the site at various times of the year. [23]

It was while visiting these two cities that a conflict started within me. I wanted to know the truth of what I saw in those places. Why were restrictions placed upon the Palestinians? Why is there apparent bullying towards the members of this minority group? Was our Palestinian guide for that day's trip telling us the truth, that the electricity supply is frequently and randomly cut off, not because the electricity bill is unpaid by the Palestinian Authority (as my friend before the trip had told me), but because the Israeli authorities want to make life harder for Palestinians. I had so many questions. I felt it was time to seek the truth and find answers if possible. Little did I know that two years from then, I would start finding answers to my questions that day.

The summer was hot and dry that year, so floating in the Dead Sea was a pleasure. Floating in the Dead Sea is easy because it contains 34 percent salt. It also means no sea creatures or organisms can live in it, hence the name. Looking across the Dead Sea, I could see into Jordan. I wanted to go there. I wanted to visit. I considered going to Jordan on our free day, but it would take a lot of work for me as a foreigner to organise it on such short notice. Plus, our lecturers told us that we were not allowed to go anywhere by ourselves; there always had to be at least two of us together.

ABOUT ME

During our trip, we also visited areas of Jewish and Israeli significance, including Masada, which was the site of the last battle between the Jews and the Romans after the fall of Jerusalem to the Romans in 70 CE, the Western Wall, the Israel Museum, and Yad Vashem a memorial and reminder of the Holocaust. Shortly after entering Yad Vashem, I had to exit prematurely because I was crying so much, seeing the horrors that had been perpetrated against the Jewish people under the hands of Germany during World War II. I now find it unfathomable that a people group who was mistreated by others can then treat the Palestinian people in such a terrible way.

DISCOVERING MY TRUE HERITAGE

Even though I was born in England and spent nearly five years there, I have always felt more connected to the Middle East through my mum. She brought into our home and family (and still does) aspects of the culture, primarily through food, music, and language, which I continue to love. My mum shares memories of special events their family was involved in and their daily lives.

Easter was significant while my mum was growing up since my grandmother's Christian beliefs were Roman Catholic, and my grandfather's Christian beliefs were Greek Orthodox. Immediate and extended family members, along with the broader Christian community, would gather together every year and re-enact the death and resurrection of Jesus Christ through the streets of Amman, which would culminate just before dawn at one of the churches where someone would knock on the church door looking for Jesus, to be told that He was not there but had risen.

Hearing stories about my mum's life in Amman is always a joy. One of her aunties was the only relative who owned an outdoor oven in her backyard so she could bake bread. Mum's family home did not have an oven, and she often remembers taking the bread dough my grandma had prepared that morning to the community baker on the way to school. She would then collect the baked bread at lunchtime and take it home. Mum then reminisced with joy, telling of the vendors going through the streets selling door to door. There would be vendors selling eggs. Others would sell fruit and vegetables from trays perched on their heads. Goats were milked as they were led through the streets, with fresh milk going directly into customers' jugs. The goat cheese was preserved in oil and sold. There was no need for refrigerated milk trucks in those days. Homewares such as pots and pans were also sold door to door.

Mum also shared that my grandfather became a builder after finishing his job as the British Ambassador's chauffeur. Once, they had just finished pouring the concrete for the roof (always the last job of any house build) of a house they had been building. My grandfather bought a couple of lambs, a sack of apricots, and tea to share with the workers and their families to celebrate the job's end and thank them for their hard work. Before preparing the feast, one of the ram lambs only had the stumps of its horns remaining and chased my mum (around eight years old) down the long row of 104 steps just outside their home. She stopped running, turned, faced the lamb, grabbed both stumps in her hands, and started screaming. My grandma came out of the house, saw what my mum was doing, and laughed. Grandma later commented that my mum would be the only one to think of doing such a thing.

The children enjoyed collecting the apricot seeds thrown on the ground after the apricots were consumed. They would break open the seed and eat the sweet kernel, unlike the bitter kernels of apricots here in Australia. Remembering this reminded me that my mum and her youngest brother regularly climbed almond trees to pick and eat the small, green pods. It was rare that they were left to develop into nuts.

ABOUT ME

From the time I was young, I had always considered myself half Jordanian Arab through my mum and half English through my dad because of where they were born. Growing up, I soon realised that "Where were you born?" was expected when writing school assignments, filling in forms, or being asked by others through everyday conversation. I was sure it is also a common question in every other country. It was not until many years later that I understood that it was customary within some cultures to link your identity to heritage rather than where you were born.

I see a practical yet simple way to illustrate the importance of heritage. Suppose an individual wants to get a passport or live in a country where they were not born but where one or two of their parents or even a grandparent might have been born. In that case, the governing authorities usually go back one or two generations when determining whether an individual can get a passport or residency. A further delineation could also be based on which parent or grandparent was born in the country.

Out of curiosity, while working on this book, I searched the internet to see whether I could get a Jordanian passport or an easy pathway to residency. I found that I did not meet the criterion for either because in Jordan (like in other Middle Eastern countries), paternity is dominant, meaning that my dad needed to have been born in Jordan rather than my mum. I also investigated whether I could get a Palestinian passport or residency in Palestine based on my grandparents. The criterion for Palestine was more robust. It did not matter that my grandparents were both born and raised in Nazareth, Palestine. Being born there yourself and being able to prove such with a birth certificate was the only way one may potentially get a passport. As for living in Palestine, it is virtually impossible to do so, according to the regulations of the Israeli government, as there is 'no right of return' for Palestinians.

CROSSING OVER

These governmental attitudes did not surprise me, especially considering what is happening in various countries in the Middle East with division between people. Some call it an entitlement issue, a political issue, while others call it a religious issue. Whatever people think it is, talking about the Middle East can be an emotive topic that can bring out the best and worst in people, depending on what you believe and which group you side with. Even today, I select carefully with whom I have an open discussion, knowing that talking about the Middle East, let alone what is happening in Palestine, can be very divisive.

In late June to early July 2014, during a semester study break while at Malyon College, I was told by one of my sisters-in-law that I must read *'The General's Son'* by Miko Peled (who some people call a self-hating Jew), so I ordered the book and read it. The book is about a prominent Israeli family, the Peled family, that had moved from Babruysk in Belarus to Palestine in 1923 to help build a Jewish state.[24] Miko's grandfather, Dr Avraham Katznelson, signed the Israeli Declaration of Independence in 1948 when the State of Israel was birthed. Miko's father was a general in the Israeli army who later resigned and became a powerful advocate for the Palestinians. Miko also became an advocate for the Palestinians and continues to speak globally about the Israeli government, which more and more people consider to be an apartheid regime, because of the ongoing injustices perpetrated against the Palestinians. He desires to see the international community support the Palestinians to gain justice for the injustices they have had to endure over many decades.

Miko's description of the events surrounding the 2000 Camp David Summit, hosted by United States President Bill Clinton, was the start of a permanent change in my life. It is enough to say here that discussions were to be held and agreements signed between Israeli Prime Minister Ehud Barak and Palestinian leader Yasser Arafat, which would finally provide the mechanisms and building blocks for peace between the two people groups. Unfortunately, the meetings concluded with no agreement or the signing of any documents.[25] What Miko shared next arrested me:

> ... I knew that Yasser Arafat had been consistent for years. For the sake of peace, he was willing to give up the dream of all Palestinians to return to their homes and their land in Palestine. He was willing to recognise Israel, the state that had destroyed Palestine, took his people's land, and turned them into a nation of refugees. He was ready to establish an independent Palestinian state in the West Bank and Gaza - which make up only 22 percent of the Palestinian home - with Arab East Jerusalem as its capital... It was clear that what the Israelis demanded at Camp David was tantamount to total Palestinian surrender... Barak demanded that Arafat sign an agreement to end the conflict forever. In return, he would be permitted to establish a Palestinian state on an area of land that could not be defined clearly because it was broken into pockets with no geographical continuity. Instead of Arab East Jerusalem, he would receive a small suburb of East Jerusalem as his capital. To that, Yasser Arafat refused to agree.[26]

Seeing for the first time that it was the Israeli government that did not want peace and a two-state solution, rather than the Palestinian leadership, shocked me. Someone who had nothing to lose wrote this. I knew little about what was happening in Palestine because I had not been following any news. I had heard enough to know that Palestinians were consistently blamed for preventing a two-state solution, one for the Jews and one for the Palestinians.

While reading the book, I also realised I am Palestinian rather than a Jordanian Arab because of my maternal grandparents being born and raised in Nazareth. I instantly felt a solid connection and a total sense of belonging to the Palestinian people. I also felt an enormous sense of pain for what Palestinians, especially in Palestine, have endured over many years and continue to endure today.

I felt I had been lied to because of the little I had heard from the media, which seemed only to portray the Israeli side of the narrative. I cried and sobbed when reading the book as I saw for the first time what I believed to be the truth. I binged on 250g blocks of chocolate and 250g packets of chips for weeks because of the sad truth I was reading.

For a time, I had to overcome animosity towards the Israelis whenever I saw a picture or article of the Israeli Prime Minister, Benjamin Netanyahu. He was and still is the current face of the Zionist Israeli government that mistreats the Palestinian people, my people.[27] For several months, whenever I reflected on the book's impact on my life, I could hardly speak of the situation without getting emotional.

I am different from most others because sometimes I immediately accept what I have heard or read about, even if it is new to me, and then research to find out the details later. Reading Miko's book was such a case. It led me to read more books and search the internet to learn everything that I could about Palestine over the subsequent years. I also began talking to others who knew much more than I did about Palestine.

The more I learned, the more it quickly became clear to me that in Palestine, the Palestinian community, whether they are Muslim, Christian, follow another religion or secular, help and support each other in their daily lives and through each other's suffering. They live as if there is no division within their community because most of the people are hurting most of the time for whatever reason. I cannot remember where I read the following recently, but I felt it encapsulates the heart of Palestinians. "My older sister, who is sheltering at a church in Gaza, told me today that the mosque next to them provides them with water from their well, and the church provides them with electricity when it can generate it and food to the Muslim neighbours. This is our Palestine."

Six months later, after stumbling on the truth of my heritage, a cousin (who is a Professor of Refugee Law and an Associate Professor at a university in England) and her fiancée (now her husband) came out from England to Australia as they were both undertaking some lecturing here in their respective fields. My mum, our youngest son, and I met them in Brisbane for a meal. Walking to the restaurant, I was excited to tell my cousin about my recent heritage discoveries. She confirmed, "Yes, we are Palestinian." It made my day.

I wondered how far back my family history went to the people in Palestine. I started digging further, and what I found was interesting.

FAMILY LINK TO THE PAST

A little while after discovering that I am Palestinian, I watched a documentary about Palestinian families who were living in the West Bank that could trace their heritage back to the Jewish people living in Palestine after the Roman conquest of 70 CE and long before the State of Israel was created. Depending on the conqueror, these families changed their names and religion to Islam or Christianity. The Star of David, commonly chiselled above the door of Jewish homes, was purposely defaced.[28] This provided these families with ongoing protection by hiding their original identity. Only those with knowledge could see remains of the defaced Star. Even today, some of these families still secretly undertake Jewish rituals and possess some ornaments and icons, including the menorah of the Jewish religion,

Judaism. Watching this caused me to wonder how far back our family line goes.

Many of us do not ask our loved ones enough questions while they are still alive, especially regarding generational family history and connections. I asked my mum for information regarding the names of the previous generations in the family. During conversations between my mum, her eldest sister and one of their cousins, I had some names. On my grandfather's side my great-great grandfather was Salman Maaloof. My great-grandfather and great-grandmother's names were Saleh A H Salman and Hanna Laham, and my grandfather was Diab Salman. On my grandmother's side, my great-grandfather was Youssef Laham, and my grandmother was Mahdieh Laham. I was a little surprised to see the change from Maaloof to Salman on my grandfather's side. There was no known reason for the surname change. I concluded that maybe somewhere in the past, there was a change of surname to hide their identity and protect themselves from potential persecution or even death from the country's conquerors who were ruling at the time. Whether that was the case, I will never know.

My search had to proceed beyond the family, which would take work. Finding further information would be more like looking for a needle in a haystack. I had seen numerous advertisements for a very popular and heavily promoted ancestry website, so that would be the best place to start. My search finished before it began. I quickly discovered little to no information for those looking for family connections and links to the Middle East. Ancestry sites, including those I used, were only valuable for connections within the United States, the United Kingdom, the European Union, and their offshoots.

Consequently, I only found my grandparent's names recorded in the United States, as they immigrated there from Jordan. First, my grandmother and youngest uncle (who remained single and supported my grandparents)

ABOUT ME

in 1969, with my granddad following once their properties in Amman were sold. Beyond that, no information was found.

General internet searching was the next place I started looking. I started putting in the names I had. Eventually, I found that the Maaloof family name is linked to a Christian clan, the Ghassanids founded in Arabia in approximately 220 CE during the Byzantine occupation.[29]

I also listened to a talk by Palestinian theologian Pastor Munther Isaac from Bethlehem in the West Bank who spoke at the 2012 Christ at The Checkpoint conference.[30] During his talk, he mentioned that he could trace his family history to the Ghassanids, an Arabian Christian tribe, which confirmed my findings and satisfied my curiosity.[31]

I have since connected with a serious researcher of 12 years who has been investigating the history of Christians in Lebanon and Palestine. Through our conversation, it was interesting to learn the vast majority of indigenous ethnoreligious Palestinian Christians, and more widely Levantine Christians, in general, are not connected with Arabia in family history research and not in genetic genealogical DNA testing. It is all 100% Levantine DNA, 0% Arabian. Since the entire Middle East and North Africa were Arabicised, some Palestinians had chosen to start mentioning a connection to the Ghassanids as a way to protect themselves, much like the Jewish people protecting themselves by hiding their identity.

Although I did not discover further family history, I have not given up. A friend recently gave me the name of a person to contact in Nazareth. After speaking with him, it turns out that he knows someone else living in Nazareth who has known the history of the Laham family name for the last 300 years. Unfortunately, due to personal circumstances, the person has been unwell. My contact is waiting for him to be recovered enough so he can be visited. I eagerly await further news.

FURTHER ACADEMIC STUDY

Miko's book began challenging the teaching I had received and reinforced over thirty years within the Christian churches I was connected to. I wanted to learn more, so I searched the internet for more information. I started reading books on the issue, initially and predominantly from a Christian perspective, to gain clarity. I then deviated to look at the issue more broadly. At the time, I did not own many books on what was happening between the Israelis and Palestinians. I also suspected I needed a more formal education to learn more. In early 2015, I realised my current study at Malyon College would not end my formal study. I wondered whether I could undertake further academic study to learn about the Middle East, especially what was happening in Palestine.

I researched to see if any university in Australia offered Middle Eastern study. In 2015, I found that Deakin University in Melbourne, Victoria, was the primary university offering such a course. Thankfully, they also provided a distance mode of study, enabling me to undertake the course entirely online, as I lived in Brisbane. I applied and was thrilled to be invited to start a Bachelor of International Studies, with Middle East and Arabic Language as my majors, in March 2016, five months after I was due to finish a Bachelor of Ministry at Malyon College in Brisbane. In 2020, I dropped the Arabic Language as my second major, as I found the pace too fast to learn the required amount quickly. Without intentionally doing so, I discovered I had completed enough International Relations units to finish it as a major in the remaining time frame, so I added it instead. I finished that degree in November 2021.

2

TWO COVENANTS

According to the Old Testament, God created everything, including our Earth. The creation included all the land and vegetation, sea, air creatures, and land animals. Lastly, God created humanity, which was the pinnacle of His creation. God created Adam first, and then Eve was made from a part of Adam a little later because Adam was lonely without a companion like him. God planned to have an ongoing relationship with His human creation. God would join Adam and Eve for a walk in the garden amidst the creation. However, this relationship only lasted for a relatively short time because man disobeyed God's directive by choosing to eat the produce from a specific tree they were told not to eat:

> The LORD God took the man and put him in the garden of Eden to work it and keep it. And the LORD God commanded the man, saying, "You may surely eat of every tree of the garden, but of the tree of the knowledge of good and evil you shall not eat, for in the day that you eat of it you shall surely die."[32]

This disobedience meant that the relationship between God and humanity ended dramatically, with Adam and Eve being thrown out of the Garden of Eden. From that time, God enacted His plan to reconcile the broken relationship between humanity and Himself. For any form of reconciliation to occur, a Messiah had to be born into the world and killed sacrificially. Through the Messiah's death, humanity's broken relationship with God could be restored.

As mentioned earlier, the Christian Bible is divided into two major parts: the Old and New Testaments. In Judaism, the first five books of the Old Testament are also called the Torah and are in the Jewish Tanakh. Therefore, both the Old Testament and Tanakh contain the first covenant. The first covenant was made between God and one man, Abraham. Then, God reiterated the covenant to Abraham's direct son and subsequent descendants, who became known as the children of Israel. The New Testament contains the second covenant. It gives us the account of the Messiah whom God chose, Jesus, God's son. Through Jesus, the peoples of all the nations could have their broken relationship with God restored. The significant difference between the two covenants is that people under the second covenant are no longer required to live under the same conditions as under the first covenant.

The first covenant provides the text that is used as proof that the Israelis of today are the only ones who have rights to Palestine, through to today and into the future. Therefore, I needed to look at the first covenant.

FIRST COVENANT

The first covenant is predominantly about the children of Israel, the lineage of people that God would use to bring forth the Messiah, who would enable a restoration between humanity and God. It reveals God's laws and ways and how the people should live in obedience to Him so they can receive mercy and blessings and be caretakers of a particular area of land. The people were also warned many times about the suffering they would endure during their lives if they failed to live in obedience to God.

Approximately three to four months after I read Miko Peled's book, I was still feeling very raw about discovering that the Israeli government does not want a two-state solution. However, I was still very excited, having realised that I was half-Palestinian. One day, something happened that surprised me because I was certainly not ready for what I was about to hear.

"But it is Israel's Land"

I went to clean the home of one of my clients. I began sharing excitedly about my Palestinian heritage. My client listened intently, then blurted out, "But it's Israel's land." I kept talking, and she again repeated, "But it's Israel's land." Her gentle yet outspoken attitude stopped me in my tracks. It was the last thing I expected to come out of her mouth. It took all the energy I could muster to avoid tears. The conversation changed quickly after that, and then I left.

I reflected on the conversation later that afternoon and on my client's declaration that the land only belongs to Israel, even today and into the future. This was also the teaching I had received and was grounded within the Christian church I attended for over thirty years. Fortunately, I only partially believed what I was taught as I had doubts that the land was to only belong to the State of Israel. I had read Bible passages linking ownership of the land to obedience, which was rarely preached.

Teaching within sections of Christianity in the United States was clear that only the State of Israel is the rightful owner of the land. That same teaching spread and proliferated sections of the Christian church in Australia and other parts of the world.

Knowing the truth was essential. I had to investigate God's promise to Abraham. Was the State of Israel's claim to all the land of Palestine valid today? Suppose all of Palestine is to belong only to them. Do they also have the divine authority to push any Palestinians permanently out of Palestine by any means possible, whether voluntarily or forced? Worse than that, do they have the divine authority to kill the Palestinians if they refuse to leave?

Two reoccurring assumptions exist when I read some books and articles written by clergy, biblical authors, and academics about the ownership of that specific piece of land. That land retention by Abraham's descendants is forever, and land retention is unconditional. The teaching that Palestine only belongs to Abraham's descendants, and therefore the State of Israel today, originates based on a promise recorded in the book of Genesis in the Old Testament that God originally made to Abraham within the first covenant. This is where it all begins.

Promise to Abraham

Before delving into the promise to Abraham, I found a valuable piece of general advice from Stephen Sizer during some reading.[33] He says we must determine how we understand the writings when looking at religious books. Within Catholicism and before the Protestant Reformation, the content of the Christian Bible was to be interpreted allegorically. After the Reformation, a shift happened so that portions of text would be viewed and understood more literally.[34] This interpretational change has ensured that a tug of war exists, especially in determining how critical passages are viewed and understood by people within the Christian community. Those predominantly within orthodoxy continue to view the Biblical text more allegorically, while those within evangelicalism view the Biblical text more literally. I found this to be the case in the churches I attended.

TWO COVENANTS

Also, throughout the years of listening to many sermons, land ownership is a common theme within the Old Testament. With just a cursory look at the promise, the entire land of Palestine, which currently encompasses the Golan Heights, the State of Israel, the West Bank and Gaza, is to only ever belong to the Jewish people:

> Now the Lord said to Abram, "Go from your country and your kindred and your father's house to the land that I will show you. And I will make of you a great nation, and I will bless you and make your name great, so that you will be a blessing. I will bless those who bless you, and him who dishonours you I will curse, and in you all the families of the earth shall be blessed."
>
> So, Abram went, as the Lord had told him, and Lot went with him. Abram was seventy-five years old when he departed from Haran. And Abram took Sarai, his wife, and Lot his brother's son, and all their possessions that they had gathered, and the people that they had acquired in Haran, and they set out to go to the land of Canaan. When they came to the land of Canaan.
>
> "Then the Lord appeared to Abram and said, "To your offspring I will give this land."[35]
>
> On that day the Lord made a covenant with Abram, saying, "To your offspring I give this land, from the river of Egypt to the great river, the river Euphrates.
>
> And I will give to you and to your offspring after you the land of your sojourning, all the land of Canaan, for an everlasting possession, and I will be their God."[36]

These verses form the foundational teaching and belief within many Christian churches and the State of Israel. This belief is that only the Jewish Israelis may own the land of Palestine and even beyond as an everlasting possession.

However, according to Stephen Sizer, words such as 'everlasting' and 'forever' are not always to be taken literally but are sometimes used for emphasis rather than necessarily to show something eternal. "In Genesis 17:13, for example, circumcision is described as an 'everlasting' covenant, while in Psalm 74:3, the destroyed temple is described as 'everlasting' ruins. The context often shows that a very long time is intended."[37]

For this promise to become a reality, Abraham had to leave his home country, which was Ur of the Chaldees (which was in modern-day Iraq), and go to Canaan:

> Terah took Abram, his son, and Lot the son of Haran, his grandson, and Sarai his daughter-in-law, his son Abram's wife, and they went forth together from Ur of the Chaldeans to go into the land of Canaan, but when they came to Haran, they settled there.[38]

I could see that a great nation would come from Abram, which was fulfilled through the birth of Isaac and subsequent generations. "Now Abraham was one hundred years old when his son Isaac was born to him."[39] Abram was also going to become wealthy:

> Abraham was old, well advanced in age; and the LORD had blessed Abraham in all things. The LORD has greatly blessed my master, and he has become great. He has given him flocks and herds, silver and gold, male servants and female servants, camels, and donkeys.[40]

TWO COVENANTS

More than just becoming wealthy, Abram's name would be great, which it is. The three monotheistic faiths of Islam, Judaism and Christianity hold Abraham in high esteem, with Bruce Feiler cited in Bakhos, "[Abraham], the great patriarch of the Hebrew Bible, is also the spiritual forefather of the New Testament and the grand holy architect of the Koran."[41] And similarly, Bakhos states that according to all three traditions:

> [H]e [Abraham] is the father of monotheism... [and] in each faith he plays a major role as well. To Jews, Avraham (the Hebrew name) is the father of the Jewish people; to Christians, Abraham is the father of the Christian family of faith; and to Muslims, Ibrahim (Arabic) is the father of prophets in Islam.[42]

The phrase 'I will bless those who bless you' means that those who bless Abram, *specifically in person* (emphasis added) at the time, will be blessed, but there is undoubtedly no inference that those who bless the current State of Israel will be blessed some 2000 years later.[43] Similarly, 'And I will curse him who curses you' means that those who curse Abram *specifically in person* (emphasis added) will be cursed at the time. The phrase 'And in you all the families of the earth shall be blessed' can be taken to mean that *through Abraham's lineage, Jesus will come. His birth, death, and resurrection will provide the means for the relationship between God and humanity to be restored*, and there is access to heaven for all humanity, whether they are Jews or Gentiles.[44]

Based on 'Then the LORD appeared to Abram and said, "To your descendants, I will give this land" and "to your descendants, I give this land, from the river of Egypt to the great river, the Euphrates."[45] Abram's direct descendants were to gain the entire land of Canaan as an everlasting possession. In Genesis 17:8, God repeated that the whole land of Canaan is to be an everlasting possession, but possession of the land is based on conditional obedience.

This promise of the land is later confirmed to Isaac, Abraham's son:

> And the LORD appeared to him and said, "Do not go down to Egypt; dwell in the land of which I shall tell you. Sojourn in this land, and I will be with you and will bless you, for to you and to your offspring I will give all these lands, and I will establish the oath that I swore to Abraham your father. I will multiply your offspring as the stars of heaven and will give to your offspring all these lands. And in your offspring, all the nations of the earth shall be blessed, because Abraham obeyed my voice and kept my charge, my commandments, my statutes, and my laws." So Isaac settled in Gerar.[46]

These verses iterate the promise given to Abraham, which included land possession and the potential future restoration of humankind with God for all through the seed of Isaac. I found verse five to be extremely clear that it is because of the ongoing obedience of Abraham to the commandments, the statutes, and the laws of God that God was going to abide by the promise. The promise was then given to Isaac's son Jacob:

> And he dreamed, and behold, there was a ladder set up on the earth, and the top of it reached to heaven. And behold, the angels of God were ascending and descending on it! And behold, the Lord stood above it and said, "I am the Lord, the God of Abraham, your father and the God of Isaac. The land on which you lie I will give to you and to your offspring. Your offspring shall be like the dust of the

TWO COVENANTS

earth, and you shall spread abroad to the west and to the east and to the north and to the south, and in you and your offspring shall all the families of the earth be blessed."[47]

There is nothing new in the promise given to Jacob in the dream. With ownership of the land given to Jacob and his descendants, the number of descendants will be like dust, and lastly, through his seed, all the families of the earth will be blessed. However, I found this interesting:

> "Behold, I am with you and will keep you wherever you go, and will bring you back to this land. For I will not leave you until I have done what I have promised you." Then Jacob awoke from his sleep and said, "Surely the LORD is in this place, and I did not know it." And he was afraid and said, "How awesome is this place! This is none other than the house of God, and this is the gate of heaven."
>
> So early in the morning Jacob took the stone that he had put under his head and set it up for a pillar and poured oil on the top of it. He called the name of that place Bethel, but the name of the city was Luz at the first. Then Jacob made a vow, saying, "If God will be with me and will keep me in this way that I go, and will give me bread to eat and clothing to wear, so that I come again to my father's house in peace, then the Lord shall be my God."[48]

God would look after Jacob, bring him back to the land, and not leave him. Upon waking, Jacob vowed that if God would be with him and provide his needs on his way back to his father's house, the Lord would be his God. God started caring for Jacob, and Jacob then reciprocated that the

Lord would be his God. One could say that God had already made his point through His altercation with Jacob in the dream and the resulting injury to Jacob's hip. The previous interactions clarified that those receiving the promises had to ensure God was their God and were obedient to Him.

Depending on how one looks at these Biblical texts, and even if one is unfamiliar with them, it is easy to see that land possession is conditional and based on the recipient's obedience. Beyond that, one must remember that the land belongs to God, "The earth is the Lord's and the fullness thereof the world and those who dwell therein."[49] So, the covenant could refer to a 'caretaker position', which is how I see it. "The land is Mine; for you are strangers and sojourners with Me."[50] Also, "The land shall not be sold in perpetuity."[51] So, along with 'possessing and keeping' the land, which is conditional on obedience, it was never to remain theirs permanently. The year of Jubilee ensured that if any land exchanged hands, it went back to the one who originally sold it:

> "In this year of jubilee each of you shall return to his property. And if you make a sale to your neighbour or buy from your neighbour, you shall not wrong one another. You shall pay your neighbour according to the number of years after the jubilee, and he shall sell to you according to the number of years for crops."[52]

So, every fifty years, there was to be an economic refresh. Property was returned to those who owned it, debts were cancelled, and enslaved people were released. Also, crops were not harvested that year, meaning the land was given a good rest. The year of Jubilee was never realised.

TWO COVENANTS

Temporary Land Retention and Obedience

I have always considered that wealthy families worldwide are good at keeping what they have worked hard to accumulate, whether by fair or foul means. These families are not about to see their fortune fall into the hands of the next generation, who might foolishly flit it away. It would not surprise me if they intentionally added certain restrictions to ensure this does not happen. Such stipulations could include age restrictions, getting involved in and working up the family business ranks, or marrying within certain circles of society. Whatever methods are used, gaining access to the family fortune takes time and is usually conditional. This is a somewhat familiar scenario.

Apart from the repeated theme of land ownership within the Bible, many verses provide guidelines on how Abraham's descendants were to live. They describe the subsequent rewards they would receive for their obedience and punishments for disobedience.

Recently, while listening again to a sizeable chunk of biblical text, I found it easy to pick up the recurring theme of possession of land being connected to obedience to God. Six small words must be remembered, "*… and I will be their God* (emphasis added).''[53] But that is not all because God says, *"I will dwell among the children of Israel* (emphasis added).[54]

It does not matter how hard one tries to ignore the six words 'and I will be their God'; they cannot be ignored. The descendants of Abraham were to have God as their God. This strongly infers that Abraham's descendants' possession of the land is connected to their obedience to God and His ways. So, this promise is very much conditional, as seen mainly within the Old Testament books of Leviticus and Deuteronomy, which come under the Mosaic covenant but are associated with the Abrahamic covenant.[55] One does not have to read too many verses to see that obedience and its connection to the retention of the land of promise are related. Within these two books, there are many warnings of the consequences of disobedience if Abram's descendants rebelled and were disobedient to God and His ways.[56] Such verses include not only "… lest the land vomit you out when you make it unclean, as it vomited out the nation that was before you", and, "You shall therefore keep all my statutes and all my rules and do them, that the land where I am bringing you to live may not vomit you out."[57] As shown in other passages throughout the Old Testament, obedience is critical in obtaining and keeping the land of promise.

Assault by Assyrians and Babylonians

There is an understanding within some church teachings that the ten northern tribes of the children of Israel were taken captive by the Assyrians because of their ongoing disobedience, with none of them remaining. However, "in his invasion of the Northern kingdom, Tiglath-Pileser III left numerous destroyed towns and cities behind him and took some of the Israelite population into exile."[58] The suggestion is that 27,000 were taken, with the rest remaining.[59] The children of Israel were warned that this was going to happen:

> Hear this word that I take up over you in lamentation, O house of Israel:
> "Fallen, no more to rise,
> is the virgin Israel;
> forsaken on her land,
> with none to raise her up."[60]

The children of Israel, as a people group, were going to suffer. But they would survive:

> For thus says the Lord God:

"The city that went out a thousand
shall have a hundred left,
and that which went out a hundred
shall have ten left
to the house of Israel."⁶¹
"In that day I will raise up
the booth of David that is fallen
and repair its breaches,
and raise up its ruins
and rebuild it as in the days of old,
that they may possess the remnant of Edom
and all the nations who are called by my name,"
declares the Lord who does this.⁶²

David was a king who ruled over the children of Israel. God told David that his throne would endure forever:

> Now when David lived in his house, David said to Nathan the prophet, "Behold, I dwell in a house of cedar, but the ark of the covenant of the LORD is under a tent." And Nathan said to David, "Do all that is in your heart, for God is with you."
>
> ... [F]rom the time that I appointed judges over my people Israel. And I will subdue all your enemies. Moreover, I declare to you that the Lord will build you a house. When your days are fulfilled to walk with your fathers, I will raise up your offspring after you, one of your own sons, and I will establish his kingdom. He shall build a house for me, and I will establish his throne forever. I will be to him a

father, and he shall be to me a son. I will not take my steadfast love from him, as I took it from him who was before you, but I will confirm him in my house and in my kingdom forever, and his throne shall be established forever."[63]

Approximately 250 years after the Assyrian assault on the ten northern tribes, the two remaining tribes of the children of Israel would suffer. This was again because of their ongoing disobedience to God's ways. The fall of Jerusalem by the Babylonians, with Jerusalem falling in September 586 BCE (2 Kings 25:8), resulted in a sizable number of its significant inhabitants being taken to Babylon.[64]

As with the previous assault of the ten northern tribes by the Assyrians, God forewarned the two remaining tribes it was going to happen. But unlike what happened in the north, they were told to buy land:

> Behold, Hanamel, the son of Shallum, your uncle, will come to you and say, 'Buy my field that is at Anathoth, for the right of redemption by purchase is yours.'

> 'Thus says the Lord of hosts, the God of Israel: Take these deeds, both this sealed deed of purchase and this open deed, and put them in an earthenware vessel, that they may last for a long time. For thus says the Lord of hosts, the God of Israel: Houses and fields and vineyards shall again be bought in this land.'[65]

They were told to purchase land because God intended for the leaders who were taken to return to the land. Upon their repentance, most of them eventually returned and promised to follow God and His ways again.

TWO COVENANTS

Roman Occupation Force

From 63 BCE ancient Palestine was under the occupation of the Roman Empire. However, their disobedience led to another attack by an occupation force, with Jesus warning the Jewish people about this upcoming attack, as recorded in the New Testament:

> Jesus left the temple and was going away, when his disciples came to point out to him the buildings of the temple. But he answered them, "You see all these, do you not? Truly, I say to you, there will not be left here one stone upon another that will not be thrown down."[66]

This refers to the Roman attack after the Jewish revolt, which ended in 70 CE, as Jesus prewarned, as recorded in the New Testament.

SECOND COVENANT

The first covenant was primarily between God and one group of people, which originated from one man, Abraham. It relied on strict obedience and following a specific set of rules that God set out. Since they were also to be caretakers of the land, the people needed to live on the land physically. God would also dwell with them. During ancient times, there was a belief that deities were connected to a specific geographical location. This is why, as recorded in the Bible, when Naaman, a Gentile army commander, went to Palestine from Syria to seek healing from leprosy, he returned home, taking two mule-loads of dirt with him.[67] He believed that taking dirt from Palestine to Syria would let him worship God there.

During the first century of the Common Era, all the people who lived in historic Palestine were under Roman occupation. Under this occupation, the second covenant, as recorded in the New Testament, was enacted. I mentioned earlier that King David's throne would be "established forever." Because Jesus was from the line of King David, He would become the one sitting on the throne. Under this new covenant, genuine belief in the historicity of Jesus through His birth, life, death, and resurrection is *all one requires to have a restored relationship with God and* enter heaven when one dies. People no longer needed to live on a specific land to worship God, as they could worship God wherever they were.

Due to an uprising and revolt by the Jewish people against the occupation of the Roman Empire, Jerusalem was besieged for forty-two months, ending in 70 CE. Also, during this time, the city experienced terrible famine. Historian Josephus recorded that at least one woman ate her children to survive.[68] Contrary to popular belief within some Christian circles, although some Jewish people chose to leave historic Palestine at this time, according to Roman documents and local sources, the majority decided to remain.[69] However, in 135 CE, the Bar Kokhba Revolt against the Roman occupation, did see Jewish people leave historic Palestine.

The temple's destruction during the siege reinforced the second covenant that it was no longer necessary for the Jewish people to live on the land to worship God. However, they could continue to provide sustenance for themselves and their families by living and working there. Most of them did so while living alongside other groups.

State of Israel and the Land

The primary verses from the Old Testament or Tanakh that are used to prove that the current Jewish Israelis in the State of Israel are entitled to the land and will be restored to the land is:

> "I will restore the fortunes of my people Israel, and they
> shall rebuild the ruined cities and inhabit them;
> they shall plant vineyards and drink their wine, and they
> shall make gardens and eat their fruit.
> I will plant them on their land,
> and they shall never again be uprooted
> out of the land that I have given them,"
> says the Lord your God.[70]

However, as with previous verses, I learned these verses could also refer to the Assyrian attack of the ten northern tribes in 721 BCE. Restoration would come later. The promise of restoration, as mentioned previously, was:

> "In that day I will raise up
> the booth of David that is fallen
> and repair its breaches,
> and raise up its ruins
> and rebuild it as in the days of old,
> that they may possess the remnant of Edom
> and all the nations who are called by my name,"
> declares the Lord who does this.[71]

The restoration became a reality in the first century before the Roman siege of Jerusalem in 70 CE when Jews and Gentiles were coming to believe in Jesus as their Messiah. Physical restoration of the temple was no longer the focus, as there was no longer a need for animals to be sacrificed for sin. A physical restoration changed to a spiritual restoration, as seen in the New Testament Book of Acts:

And with this the words of the prophets agree, just as it is written,

"'After this I will return,
and I will rebuild the tent of David that has fallen;
I will rebuild its ruins, and I will restore it,
that the remnant of mankind may seek the Lord, and all the Gentiles who are called by my name, says the Lord, who makes these things known from of old'.[72]

After Jesus ascended to heaven, His Jewish apostles and disciples spread the message of reconciliation between humankind and God. Along with Jews accepting Jesus as Messiah, Gentiles embraced Him, with Middle Eastern Arab Jews continuing to live in the land. There have always been Arab Jews who have lived alongside Arab Christians and, later, alongside Arab Muslims within historical Palestine.

However, it is the European Zionist Jews who immigrated to Palestine starting in the late 1880s who were not content to live alongside those who were already living in the land. They intended to take over the whole of Palestine, which they are still in the process of doing today.

3

DEAKIN UNIVERSITY

I was chaffing at the bit with excitement to learn about the Middle East at Deakin University, starting in March 2016. However, it was not until 2017 that I could undertake my first unit, specifically about the Middle East, so I had to be patient. One of my first general but compulsory units was Intercultural Communication, where I learned about the 'Other'.

THE OTHER

Philosopher and activist Edward W Said explains that the concept or term 'Other' "originated from differences between the people of the 'Occident' and 'Orient'." The Occident encompasses Britain, France and the United States of America.[73] The 'Orient' represents the people of present-day Turkey, Greece, the Middle East, and North Africa.[74] He explains the difference between the two groups, "Arabs, for example, are thought of as camel-riding, terroristic, hook-nosed, venal lechers whose undeserved wealth is an affront to real civilisation. Always there lurks the assumption that although the Western consumer belongs to a numerical minority, he is entitled either to own or to expend (or both) the majority of the world's resources. Why? Because he, unlike the Oriental, is a true human being."[75]

Said further considers that "A very large mass of writers, among whom are poets, novelists, philosophers, political theorists, economists, and imperial administrators, have accepted the basic distinction between East and West as the starting point for elaborate theories, epics, novels, social descriptions, and political accounts concerning the Orient, its people, customs, "mind", destiny, and so on."[76] Because of this line of thinking, 'anyone who lived outside of European society was seen as 'less civilised', 'barbaric', 'primitive', and lacking 'culture'. This became the primary thinking behind domination and colonisation.[77]

Our culture determines how we see people as similar or different. Culture, according to Sorrells, which is based on the work of anthropologist Clifford Geertz, is:

> "a system of shared meanings that are passed from generation to generation through symbols that allow human beings to communicate, maintain, and develop an approach and understanding of life… [or] make sense, express, and give meaning to our lives."[78]

Our view and understanding of culture determine how we look at people groups and decide whether or not they are 'like' us or the 'other'. This is based on "socially constructed hierarchy such as culture, race, class, gender, nationality, religion, age and physical abilities among others."[79] I did not know before this unit that there is an underlying cultural bias that may even be unknown to individuals, which can cause people to be discriminatory in their thinking and actions towards other people groups. While in shops, my husband hears staff talking down to or ignoring customers who do not originate from a predominantly 'white' based country, which disgusts him.

I remember learning that 'Other' thinking also made it acceptable for indigenous populations to be targeted and potentially killed, to where they can become close to being extinct or extinct. The Spanish colonisers developed a racial hierarchy. Being white, they placed themselves at the top of the ladder and then put other people groups on it based on their skin colour. To them, the whiteness of a person determined racial purity.

One point that stood out above all the others was a statement by Lopez stating, "This hierarchical system developed to the stage where in North America, European Americans or Whites instituted the 'one drop' rule, where if one had just one drop of non-white blood, they were not White."[80] Hearing this shocked me, and I have not forgotten it. I have watched movies over the years, including the 1977 mini-series Roots. As a young teen, I was certainly unaware that the 'other' is the origin of such deplorable treatment as slavery. I also learned that among some Christians, when slavery was expected, they considered it acceptable.

Although learning about the 'other' was emotionally hard, I finally understood just a little about the reasoning behind the inhumane treatment and even the killing of Indigenous people groups, not only here in Australia but in many other countries. It also proved invaluable when immersed in the university unit, Historical Foundations of the Middle East. I quickly came to understand why people of the Middle East are treated with such disdain, even today. It is because white Europeans were the ones who predominantly explored the world, and the peoples of the Middle East are various shades of brown. Therefore, people from the Middle East would not be treated as equals based on this hierarchical system. Before this unit of study, I had only learned a little about Mesopotamia and Sumer in the Middle East while in lower high school.

I remember thinking that my university studies would help fill a big hole in my knowledge of history. Since Australia is part of the British colony, the history that is predominantly taught throughout the primary and high school education system is British and European-centric-at least when I went through school. I realised that anyone who wants to learn a different history must seek it out through higher academic learning or private research, which I did and continue to do.

I was excited and encouraged to learn that when Europe was going through the Dark Ages, which was predominantly when the Roman Catholic church authorities were burning books that were not religiously based, it was the Arabs, and particularly the Muslims, who kept civilisation alive by moving books to Spain. They even translated some of the books from Latin and Ancient Greek.[81] But I was angry and upset when I learned through a lecture on Orientalism that European explorers and historians portrayed Arabs as uneducated, filthy, thieving, and worse than animals.[82]

As a people group, Palestinians are easily considered the 'other' because they are different to the Europeans, not only because of the 'one drop' rule but also because they are seen as being uncultured and not as highly educated as Europeans. The European Jews who migrated to Palestine and then to the declared State of Israel after 1948 would have considered the Palestinians as uneducated and an unwanted group of people in the land. Therefore, as a people group, it had to be eliminated.

Through much reading, I have concluded that not only do the Palestinian people of today suffer under colonialism, but thousands of years ago, the non-Jewish Arab people groups in ancient Palestine also suffered at the hands of the Jewish Arabs, as they were then known.

COLONIALISM

While researching the internet and reading through sections of the Old Testament, I saw similarities to what I learned about modern-day colonialism. Since the 1500s, various kingdoms and nations have undertaken modern colonialist exploits. These include the British Empire's initial push into four African areas: Gambia, the Gold Coast, Sierra Leone and Cape Colony.[83] Later, the British spread further to other regions, with Egypt, Northern and Southern Rhodesia, Nyasaland, Nigeria and British East Africa all becoming part of the British Empire.[84] The British also infiltrated China, beginning with the Opium Wars of 1839-1842, which forced trade between the British Empire and China.[85]

Our youngest son studied Chinese history at university and came home telling us information about the Opium Wars. During his conversations with Chinese peers and friends, he found that many knew little about their history or the knowledge he tried to share. To me, the Chinese government intentionally hides the truth from their people. We could not decide why they would hide such important history from its citizens. Eventually, we concluded, rightly or otherwise, that by not telling their people this vital part of their history, the Chinese government might have been pushing aside their country's perceived humiliation, which was aroused by their defeat. Remembering back to my university studies, and while doing the unit on China in 2020, I learned that after the Opium Wars, the Chinese had to pay reparations to the British, even though the British had invaded China, and worse. An incredible injustice.

The Spanish invaded South America, which began with Christopher Columbus 'discovering' what became the Bahamas in 1492. The suffering of Indigenous people groups is widespread in many nations. Just a few of these countries include Canada, the United States, Australia, South America and the Caribbean.

The Middle East has predominantly suffered under the colonial exploits of the French, British, and Russians. In recent years, the region has endured under the influence and meddling of the United States because of its abundance of oil, a valuable commodity.

These empires assumed they had the right to think they were better than anyone else. Even religion has validated the killing off and dispossession of people groups, including Christians under Catholicism, Muslims under Islam, and Jews under early Judaism in ancient Palestine.[86]

Further, the West Papuans and Palestinians are just two people groups that are continuing to suffer because of living under colonialism, with both peoples still trying to gain their freedom and independence to establish a state of their own. Through my learning, the apparent main issue at hand with colonialist activities is that "the people living in these regions were largely neglected and ignored before occupation."[87]

ANCIENT ISRAEL AND COLONIALISM

In ancient times, and with the promise of gaining the land that encompasses the whole of the current area of Palestine and further beyond, ongoing obedience to God was required. This obedience meant living in a certain way, and it also meant killing various people groups that were already living in the land. One day, I applied what I had learned from my university studies to what I understood about the events recorded in the Bible, which were based on my reading and hearing years of sermons being preached. I could see that the events recorded in the Old Testament appeared no different from any other colonial exploits undertaken by various European nations and the British Empire. The children of Israel would invade cities, and at times, they would kill all men, women, children, and livestock.

When I contemplated these killings, something did not seem right. After talking to a cleric friend, I realised I was looking at the events in the Bible as historical facts, a practice encouraged within sections of the Christian church. I mentioned this earlier when I referred to Stephen Sizer and his thoughts on how we should look at religious texts. The churches I belonged to encouraged a literal reading of the Bible. However, Biblical authors did not intend to provide literal historical information, which was confirmed by archaeological evidence. This suggests that the Old Testament and Torah were not to be taken literally or understood as historically accurate texts but as lessons and metaphors for human connection to the spiritual world.[88]

The Bible was written when the children of Israel were in Babylon in exile. They were losing their faith in God and needed encouragement not to lose hope. My friend implied that although the events of the Bible were not recorded to provide an accurate historical account, we can still accept them as gifts from God. Also, since books are ancient and oriental, the intended meaning of what is written may differ from our understanding of the modern use of the same words.

Also, the events throughout Scripture that are considered historical were based on oral tradition because most of the population were illiterate. As many of us know, we must record events when they occur; otherwise, we may forget details, causing the recollection of the event to become inaccurate. A classic example that shows this well is when children play the game called Chinese Whispers. By the time the original story has gone through all the children, it is different to what was told to the first child at the beginning of the game. This is even with no deliberate additions or changes by a mischievous child.

With an emphasis placed on the literal understanding of Biblical texts, I understand that today, some Palestinian Christians within evangelical churches ignore significant chunks of the Old Testament. This is because of the recorded killings of people groups within its pages. They read those sections literally and as an absolute fact. For them, reading it is too painful. All it does is reinforce in their minds, at least, that their end will be the same, that the Israeli government will eventually kill them off or force them to leave Palestine permanently, never to return. What a cruel way to have to live. Live in fear that one day your life will be taken away from you or you will be forced out of your home, all because of words on a page of a religious book that people believe is historical fact.

The central event in the last one hundred years that has brought pain and suffering to the Palestinian people is the Al Nakba.

AL NAKBA

David Ben-Gurion, the head of the Jewish Agency, declared on 14 May 1948 in Tel-Aviv that the State of Israel was a nation. The Jewish Agency was set up in 1929 to help establish a Jewish homeland within the parameters of Zionism.[89] The following day, 15 May 1948, Al Nakba or 'The Catastrophe' began what has remained a significant date on the Palestinian calendar. On this day, the Israeli authorities began the forced expulsion of Palestinian Arabs from their homes, villages, and towns. Within a short time, between "750,000 and 800,000 men, women and children were forced out of their homes. There were also 80 massacres, with 15,000 killed."[90] Many Palestinians expected to return home within a few weeks. Unfortunately, the weeks extended to months, which has extended to years, with expulsions continuing today, 76 years later. The events in Gaza since 8 October 2023 are being called a second Nakba as 75 percent of the 2.2 million Palestinians were forced out of their homes and pushed towards Rafah. Israel's endgame is to make them exit through the Rafah Crossing into Egypt.[91] As of 8 February 2024, Egypt has resisted Israel's determination.

In the early days of the 1948 expulsions, many Palestinians only took a few possessions with them. One possession that they kept with them was the key to their home. Today, decades later, many still hope that they, or at least their surviving generations, will be able to return.

As many Palestinians fled their homes, European Jewish families who were pouring into the new state in the aftermath of World War II took over the ownership of the homes. However, any permanently vacated homes underwent demolition. Often, towns were entirely and utterly erased from the land, with no structures remaining. Towns were renamed if they survived erasure, which 531 did not.[92] Eighty-five percent of the Palestinian population suffered displacement.[93] Miko Peled's family could have lived in one of these 'vacated' homes. However, his mother refused to accept it as "it was unbearable to her that she might sit sipping coffee in the home of another woman who was now, with her frightened or wounded family, sitting, hungry and miserable, in a refugee camp."[94] Many other families put aside their conscience and accepted any home given.

A second significant dispossession happened in 1967, with somewhere between 250,000-300,000 Palestinians being thrown out of their homes. For some, this was their second dispossession.[95] I have extended family members directly affected by the 1948 Al-Nakba or the 1967 Al-Naksa dispossessions.

My grandparents were engaged in 1928 and were married the following year, 1929. Over the years, my mum has told me a few times that my grandfather was a progressive thinker. With the influx of Zionist Jews from various European countries into historical Palestine, and with the Balfour Declaration in 1917, with the Jews being promised a state, it was only a matter of time before it would become a reality. My grandfather would have expected that life for the indigenous Palestinians was going to become even more challenging than it had already become. He would have also been looking ahead to when he would have a family and how the future would be for his children. The same year they were married, they left

CROSSING OVER

Nazareth for Amman, Jordan, after my grandfather secured employment as the chauffeur for the British Ambassador to Jordan. My mother and all her siblings were born in Amman, with my mum being the second youngest of seven children, four boys and three girls.

A first cousin and their family sought refuge with their aunt and uncle (my grandparents) when they were forced to leave Jerusalem in 1948. Mum recently spoke with her cousin, who said that their father expected they would be able to return home within two weeks, but as history has shown us, returning home has never been permitted by the Israeli government since that time. This family of cousins lived with them for three to six months until they could find work and a place for their family to live in Amman. The house was full of people during that time. One of my mum's cousins eventually emigrated, and one now lives in Melbourne, Australia. Sadly, other relatives had to seek refuge within my grandparents' welcoming home during those early years of the dispossession. Some stayed in Jordan, while others left the Middle East altogether, seeking a new life afield.

Another of my mum's cousins ended up living in the United States after his family was forced to flee Palestine in 1948. He died in February 2023. When his children were sorting through his possessions, they found their father's original key to his home in Palestine.

During the middle of May 2023, not long after hearing of the death of my mum's cousin, I heard about a four-part mini-series called 'The Promise', which is based on a true story. I watched it in one sitting. The series was about a British officer, Len, stationed in Palestine during the years leading up to and shortly after Israel became a state. He became friends with a Palestinian Arab man, Abu Hassan Mohammed, who with his family was forced to leave their home in 1948. Before they left their home, Abu Hassan Mohammed gave their house key to his son Hassan to look after. During their departure, Hassan ends up separated from his family. Len looks for him and eventually finds him and other Arabs fighting some Jews. Hassan gets shot, but before he dies, he gives the house key to Len, who promises to return it to his friend. Unfortunately, Len could not find his friend to return his key, which haunted him for the rest of his life.

Had my grandparents chosen to remain in Nazareth, their fate would have been somewhat precarious as Nazareth became occupied on 16 July 1948.[96] However, due to Nazareth being a significant religious town and to boost international support for the new state, the Israeli government did not cleanse the city of Palestinians.[97] Nazareth was under military rule from 1948 to 1966, much like the Occupied Territories is today. The Palestinians in Nazareth were eventually given Israeli citizenship, which was second-class citizenship, as they were not given the same privileges as Jewish Israeli citizens, even today.

Annually during May, Palestinians (and those who want to stand in solidarity with them) hold rallies and marches in various cities around the world, calling for justice and freedom for Palestinians in Palestine and for the ability of those in the diaspora to be able to return home if they want to do so. Palestinians are currently prevented from returning by the Israeli government. These gatherings are usually mentioned in the news, even in a small way. I have noticed that it seems to be the one time in the year when Palestinians can demonstrate and hold rallies without suffering adverse reactions from others.

Nobody ever wants to suffer from expressing what they believe. Even throughout the last ten years, since discovering that I am half Palestinian, I have chosen carefully who I share that information with. I shared earlier about the time I was cleaning in a client's home, and she made it quite clear that she believed the land was only to belong to Israel. As time progresses, I am becoming bolder in sharing this knowledge.

CROSSING OVER

When I heard about what appeared to be the blatant and targeted killing of Al Jazeera journalist Shireen Abu Akleh on Wednesday, 11 May 2022, I was momentarily shocked but not surprised to hear 20 journalists, who included 18 Palestinians and two foreign correspondents up to then, had been targeted and killed by the Israeli government since 2000, with no charges being laid.[98] A few days later, on Saturday, 14 May 2022, the Brisbane city Al-Nakba remembrance rally was held. It also became a time to collectively remember Shireen, who was greatly loved not only by all Palestinians, whether Christian or Muslim, but by many others, particularly in the Middle East. Shireen had worked for many years to provide truthful news of what was occurring in Palestine and other regional areas. She was also described as a fantastic role model for the upcoming generation.

Although my husband and I had previously attended fundraising events to help Palestinians in Palestine, particularly for those living in Gaza, where life is the hardest, it was the first time that we had attended an Al-Nakba rally. Due to the potentially rainy weather, the number of people who participated in the Brisbane rally was less than usual. After listening to spokespeople from various organisations that advocate for Palestinians and from Palestinians who have been directly or indirectly affected by the Al-Nakba, it was time for a peaceful march. With those leading the procession holding banners and those following holding flags up high, we began our march. Our voices rang out in unison, declaring the future hope for Palestine. Members of the Police Force shortened the distance of the march. They would only let it proceed for approximately 400m, so the march finished prematurely. Shortly afterwards, everyone in attendance disbanded and headed for home. During the rally, my husband and I decided that we would attend as many future rallies as possible that are related to the Palestinians, whether it is in Brisbane, where we are now, or elsewhere.

Thinking back ten years at the time of writing, I would never have thought I would be involved in such events one day. For me, discovering I am Palestinian, as well as seeing what I believe to be the truth as seen in the Bible, had propelled me to march the streets to see freedom for my people who have been oppressed for so long.

Upon returning home, news of Shireen Abu Akleh's funeral procession was broadcast. Unlike an average funeral procession, news reports showed the pallbearers being beaten by members of the Israeli Police Force, with the coffin nearly being dropped. It was also the first time that both the Muslim and Christian communities joined together for a funeral. This was because of the high regard both communities had for Shireen. Many people from across the globe have rightly expressed their disgust at the Israeli police actions.

We attended the next Nakba commemoration rally in May 2023. Then, in light of what has been occurring in Gaza since 8 October 2023, we have attended most of the rallies held in Brisbane and will continue to join with thousands of others as often as we can, with only work commitments or sickness preventing our attendance. In the early weeks since that date, and due to the ferocity being unleashed upon Palestinians by Israel, the word Nakba is again being mentioned. Once again, Palestinians were being displaced from their homes and being forced to move elsewhere. When will it end, and when will there be justice and freedom for Palestinians in Palestine?

On Sunday, 19 May 2024, we again gathered in the city for a rally and a march. We listened to numerous testimonies of the effects that the 1948 Nakba had on people's families and lives. Only this time, thousands of people gathered together. It was officially declared the biggest Nakba rally held in Brisbane. The day was emotionally heavy as, once again, Palestinians in Gaza are going through another Nakba, as they have been told many times over the last seven and a half months to move. Initially from their homes, then from shelters in schools, hospitals, with other friends and relatives and then tents. All of the places that should have been safe for them to move to have been bombed by the Israeli Defence Forces.

4

PALESTINE AND PALESTINIANS

Throughout my adult life, I heard prominent opinions regarding historical Palestine and Palestinians: that as a nation-state, they have never existed or they never had independent borders or a proper ruling government like a real nation-state; that as a people, they did not exist. Even within sections of the Christian church, it was common to hear that Palestinians were just another name for the Philistines of the Bible.

I had never really spent any decent amount of time researching this people group I belonged to, so I was determined to do so. During one of the weekly online university seminars for the unit Key Concepts in International Relations in 2021, the bookshelf behind the lecturer attracted my attention. Many of the book spines' titles needed clarification, but I recognised one book on Gaza because I already owned it. I could also make out the word 'Palestine' on the spine of another book. Naturally, I had to own any book with the word Palestine. Plus, since my lecturer owned it, I assumed the book must be worth reading. I contacted him to get the book details and ordered a copy of 'Palestine: A Four Thousand Year History' by

Nur Masalha. Since I only had one trimester of my degree to complete, I did not start reading it until early 2022, but I am so glad that I did, as I have learned so much history about Palestine and the Palestinian people. It is a book I will keep referring to as it contains so much information that I consider worthwhile.

When I started reading Masalha's book, I had already intended to undertake this project, even though the initial seed thought was planted in 2014 while reading Miko Peled's book because of the truth it contained and its profound impact on my life.

A PLACE CALLED PALESTINE

Whenever the place called Palestine is mentioned, I have often found that there is little mention of the land before the time of the Roman Empire, which is considered to be the time when it received its name. However, the name 'Palestine' was commonly used from 1300 BC, according to historian Nur Masalha. The name Palestine came from the word Peleset, first used in Egyptian sources relating to the reign of Ramesses II and III during the Late Bronze Age.[99] Masalha further explains that before the Egyptian use of the name Palestine, the area:

> [W]as referred to by its traditional names of Renetu and Djahi, with Retenu used to refer to the region along the eastern shore of the Mediterranean, and was divided into three sub-regions: Amurru, in the north, Lebanon sometimes referred to as Upper Retenu, which lay south of Amurru and north of the Litani river, and Djahi the southernmost part of the Retenu, which referred to the

region south of the Litani to Ascalon, as far as the Rift Valley to the east.[100]

Peleset was a commonly used name. Then, from the late Bronze Era, Palestine began to be used, as seen in Assyrian inscriptions after the Egyptians used the name.[101] Palestine was used administratively during Roman rule, but "by that time, the name 'Palestine' was more than a millennium old and had subsequent currency."[102] I can finally refute the claims that the Romans initiated the name Palestine. The name Palestine remained and only changed once the State of Israel existed.

Until I went to university, I had never realised that nation-states like those which exist today are relatively new. European Imperialism brought about the global spread of nation-states and the signing of numerous treaties, including the Treaty of Westphalia of 1648, which ended thirty years of war in Europe. Eventually, these treaties between nation-states led to the forming of the United Nations and the system we have today.[103] Contrary to some belief, Palestine was legitimate, and it did have a government and authority:

> "Palestine was a distinct administrative unit and a formal province for over a millennium. This was first as the joint Roman province of 'Syria Palestina' three Palestina (135-390 A.D.) and subsequently as a province separate from Syria, in the form of three administrative presences of a Byzantine Palestine: Palaestina Prima or Palastine I, Palaestina Secunda and Palaestina Salutaris or Palaestina Terria. Moreover, these three provinces were effectively governed politically, militarily and religiously from Palaestina Prima as a 'three-in-one' polity from the 4th century until the early 7th century. And once again

> Palestine existed as a separate administrative entity, in the form of the administrative Arab Muslim province of Jund Filastin, [which] existed for nearly four and a half centuries from the Muslim conquest of Palestine and 637-638, until the Latin Crusade invasion of 1099 AD."[104]

Through this discovery, I realised that Palestine was not unlike any other patch of land that has undergone countless invasions and conquests over centuries. Consequently, it had been virtually impossible for the indigenous people living there to form an independent governing authority. I also concluded that the current ruling government in the State of Israel and its Occupied Territories is the most current conqueror and victor and currently controls the narrative.

PALESTINIANS

I often hear it said, "Palestinians do not exist. They are an invented group of people that Yasser Arafat created to encourage some fake nationalism." Or they are simply another name for the Philistines. Yes, Yasser Arafat started a movement in modern times to increase momentum for the dream of an independent Arab state in Palestine. However, the Philistines are just one group of people who lived in Palestine.

Palestinian Arabs are Jewish, Muslim and Christian

There was always a mixture of different groups living within Palestine with varying religious beliefs. These groups, to name a few, not exclusively, include the Philistines, Jebusites, Hittites, Nabateans, and Hebrews, who lived relatively peacefully with each other as neighbours.[105] With the conquests of the land over the years and into more recent centuries, there was a need for groups to preserve one's life. The groups morphed and became associated with the more dominant groups of Arab Muslims, Christians, and Jews, with Christians being the minority group.

My mum grew up in the Middle East during the 1940s and 1950s, and hearing stories from her, I knew that there was a mixture of Christians and Muslims living in the area where their family lived. However, based on what I have heard, and particularly within Western opinion, non-Jewish people within the Middle East are Arab and, therefore, Muslim, which I consider to be an incorrect assumption. Yes, the number of Christians within the Middle East has severely diminished and is continuing to diminish, but they remain in the Middle East.

Such thinking also pervades the Christian church. I often heard the same thing mentioned in sermons when Isaac and Ismael were mentioned. Congregants learned that the people in the Middle East were connected either to Isaac or to Ishmael, with Isaac being connected to the Jews, Judaism, and today's State of Israel, and Ishmael being connected to Arabs and Islam. Yes, most of the Arab people in the Middle East are Muslim, but not all. The Ishmael connection is one construction.

Within Palestine alone, 85 percent of the non-Jewish population practises Islam and six percent practise Christianity. In the State of Israel in 2022, 18.1 percent, or 1.7 million residents, were Muslim, and 2 percent, or 170,000, were Christian.[106] For those in the Occupied Territories, it is sometimes hard to find accurate numbers regarding its population status. From what I could see, 85.2 percent of the population is Muslim, and approximately 4 percent is Christian.[107]

Because of the false assumption that people within the Middle East are Jewish or Muslim, it may not even occur to many people who live beyond the Middle East that there is a small group of Christians in the Middle East, let alone within the Palestinian community.

CROSSING OVER

Foreigners in the Land

Benjamin Netanyahu, the current Israeli Prime Minister, believes that all of Palestine belongs to the Jewish Israelis, based on what he sees as the Jewish people's connection to Abraham. In his speech at the Begin-Sadat Centre at Bar-University on June 14, 2009, he said:

> But let me first say that the connection between the Jewish people and the Land of Israel has lasted for more than 3500 years. Judea and Samaria, the places where Abraham, Isaac, and Jacob, David and Solomon, and Isaiah and Jeremiah lived, are not alien to us. This is the land of our forefathers.[108]

Prime Minister Netanyahu continues to use passages from within the first covenant to justify this belief in action on the ground against Palestinians. During Operation Swords of Iron, which began on 8 October 2023, he reminded the soldiers before they started their ground offensive into Gaza. He said, "You must remember what Amalek has done to you, says our Holy Bible." Prime Minister Netanyahu was referring to 1 Samuel 15:3 Now go and smite Amalek, and utterly destroy all that they have, and spare them not; but slay both man and woman, infant and suckling, ox and sheep, camel and asses.[109]

Likewise, the Likud ruling party's original platform of 1977 also believes the Jewish people's right to the land of Israel is eternal and indisputable and linked with the right to security and peace. "Any part between the Sea and the Jordan River will not be relinquished to any foreign administration; it will only be under Israeli sovereignty."[110]

Consequently, since Palestinians are not Jewish and considered 'foreigners', they are also not welcome. With 85 percent of Palestinians within

Palestine being Muslim, it appears easy for the Israeli government to frame what is happening in Palestine as a religious struggle rather than their unwillingness to share the land with any people group other than their own. Especially now, since 98 to 99 percent of the population in Gaza is Muslim, it is advantageous for the Israeli government to make this a religious war where it is Jews versus Muslims.[111] That narrative was reinforced when Israeli Ambassador to the UN Gilad Erdan the attack in Israel on 7 October 2023 to the attack in the United States on 11 September 2001 by Muslims, saying, "This is Israel's 9/11."[112] This statement was made as it was referred to as the worst day of Israeli deaths since the Holocaust, and there were more deaths per capita than what happened on 11 September 2001.[113]

Since Palestinians are Muslims, Christians, belong to another faith, or hold no belief, they are to be removed from the land by any means possible. The Bible is quoted to justify the Israeli government's position of being able to eliminate the Palestinian people. However, it appears they conveniently forget verses from the Old Testament, which say the total opposite:

> "When a foreigner resides among you in your land, do not mistreat them. The foreigner residing among you must be treated as your native-born. Love them as yourself, for you were foreigners in Egypt. I am the Lord your God."[114]

I believe in following the Golden Rule, "So whatever you wish that others would do to you, do also to them…" which means treating others the same way you would want to be treated.[115] Professor Mazin Qumsiyeh, a Christian, has extensively studied many religions and found that many have a similar ethic, with none outworking it more than those of the Muslim faith.

I accept his conclusion based on my experience as a Christian of being welcomed and accepted by Muslims without any underhanded or ulterior motives. I said to my husband recently that I feel more comfortable being around Muslims than most of the Christians I know. Furthermore, I feel embarrassed about the way that some Christians treat others. They appear only interested in getting converts.

Unfortunately, the portrayal of those from the Orient is less than favourable, as previously discussed. Also, if one looks at how individuals are treated in some predominantly Muslim-governed countries, it does not inspire anyone to consider that religion. I think especially of the way that women in some countries are treated in such a demeaning way. There needs to be more equality between men and women. In some countries, girls are not permitted to be educated. Women must be escorted and cannot be seen alone with males apart from family members. If a woman marries a man from a specific country, she may be dissuaded from visiting their husband's country since there have been cases where the husband decided to stay, and the wives were not allowed to leave.

Also, the activities of isolated extremist groups of Muslims who are accused of undertaking activities that are contrary to the way most Muslims live cause all Muslims to be wrongfully charged as being deceivers with suspect motives.

I consider some Christians today to be extremists. Their theology thrusts them to endorse the current genocide, which started on 8 October 2023. Yet, strangely, I do not see them devalued as humans like Muslims appear to be.

Based on the Golden Rule, all Palestinians within the whole of Palestine and throughout the diaspora should be welcomed by the Israeli government and the Jewish Israelis, and they should be treated equally. However, they and those who support the State of Israel ignore those verses. Some individuals would rather believe the theology they have been taught about gaining an easy life rather than treating others well, which should be a priority above narrow theology.

In 2015, while reading the book Through My Enemy's Eyes, I realised that Palestinians have due cause to, "… take offence at the notion that according to certain extreme rabbinical attitudes, Messianic Jews and others sometimes regard them as strangers in the land… and they have to justify their presence in their homeland."[116]

All Palestinians believe that they have a right to live in Palestine, whether they are Christian, Muslim, have another belief, or are secular. They are all humans and have the right to be treated like everyone else, not as second-class people.

5

PALESTINE AND JEWISH ISRAELIS

My husband was working for a community radio station approximately fifteen years ago. He was away installing a low-band radio transmitter in Wee Waa in New South Wales. While staying with a farmer, he met and spoke with two Jewish Israeli men who would periodically come to Australia from Israel to work on the farm. During the conversation, my husband said, "You've got fans in the Christian church", to which a quick retort came back, "Haha, chosen people." These Israelis believe such a more accurate statement could not have been said.

I thought about the Palestinians continuing to live as an occupied people, which is now in its 77th year. The conditions under which they live will not remain static, but from what I can see, they will continue to deteriorate. As they do, I wondered whether public opinion could shift away from the Jewish Israelis and towards the Palestinians. This shift would not be by the current supporters of Israel but by the younger next generation of people who do not accept that what is happening in Palestine has any moral and legal grounds for it to continue.

A significant section of the broader Christian church, and especially the Evangelical church, believes that Palestine belongs to the Jewish people. Christians belong to lobby groups, particularly in the United States, which can influence governmental policies. The United States government does not need to be influenced as it has a close relationship with the State of Israel and is holding fast to its current foreign and domestic policies within the Middle East, which prioritise Israel, security and oil.

Since I knew nothing really about the broader Christian community's thoughts about the State of Israel and the Jewish Israelis, I started hitting the computer keyboard once again. Most of the information I could find on the church's view of Israel comes from the Evangelical church's perspective. I surmised that this is probably because of the strength of the Evangelical church within the United States. I also looked to the broader population to find out the current position within the population. Surveys I found were never related to just the State of Israel and the Jewish Israelis but were always compared to the Palestinians in Palestine.

EVANGELICAL CHRISTIAN VIEW OF JEWISH ISRAELIS AND PALESTINIANS IN PALESTINE

In May 2022, Gallop conducted a poll revealing that 86% of white evangelicals said they felt warmly towards Israelis, and 68% were favourable towards the Israeli government. Some 70% also believe that God gave the land of Palestine to the Jewish people, while only 32% of the United States Jews felt God gave the land to the Jewish people. They were only 37% favourable towards the Palestinians, even though some are also fellow Christians.[117] Two months later, a Pew Research poll revealed that 80%

of white evangelicals felt warmly towards Israel, compared with 61% of white non-evangelicals and Black protestants was 43%.[118] Based on my own experience and these figures, it is apparent that significant numbers of white people within Christian Evangelicalism eagerly believe what they hear preached without question.

The modern State of Israel is a secular state. One of its biggest Christian Evangelical supporters is the United States Cornerstone's Pastor John Hagee.[119] He also heads Christians United for Israel, a Christian Zionist organisation. The group is also one of the most prominent groups that lobby the United States government, "with over 10 million members, who are predominantly white evangelicals and make up around 14 percent of the United States population."[120] The primary and simple rationale for his emphatic support of the State of Israel originates (as previously discussed) from Genesis 12:1-3 and some fundamental core beliefs that exist.

First, the entire land promised to Abraham and his descendants is a perpetual and 'everlasting' promise. However, Stephen Sizer suggests that "within Evangelicalism, words such as 'everlasting', 'eternal' and 'forever' are mainly used literally when there is a reference to the giving of land, Jerusalem, or the temple to the Jewish people."[121] I reiterate Stephen Sizer's suggestion that "sometimes the immediate context of a passage shows that a 'forever', 'eternal', and 'forever' is not always to be taken literally with context often showing that a very long time is intended."[122]

Again, God gave the land as a gift in the first place. The land was God's land, and the children of Israel were to share it with others because, according to Leviticus 25:23, "The land is Mine; and you are strangers and sojourners with Me."[123] Berry states, "The Promised Land is not a permanent gift. It is 'given', but only for a time…"[124]

Second, I would argue that the blessings and curses related directly to Abraham are not to be applied directly to all their descendants, up to the establishment of the State of Israel, through to today, and even into the future.

Last, according to Christians United for Israel's eschatology, the group promotes a belief that "the modern state of Israel and the gathering of millions of Jewish people [from around the world] are signs that Jesus will soon return to Jerusalem."[125] Journalist Grace Halsell believed that Zionism was a cult.[126] She went twice to Israel as a part of Jerry Falwell-led pilgrimages in 1983 and 1985.[127] Grace quotes a pilgrim on the trip, "The Jews must own all of the land promised by God before Christ can return. The Arabs have to leave this land because this land belongs only to the Jews. God gave all of this to the Jews."[128] I have heard portions of this quote or versions of it within the Evangelical church many times.

Consequently, "[Christian] Zionism functions to justify and support the ongoing humiliation and dispossession, not primarily for the sake of the Jews, but to hasten the return of Christ and the apocalyptic 'End Times', in which Jews will be given their last opportunity to convert to Christ and be saved or to be condemned to Hell."[129] Therefore "acts that excuse or accept Israeli settler colonialism, such as the Abraham Accords and the 2018 decision to move the United States Embassy from Tel Aviv to Jerusalem, are to be applauded."[130] Whether these Christians are aware of it or not, this dogged support of the State of Israel means that all Palestinians are to be ethnically cleansed from the land to make room for the Jewish people immigrating to Palestine.

When Palestinians in Palestine and others question Zionist Christian beliefs, supporters of Israel may think Palestinians and their supporters want the state of Israel destroyed. When I was reading the book The Other Side of The Wall by Munther Isaac, he answers this type of thinking by saying, "Just because Israel believes that it has a divine right to the land

and prophecy is being fulfilled, which is based on their interpretation of the Bible, it does not mean that there is a call for the destruction and eradication of the State of Israel. Palestinians are asking that international law and human rights be applied."[131] He does not consider he is asking for too much.

Furthermore, while attending an event in Brisbane on 16 December 2023, the Palestinian Ambassador in Australia, Izzat Salah Abdulhadi, who was born and raised in Nablus, spoke about the continued desire to have peace within all Palestine with ongoing work with the hope that there will be a separate Palestinian State alongside the State of Israel. I do not find that any Palestinians speak about a desire to eradicate Israelis or their State. I consider it a false assumption that for Palestinians to want peace and justice means the destruction of Israel.

I wonder whether Evangelical Christians who support the State of Israel fully understand what is happening in Palestine. I did not, so I suspect that many others do not. I did not know that land was being appropriated from Palestinians for the building of Jewish settlements. I did not realise houses were being demolished and villages were being razed. I did not realise that checkpoints, restrictions on travel, night raids and administrative detentions are occurring. I did not know that an ethnic cleansing at best or a slow genocide at worst is happening to the Palestinian people as a whole. All I heard was that a giant wall was built that divided two people groups to stop suicide bombers.

I also wanted to know the general public's thoughts about the Israelis.

PALESTINE AND JEWISH ISRAELIS

PUBLIC'S VIEW OF JEWISH ISRAELIS AND PALESTINIANS IN PALESTINE

In a Pew Research report of 11 July 2022, 55 percent of Americans view Israel favourably, while 42 percent say they do not have favourable views towards the Jewish Israelis.[132] The same report also showed support for the Israeli government, with 48 percent recorded. Regarding the Israeli people, 67 percent of those surveyed felt favourable towards them.[133]

Figures from polls that were conducted in 2022 by YouGov in Australia seemed to show that support for the Palestinian Arabs is slowly increasing. The Australian public appears to want the Australian government to change its stance relating to Israel and Palestine, with Australia Palestine Advocacy Network President Bishop George Browning stating, "Whether it's illegal Jewish settlements, recognition of Palestine, or the ongoing occupation, the Australian public wants to see their government take a moral stance in addressing the gross human rights violations committed by Israel. It's also clear these opinions cross political affiliations, with most of the Labor (62 percent), Coalition (54 percent), and Greens (79 percent) voters believing the Australian government should call on Israel to end its apartheid or work with international human rights groups for a solution."[134]

The poll also covered opinions on the Israeli settlements, with 43 percent of those surveyed saying they opposed the ongoing building of the settlements, while 18 percent supported them.[135] Relating to whether Palestine is to be an independent state, 54 percent agreed, and nine percent opposed there being a Palestinian state.[136] Regarding the ongoing occupation, 50 percent believe Israel should stop, and 13 percent think it should continue.[137]

The United States' people's overall impression of the State of Israel has remained steady with 58 percent viewing it favourably since 2001.[138]

Sympathies towards the State of Palestine sit at 25 percent.[139] However, an age breakdown showed that 13 percent of those aged between 18 and 34, 34 percent aged between 35 and 54, and 45 percent of those above 55 are more sympathetic to Israel.[140] In the May 2022 poll, according to Gallup, 55% of the population is still sympathetic towards the Israelis and 26% towards the Palestinians.[141]

CONNECTION BETWEEN CHRISTIAN & JEWISH ZIONISM IN MODERN HISTORY

The 1500s is known as the start of modern history. As previously discussed, it was during this period that colonisation began to increase. This was due to technological advancements, such as the Industrial Revolution, which birthed a desire for people to discover what was beyond their then-known world.

The Protestant Reformation also began during this time as a break away from the Roman Catholic Church. It was also after this event "which renewed interest in the Old Testament and God's dealings with the Jewish people."[142] Central to this thinking was a conflict of opinion relating to the meaning of the word Israel:

> For I do not desire, brethren, that you should be ignorant of this mystery, lest you should be wise in your own opinion, that blindness in part has happened to Israel until the fullness of the Gentiles has come in.[143]

Some chose to hold that the word Israel referred to "the church of Jewish and Gentile believers, as had the Roman Catholic Church", [while others] "preferred to apply the word to unbelieving Jews in Judaism."[144]

PALESTINE AND JEWISH ISRAELIS

According to Israeli historian Ilan Pappé, societal collective imagination was used to portray the biblical Holy Land through the Middle Ages. Palestine was frozen in time as if in Jesus' time. Later, it was imagined to be like medieval Europe. There were few Arabs or Muslims. Jesus was portrayed anywhere from being Aryan to Arab to a black Jew. Also, they imagined that the Hebrews were living in an ancient Christian land that was empty. This thinking prevailed from 70 CE [and especially after 135 CE] until the late 1800s. Because of this empty land thinking, it was easy for Christians to envisage the Jews back in their land and building a future.[145]

Also, printings of the Bible favoured the interpretation that there would be a significant conversion of the Jews, bringing blessings to all people worldwide.[146] The Puritans spread this belief throughout Britain and the American colonies. Due to the American War of Independence, the French Revolution, and the Napoleonic Wars, this belief waned, which allowed for a second Great Awakening, during which there was a belief that the world would end soon.[147]

Orientalism and an interest in the Jewish people continued due to archaeological discoveries and the writing of over 2000 authors about the Holy Land. In 1865, the Palestine Exploration Fund was formed by academics and clergy who promoted history, geology, and other sciences. However, some saw it as an opportunity to establish a way of bringing the Jews back to Palestine.[148]

The building and establishment of the British and Foreign Bible Society began on 11 June 1866 under the Society's third president, Anthony Ashley-Cooper. As a Zionist supporter, he desired to create a Jewish state in historic Palestine.[149] His belief, and the religious belief of some of the theologians that the Jews returning to Palestine would usher in the return of the Messiah, was not the only reason for the push to establish the Jewish state in historic Palestine. Also, the Ottoman Empire was declining, and the

British were looking for a way to instil itself within the Empire, which was found by encouraging and establishing a Jewish state. I began to wonder that maybe one of the reasons that Christian Zionism is so strong is because its roots run deep into previous centuries.

JEWISH HISTORY IN PALESTINE FROM MID-1800s TO 14 MAY 1948

In the mid-1800s, a secular Zionist movement started lobbying for a homeland, especially in the United Kingdom. A survey of Palestine was conducted between 1871 and 1878 by the Palestine Exploration Fund to determine the best place to establish settlements based on the available natural resources. Shortly after the opening of the Suez Canal, Thomas Cook arranged for 12,000 tourists to visit Jerusalem and the Holy Land, with his reputation reaching the highest authority in the British Palace.[150] While this happened, a nationalist movement, predominantly by secular Jews, began. They wanted to have a place for the Jewish people within historical Palestine. The land of ancient Israel surfaced because of the persecution that traditional Jews were suffering in Europe, with the first attacks occurring against them between 1881 and 1884.[151] These first groups of Jews moving to Palestine "were not technically Zionists", as they were predominantly religious rather than nationalistic. These Jews moved to newly settled agricultural areas and were supported by wealthy families, including Rothschild.[152]

The declared founder of Zionism was Theodore Herzl. Although he was born to a secular family and was an atheist, he felt that Judaism was stopping the Jewish people from progressing. With the persecution of the Jewish people increasing, he saw that leaving Europe and having a land of their own was the only way for them to survive economically, socially and politically. In 1897, he founded the World Zionist Organisation, and it did not take long for other leaders of Zionist movements to be drawn to Herzl. His ideals for a Jewish state would be modern and based on European culture. He would also oversee the building of the third temple. Although the state was not intended to be religious, there would be respect for those Jews who were. He expected many languages to be spoken, with Hebrew not necessarily one of them. He also anticipated equal rights for everyone, including the non-Jews living there. Women were to have equal voting rights, as he saw them as an essential part of society.[153] He planned to end with a large land area from the River Nile in Egypt to the Euphrates River, including the Jordan River valley, based on the Torah.[154] He intended to encourage non-Jews to leave through gentle means by helping them to secure employment in other countries while denying them employment in Palestine and buying their land from them. He intended to push the Arabs from their land quietly. Herzl was clear that although everyone was to be respected, coercion was going to be used on the Palestinians as strongly as possible to make them leave. If anyone refused to leave, they were to be left alone and the Jews would develop business elsewhere.[155]

Unlike Herzl, Zionist leaders, including Ben-Gurion and Vladimir Ze'ev Jabotinsky, went to Palestine between 1904 and 1914.[156] Although both were atheists, they used the Bible, particularly the accounts from the Book of Joshua, for their gain. They learned strategy and subjugation of the Canaanites and other peoples and utilised Joshua to justify Zionist attitudes towards the Indigenous Palestinians.[157]

Ben-Gurion stated that "the Jewish 'return' to Palestine is a 'repeat' of Joshua's conquest of ancient Palestine."[158] Jabotinsky was extremely blunt regarding the indigenous inhabitants of Palestine. He said that there are no promises to the Arabs, and Zionist colonisation must continue or end.

He saw it as hypocritical for it to be any other way.[159] With such determination to have a separate Jewish state through establishing an agricultural foundation for future Israel, the Zionist Jews kept purchasing land with the help of the Jewish National Fund, which is a part of the World Zionist Organisation.[160]

I found a good basic history regarding the establishment of the Zionist Jews in Palestine, which I will now share.[161] Even before 1900, it was clear to both Muslims and Christians that the Zionists wanted to remake the lands into a Jewish homeland. Increasing opposition occurred from 1908 and onwards when there was a call to employ Zionist workers rather than Arabs, and there were also calls for a "separate Jewish entity in Palestine." It was predominantly the Palestinian Christians who opposed the Zionist immigration, but even though most Muslims remained loyal to Ottoman authority, they supported the Christians.

By 1914, which was also the year that World War I started, there were 85,000 Jews in Palestine, with them owning over 400,000 dunams (100,000 acres) of land, and they had forty-four agricultural settlements.

The Ottomans entered the war because Jewish Zionist migration to Palestine was increasing, and the Ottoman officials could not slow it down. They also entered the war because Western imperialism wanted the Ottoman lands, which meant they had to fight for their survival, so they fought on the side of Germany.

Nearly three years into the war in 1917, there was a fear that Russia might pull out of the war because of their revolution, which brought the Bolsheviks to power. Britain started encouraging Zionism as it wanted the Russian Jews to support Russia so they would stay in the war. Britain also needed American aid and troops, so they encouraged Zionism, hoping the Jews could gain the support of President Woodrow Wilson to fight on the side of the alliance. That, coupled with the ongoing persecution of the

Jews in many countries, led to the signing of the Balfour Declaration of November 2, 1917, which promised the Jews a national home in Palestine. By the end of World War 1, Germany and its allies, including the Ottoman Empire, were defeated. The French and British shared the former Ottoman land, with the British gaining Palestine.

During the 1920s, the Zionist leadership was pushing to gain the right to all of Palestine. The number of Jewish immigrants entering Palestine increased, with 18,294 entering between 1919 and 1922. Additionally, the Zionists built an intelligence network, including having spies. They quickly gained information themselves or directly from British officials sympathetic to their cause. Because of World War 1, drought conditions, and economic reasons, many Arabs during the 1920s and 1930s had to sell or relinquish their land if it was a part of a community holding. It was the Zionist organisations who bought the land, with many Palestinian Arabs forced to leave the land altogether.

Arab Palestinians had ever-increasing employment restrictions placed on them because of British policy, which led to increased unemployment. With conditions continuing to worsen, there was an Arab revolt in 1936. With both sides pushing for a state of their own, and after an investigation that found in favour of the Zionist Jews, a decision by the British to partition the land into two separate states was thought to be the only solution. The Jews, including Ben-Gurion, saw the division as a stepping stone to gain more land in the future, with their desire not to stay within the proposed boundary. With the Jews gaining the best land and the Arabs aware of the Jewish plan to continue taking over more of the land, the Arabs started another revolt, which lasted from September 1937 to January 1939. Both the British and the Jews became targets. The British and Jewish forces of the Haganah and Irgun employed terrorist tactics, with many casualties being predominantly on the Arab side. The proposed partition being considered was abandoned, and the British kept control of all of Palestine.

From 1939, with the Zionist Jews, including Ben-Gurion, determined to have a state in all of Palestine, they increased illegal Jewish immigration. With the British again considering partition, Jewish terrorism against the British increased with the assassination of Lord Moyne in Cairo in 1942. After the conclusion of the European war on May 8, 1945, Israeli terrorist activity increased. The bombing of the King David Hotel in Jerusalem on July 22, 1946, killed 91 British, Jewish and Arab personnel and injured many more. The British decided to relinquish its hold on Palestine. The situation was brought before the United Nations, which voted for partitioning Palestine. This, in itself, did not ensure there was going to be a Jewish state.

The British continued to pull out of Palestine, and the United Nations were organising the partition. President Truman of the United States privately said he would recognise a Jewish state. The village of Deir Yasin was attacked on 9 April 1948 by the Irgun, and they "slaughtered about 115 men, women and children, whose mutilated bodies were stuffed down wells."[162] With the threat of more of the same occurring to those of other villages, 300,000 Arabs fled by 15 May 1948, the day after Ben-Gurion proclaimed the State of Israel on the borders of the United Nations partition plan.

6

BEYOND OCCUPATION

I have seen a shift in how the Israeli government is being described, with more people calling Israel an apartheid state. This is not only being said within the international sphere but also by more Israelis. Academics, including historians Ilan Pappe and Benny Morris, and human rights groups are becoming more vocal.[163] A description I read by academic Neve Gordon, which he wrote in 2009 clearly explains what is happening in Israel. "Israel is an apartheid state. For more than 42 years, Israel has control of the land between the Jordan Valley and the Mediterranean Sea. Within this area, six million Jews and five million Palestinians live."[164] He further explained there are also approximately 500,000 Jews who live in the Occupied Territories that Israel claimed in 1967. The Jews and Palestinians live under two different legal systems, with the Jews under civil law and the Palestinians under military law. The Palestinians lack fundamental human rights and do not have a state of their own, yet the Jews have everything and live just like the Jews in the State of Israel.[165] This is still true today, 76 years later, except that today, the populations are more even in number, with approximately seven million Jews and seven million Palestinians living in Palestine, and the human rights afforded to Palestinians are diminishing even more.[166]

Apart from some of Israel's citizens calling their government out, some sections of the international community, especially humanitarian-based organisations, are also calling out the Israeli government for being an apartheid state. Palestinians are being treated similarly as regards the discrimination and segregation that occurred in South Africa, which is considered a crime.[167] The International Convention on the Suppression and Punishment of the Crime of Apartheid, which entered force on July 18, 1976, and certainly applies to Palestinians, contains Article II (c) and (d) stating:

> "(c) Any legislative measures and other measures calculated to prevent a racial group or groups from participation in the political, social, economic and cultural life of the country and the deliberate creation of conditions preventing the full development of such a group or groups, in particular by denying to members of a racial group or groups basic human rights and freedoms, including the right to work, the right to form recognised trade unions, the right to education, the right to leave and to return to their country, the right to a nationality, the right to freedom of movement and residence, the right to freedom of opinion and expression, and the right to freedom of peaceful assembly and association.
>
> d) Any measures, including legislative measures, designed to divide the population along racial lines by creating separate reserves and ghettos for the members of a racial group or groups, the prohibition of mixed marriages among members of various racial groups, the appropriation

of landed property belonging to a racial group or groups or members thereof."[168]

I found so much in this statement that can relate to Palestinians in Palestine. Another controls every part of their lives. Where they live, whether it is in the State of Israel, the West Bank, or Gaza, determines how much they will suffer during their life. Palestinians living in the State of Israel, although they endure various forms of prejudice and discrimination, can come and go with relative ease, get essentials for life, and access most services. Beyond that, they are not equal to Jewish Israelis and suffer such things as verbal abuse (which I have heard from acquaintances suffering the same before they left the State of Israel), unequal employment opportunities with differing pay rates, and differing educational opportunities. It is much worse for Palestinians living in Gaza. They have been locked away for sixteen years. Many were born where they live and will more than likely also die there, having never stepped outside of the open air concentration camp in which they exist.

For Palestinians, being alive and able to live, work, go to school, eat, drink, have a home, get married and even bear children are all privileges. At any time, one or more of these 'privileges' can be snatched away from them as if they had never existed. They know this because they have seen it happen to others. They know that one day, it will be their turn. Being able to have and keep any of these privileges was never guaranteed.

STATE OF ISRAEL

Palestinian Israelis constitute 21 percent or just under two million of the population in the State of Israel as of the end of 2020.[169] They are primarily descendants of those who remained after the Arab-Israeli war of 1948 (al-Nakba) and were automatically given Israeli citizenship.[170] When comparing the demographics of the two people groups, the figures show that the Palestinian Israelis are lagging in most areas, which does not exclusively include poverty, home ownership, education - both in years studying and in the level of education attained, employment, and level of salaries.[171]

Not everyone is treated the same when considering the overall status of all Israeli citizens. Both Palestinian Israelis and Jewish Israelis live in the State of Israel and are citizens, as proven by a piece of paper they own. However, the Israeli government is always looking for ways to reinforce the reality that Palestinians 'are treated as second-class citizens' when compared to Jewish Israelis.[172] The introduction of the State Basic Law on July 19, 2018, is just one mechanism.

State Basic Law

Israel is described as being a liberal democracy [and it also sees itself as being one] because it has independent courts and a relatively extensive judicial review.[173] It also claims to follow international law.[174] In reality, it is far from being a liberal democracy. It also has strict guidelines relating to immigration, where unless one is Jewish or marries an Israeli national, one will be unlikely to get residency.[175] Coupled with this, and within the State of Israel itself, the Israeli government's ideals for a Jewish-only state continue to grow and be enforced. From 19 July 2018, the state was officially considered a Jewish-only state, with the Israeli Knesset passing the Basic Law: Israel - The Nation State of the Jewish People.[176] Some of this framework, but not exclusively, includes and specifically states:

1. Basic principles.
    (a) The Land of Israel is the historical homeland of the Jewish People, in which the State of Israel was established.

(b) The State of Israel is the nation-state of the Jewish People in which it realises its natural, cultural, religious and historical right to self-determination.

(c) The realisation of the right to national self-determination in the State of Israel is exclusive to the Jewish People.[177]

It is evident to me that there is certainly no room for Palestinian Israelis to have any self-determination, and there is certainly no room for the 'right of return' to former land and properties.

2. The capital of the State.
   The complete and united Jerusalem is the capital of Israel.[178]

Again, there is no room for any part of Jerusalem to be given to any Palestinian State, should it become a reality in the future.

3. Language.
   (a) Hebrew is the language of the State.
   (b) Arabic has a special status in the State. Regulation of the use of Arabic in state institutions or in contact with them shall be prescribed by law.
   (c) Nothing in this article shall compromise the status given to the Arabic language in practice, before this basic-law came into force.[179]

Hebrew is the state language, so Arabic could continue to be used anywhere it was already used. However, the law determines where Arabic will be used in official future settings, which means it will only be used for a few generations.

4. Jewish settlement.

    The State views the development of Jewish settlement as a national value and shall act to encourage and promote its establishment and consolidation.[180]

The ongoing building of Jewish settlements in all of historical Palestine occurs because it is of national importance.

Currently, Israel does not have a constitution, so this fundamental law provides the foundation for the legal framework. Also, this law does not change the situation for Palestinians currently living within the West Bank and Gaza, as they continue to be ruled by military law rather than civil law.[181]

WEST BANK

Barely a day passes without some reference in the media to the inhumane treatment of Palestinians by the Israeli government. The ongoing annexation of their land, particularly in the West Bank, to build more settlements, leads to house demolitions and villages being razed to the ground. Daily restriction of movements due to the Separation Wall, checkpoints, and the denial of permits to leave the West Bank or Gaza are just some ways that the Israeli government makes it extremely difficult, or even impossible, to live an everyday life.

Night raids into homes occur without notice, and administrative detention can happen to any Palestinian. Palestinians, even without charge or conviction, can be held indefinitely. Life for Palestinians can be debilitating. The results of The Palestinian Psychological Conditions Survey of 2022 showed that 58 percent of all adults in the West Bank and Gaza had some level of depression, with 71 percent in Gaza and 51 percent in the West Bank suffering.[182] Even though there are calls from the international community to the Israeli government to improve conditions for Palestinians, the Israeli government is determined to continue with its plan to have all the land.

Land Confiscations and Settlements

In an article by The Medialine from July 2023, Prime Minister Benjamin Netanyahu clearly stated that Palestinian hopes of establishing a state of their own "must be eliminated."[183] The Israeli government's agenda of building as many settlements as possible in the West Bank is speeding up, with more Palestinian land being confiscated by the Israeli government every day. A report by Peace Now revealed that on June 25, 2024, the Israeli government had seized and declared 12,700 dunams (12 km^2) of Palestinian land in the West Bank as State property, being the largest land grab in 30 years since the Oslo Accords.[184] Since the beginning of 2024, 23,700 dunams have been taken.[185] The settlements are primarily for newish migrants needing a permanent living place.

Many Palestinian families have been living and farming on their land for many generations, and long before the European Jews began immigrating to Palestine. They see it as their right to continue living and farming there. From what I have seen over the years through observing from a distance, the Israeli government is not concerned about where these families will live or how they will earn an income.

Early in my journey, land confiscation and building settlements were issues I had not considered. As the 2014 Gaza War was happening, all I saw and heard about was death and the destruction of buildings and infrastructure. Years later, when it was time for me to learn more, as with other parts of this journey, I started with a general internet search using the word 'settlement'. This automatically opened many news reports and articles about what was happening in Palestine. Initially, while skimming briefly, the Fourth Geneva Convention appeared connected to the ongoing building of settlements, which was something else that would need my attention. I remembered the Fourth Geneva Convention mentioned during my university studies, but could not remember the details.

I discovered that Henry Dunant (mentioned during my university studies) was an entrepreneur, which led him to start the International Committee of the Red Cross.[186] He also founded the 1st Geneva Convention in 1864 to protect combatants during war.[187] By the close of World War II, a lot of land was occupied by occupying powers. These occupying governments would then forcibly deport some of their citizens from their own homes to their newly gained territory to set up communities. "Historically, over 40 million people endured forced migration, evacuation, displacement, and expulsion, including 15 million Germans, 5 million Soviet citizens, and millions of Poles, Ukrainians and Hungarians."[188] During World War II, there was no international protection for these people against their government.[189] A fourth Geneva Convention on 12 August 1949 addressed such situations under *Article 49, paragraph* 6: "The Occupying Power shall not deport or transfer parts of its own civilian population into the territory it occupies."[190]

In 1958, according to the International Committee of the Red Cross, Article 49, paragraph six was published to protect not only the nationals of the occupying power who were forced to move from their homes to the occupied territory but also the native population already living in the occupied territory, as their economic situation became worse and their existence as a race was put in danger.[191]

Individuals, including Special Rapporteur Michael Lynk, said, "Article 49 paragraph 6 could apply to Palestine with the growing number of 'Unauthorized outposts' [by Jewish settlers], most of which have been established on private Palestinian land and are located deep within the occupied West Bank..."[192]

These outposts then become settlements once their application to authorities gains approval. When Australian Settler Michael Lourie's outpost gained approval after many attempts, 70 Jewish Settler families lived there. With approval, the number of families was permitted to increase to 120.[193] Along with settler-initiated settlements, land is also confiscated from Palestinians by the Israeli government to increase the number of government-initiated settlements. Whether settlers or the Israeli government initiates the construction of settlements, the Jewish settlers who move into the West Bank do so voluntarily, so the Article does not apply to them. The indigenous Palestinians are the ones who suffer, so it applies to them.[194]

However, the Rome Statute of the International Criminal Court, 17 July 1998, was introduced, establishing the International Criminal Court.[195] This gave validity and strength to the original 1949 Article 49 paragraph six, with the introduction of *Article 8 (viii) under War Crimes,* stating, "The transfer, directly or indirectly, by the Occupying Power of parts of its own civilian population into the territory it occupies, or the deportation or transfer of all or parts of the population of the occupied territory within or outside this territory."[196]

The introduction and use of the word 'indirectly' implicate the Israeli government as they encourage their citizens to move into settlements, especially within the West Bank.[197] I remember seeing giant billboards during my study trip advertising the building of settlements, with cheap home loans offered to anyone who wanted to move to one. At the time, I did not know what was happening to Palestinians, so I did not understand the implications and thought it was good for the Israeli government to have such an initiative. Even while travelling on the bus, I took photos of some settlements. Since then, I have genuinely come to understand what is happening, particularly in East Jerusalem and in the West Bank, and the devastation that settlement building is bringing to Palestinians. Approximately Jewish Israelis live in settlements in the West Bank.[198]

Even Israel's long-time ally, the United States, in a press release dated 18 June 2023, denounced the Israeli government's move to continue the planning for over 4,000 settlement units in the West Bank, which, if continued, is seen by the United States as "an obstacle to peace."[199] In 2023 and up to 31 July 2023, 12,855 new units were approved by the Israeli government, as future settlement planning is being fast-tracked.[200] Australia's Foreign Minister Penny Wong also looked to "strengthen the government's objection to settlements by affirming that they are illegal under international law and a significant obstacle to peace."[201] Furthermore, the government "will reinstate the term 'Occupied Palestinian Territories'", she said.[202]

Following Minister Wong's comments, the National Labor Conference was held in Brisbane in August 2023 without a vote or the government taking definitive action. Instead, two members were chosen to speak at the conference, with them expressing the message that friends of Israel are also friends of the Palestinian people and that peace cannot be achieved at the expense of either side. Furthermore, they expressed that both peoples should have individual states with independently recognised borders.[203] Currently, Palestinian land seems always to be under threat. Even if land is not required for the building of settlements or military use, Palestinians sometimes find that their homes must be demolished.

House Demolitions and Villages Razed

A few years ago, I naively uploaded a post to 'friends' and not even 'public' on social media about the ongoing demolition of homes belonging to Palestinians because they did not have building permits. The responding comments implied that it was their fault that their homes were demolished for not getting a permit. I did not know how to respond, so I deleted the post within two days. There had to be an underlying reason why many people would risk having their homes demolished instead of getting a building permit. Indeed, it could not be that the majority of Palestinians building any form of structures are just negligent. I discovered that they are not negligent at all. To understand the reason for the demolition of so many homes, it is helpful to know that the governance of the West Bank is unevenly shared between the Palestinian Authority and Israel.

The West Bank is divided into three areas: Area A, Area B and Area C. These divisions were one of many results achieved by negotiations at the 1995 Oslo II meetings.[204] These meetings were held between Israel's Yitzhak Rabin and Shimon Peres, as well as with the Palestinian Liberation Organisation leader, Yasser Arafat. Government leaders from the U.S., Russia, Egypt, Jordan, Norway and the European Union witnessed the meetings.[205] Currently, Area A constitutes 18 percent of the West Bank. The Palestinian Authority controls most of the affairs in this area, including internal security. Area B comprises about 21 percent of the West Bank. The Palestinian Authority controls education, health and the economy. Israeli authorities have complete external security control in both areas A and B. This means that the Israeli military retains the right to enter these areas at any time, typically to raid homes or detain individuals under the pretext of security. About 2.8 million Palestinians live in Areas A and B, where the major Palestinian cities and towns are Hebron, Ramallah, Bethlehem and Nablus.

Area C contains 60 percent of Palestinian land and is the most extensive section of the West Bank. This area was meant to be transferred to the Palestinian Authority in 1999, but the handover did not happen—consequently, security, planning, and construction remain in the hands of Israel.[206] There is also a virtual blanket rejection of any building applications. Area C has not been zoned to allow construction, including land that Palestinians undeniably own.[207] This can also mean that anyone who gets married cannot build a home. Consequently, for Palestinian newlyweds, it can be more attractive to leave Palestine and move abroad permanently.

Area C has been designated for use by the military to be used for their bases or training purposes, as a 'buffer zone' around the wall, or for settlement use, whether they are already built and require further services, or for future building of settlements, and lastly, for nature reserves.[208] In 2016-2018 alone, out of the 1485 applications submitted by Palestinians for construction permits in Area C, only 21 were approved by the Israeli Civil Administration.[209]

Because of the virtual impossibility of being legally allowed to build a home, particularly in Area C, most Palestinians build, knowing that any day and any time, their home or any other building could be demolished. In 2022 alone, 953 Palestinian structures were demolished or seized across the West Bank, including East Jerusalem, which is the highest number since 2016. There, 1,031 people were displaced, and 28,446 were affected by the demolitions.[210] In East Jerusalem, 51% of the homes were demolished by their owners, as they could not afford the cost of others demolishing their homes.[211] Palestinians in this situation demolished their own homes. Between 7 October 2023 and 7 January 2024, 444 Palestinians were also displaced from their homes in Area C and East Jerusalem.[212]

With the ability of the Israeli government to be able to take land at any time and for any reason in Area C, daily life can become precarious, not only for individuals but also for villages. One such region is Masafer Yatta near Hebron, which contains eight villages. The people are losing their fight to remain. The area was declared a military firing zone in 1981, even though the town existed before the area was rezoned.[213] On 17 November 2022, the Israeli Civil Administration issued a demolition order against the donor-funded humanitarian project Isfey al Fauqa School in Masafer Yatta, which was demolished on 23 November 2022.[214] There are also plans to relocate Palestinian Bedouin communities to urban townships.[215] According to the Colonization & Wall Resistance Commission, in the first six months of 2023, 303 Palestinian structures had been demolished, and 822 demolition orders had been handed out.[216]

House demolitions also regularly occur if the homeowner is connected to someone that the Israeli authority has deemed as being a 'terrorist'. This is considered a form of 'collective punishment'. However, there are protections against collective punishment under the 1907 Hague Convention *Article 50: Regulations,* which states, "No general penalty, pecuniary or otherwise, shall be inflicted upon the population on account of the acts of individuals for which they cannot be regarded as jointly and severally responsible."[217] Stronger language is provided that prohibits the use of collective punishment by the Fourth Geneva Convention, *Article 33 Individual responsibility, collective penalties, pillage, and reprisals.* "No protected person may be punished for an offence he or she has not personally committed. Collective penalties and likewise all measures of intimidation for terrorism are prohibited."[218]

This means that any form of collective punishment is illegal under international law. Consequently, if the Israeli government considers any individual as being a terrorist, and the home in which they are living, even if it is not their home, is demolished, they are breaking international law.[219]

When people belong to a minority group, there are various ways that they are controlled. Three of the mechanisms that the Israeli government uses to help keep the Palestinian people under subjugation are the separation wall, checkpoints and the denying of permits to travel outside of the areas where they live.

The Separation Wall

The Israeli government initiated the plan to build the 'security wall' on 23 June 2002. The position of the wall was to be inside the 1949 Armistice Line or 'Green Line', which required 10% of West Bank land to be seized.[220] According to the Israeli government, they decided to build the security fence at the height of the Second Intifada, when Palestinian suicide bombings killed Israeli civilians.[221] Israeli authorities also said the barrier was being constructed to prevent Palestinians without permits from entering Israel from the West Bank and that it was never intended to be a permanent border."[222] By the time the wall was begun the Second Intifada was almost over; thus a different motive can be seen.

The reality for Palestinians is that the separation wall has become a permanent fixture, with 85% of the wall not staying close to the Armistice line but snaking its way around the West Bank, encroaching deeply into it.[223] By 2020, 13% of the land had been seized, rather than the initial 10% required.[224] The undeclared purpose was to unofficially annex settlements and parcels of land for the building of future settlements, which it did conveniently in areas where Israel's largest blocks are located.[225] This resulted in Palestinian families and communities being divided and cut off from each other. Also, access to their farmlands was often no longer possible.[226] One family's property fence is the wall, and they must wait for hours until the Israeli army opens a gate, which was installed only after human rights agencies intervened on their behalf so that they could work on their land.[227] It seems to me that the Israeli government intends that the family will leave their home.

The Israeli government says that the reason for building the fence was to protect its citizens from external threats, including the infiltration into Israel by potential suicide bombers. I feel their aim is more sinister, especially when the barrier does not remain on the Armistice line and also annexes water sources controlled by the Israeli authorities.[228]

According to B'Tselem, the total length of the wall is 712km, covering from the planning stage to being fully completed, but if it followed the Armistice line, the total length would only be 320km. Most of the wall comprises an "electronic fence with paved paths, barbed-wire fences, and ditches flanking it on either side. The barrier is about 60 metres wide on average." About 70km of the wall exist in urban areas.[229]

Through the ongoing appropriation of land and the continuing building of settlements, it is becoming clearer by the day that the possibility of having two separate states in Palestine is becoming less viable. It has been said that the time for two separate states ended in the late 1990s. That opinion is based on the separation wall, which continues to break up the West Bank into smaller areas, with many Palestinian communities becoming fractured. Also, there is a continual building of new Israeli settlements, particularly within Area C in the West Bank.

Checkpoints

Checkpoints are usually on the borders between countries, but like the separation wall, they are inside the West Bank. The United Nations Office for the Coordination of Humanitarian Affairs undertook a survey in early 2023. There were 645 barriers in the West Bank and East Jerusalem. These include permanently staffed and occasionally staffed checkpoints, roadblocks, mounds of dirt ditches and gates. Hebron has checkpoints of its own that are constantly staffed. In their previous 2020 report, there were eight percent fewer, totalling 593 obstacles. These blocks affect every aspect of Palestinian life. Added to this, the Israelis randomly place four 'flying' checkpoints per week on roads in the West Bank.[230]

Palestinian access to work, schools, universities, hospitals, and shops is severely affected. Pregnant women are especially vulnerable, with some women denied permission to go through checkpoints, so they give birth where they stand. Between 2000 and 2007 alone, "69 births and 35 infant and five maternal deaths [occurred] at checkpoints."[231] Recording of figures after those dates has not been undertaken by the State of Israel, as the Commission on Human Rights "Condemn[s] the denial by Israel of access to hospitals for Palestinian pregnant women, which forces them to give birth at checkpoints under hostile, inhumane and humiliating conditions."[232] Such treatment is a crime under the Rome Statute of the International Criminal Court *Article 7 Crimes against humanity* (1)(k): "Other inhumane acts of a similar character are committed intentionally causing great suffering or serious injury to the body or mental or physical health."[233]

During my study trip in 2014, we went through several road checkpoints. At one of these, while stopped, an armed Israeli soldier boarded the bus. After walking up and down the aisle, he must have been satisfied by what he saw, as he left without a word. Most of us were fascinated at seeing a rifle up close rather than in a museum cabinet. I now wonder if such an incident would strike fear into the hearts of Palestinians, or is it such a commonplace that they take it in their stride?

I have discovered that checkpoints are gradually being privatised with facial recognition, so there is less interaction with individuals except for orders being barked out when necessary.[234] The day we entered the West Bank to visit Hebron and Bethlehem, we returned to Jerusalem through 'Checkpoint 300', a main military checkpoint at Bethlehem. Having read about these privatised checkpoints, I am sure that Checkpoint 300 was one of these. It was a large concrete building with revolving turnstiles at the entry and exit, so walking was the only way to pass. Once inside, what looked to be cattle gates flanked both sides of the walkway. There were visible security cameras throughout the building. There must also be hidden microphones to record conversations because our lecturers told us to remain quiet while walking through. I quickly scanned the area from where I was standing but could not see anything obvious. While going through, we occasionally heard some instructions booming through the speakers. At a booth, which is an enclosed room, there is a bulletproof glass window on one side with a small gap. We had to pass our passports there, which a staff member checked. It was also where we had to look into what would have been a facial recognition camera that was pointing down from above. It was not a busy day, so the process only took about thirty minutes to get our group through.

Being a significant and busy crossing, the wait time can be many hours. For those who have been fortunate to gain employment in the State of Israel and have managed to secure a travel permit, this is the crossing that Palestinians have to use twice a day. Exiting the checkpoint on the Jerusalem side, a row of taxis was waiting for potential passengers. Buses also drive past the checkpoint regularly. Our regular tour coaches were also waiting there for us.

I was not surprised to learn that if Palestinians are killed at checkpoints, "nobody [is] ever held accountable. Israel's shoot-to-kill policy becomes even more widely applied when the so-called security services are outsourced."[235] I wonder if Palestinians ever think about whether they will get through a checkpoint alive or not. Such is the fragility of life there.

Restricting Movement

Up until 1991, Palestinians could travel freely throughout the whole of Israel. However, the Israeli government changed its policy, requiring all Palestinians to obtain a permit to travel from Palestinian East Jerusalem and into the State of Israel. Then, they changed the rules again by splitting East Jerusalem, West Bank, and Gaza into three separate travel areas. This meant permits were required to travel between the areas of the Occupied Territories. Over time, permits to these areas were reduced significantly, with the travel permits being stopped altogether after Palestinians killed nine Israeli civilians and six members of the Israel Security Forces in March 1993.[236] This was during the time of the First Intifada, which began in December 1987 after an Israeli army vehicle in the Jabalya refugee camp in Gaza crashed into two cars, killing four Palestinians.[237] The First Intifada ended at the Oslo Accords on 1 September 1993.[238]

Palestinian farmers began requiring extra permits because the wall prevented them from accessing their farms.[239] For Palestinians unable to get permits to farm their land and plant food, it is a struggle for survival.[240]

In October 2022, the Israeli government introduced measures to make it harder for foreigners to teach, study, volunteer, work, or live in the West Bank. This also means that if family members do not have a West Bank Identity card, they cannot spend time there with their family.[241] Regarding this latest move, Eric Goldstein, deputy Middle East director at Human Rights Watch, said that this move by the Israeli government breaks the ties that Palestinians try to hold on to with the outside world. This will make it harder for people to spend time in the West Bank. It is essentially making the West Bank more like Gaza, with over two million Palestinians being cut off from the outside world for 15 years.[242]

I see this situation as simply another case of the frog in the pot on the stove. The water in the pot is getting hotter and hotter. Once the water is too hot, and the frog cannot move, it dies. If the international community continues to sit on their hands and does nothing to bring the Israeli government to account for all of their actions against the Palestinians, who are supposed to be under their care and protection, then this could be the end scenario of the Palestinians in the West Bank.

Night Raids

Another part of everyday life for Palestinians is night raids, which Israeli soldiers conduct.

Raids occur at night and for several reasons, which can include detaining Palestinians for questioning, delivering home demolition notices and confiscating work permits. They also detain Palestinians, who may be thought to be Hamas operatives or suspected of illegal activities. These raids can involve anywhere from several hundred soldiers being involved in the arrest of one man to 1,500 or more soldiers if they raid an entire camp.[243]

Since the 1993 Oslo Accords, the destruction of Palestinian belongings during house raids has increased significantly. Also, soldiers injure, kill and beat children in front of their parents.[244] Soldiers also remove children during these night raids. In 2022, in the Palestinian town of Beit Fajjar, near Bethlehem, at 3 am, soldiers blew up the front door of a Palestinian home. After smashing furniture and belongings, they ushered the seven family members into one room. Determining who was Hasam, they then dragged the 15-year-old boy away while he was in his pyjamas, blindfolded and handcuffed.[245]

Unfortunately, this kind of scenario is the reality for so many Palestinians. It can be for no apparent reason other than to instill fear into the hearts and lives of whoever the occupation authority can, especially children.[246] Anyone could suffer this fate. Young children, men, women. No one is exempt.

Unfortunately, children are the ones who suffer most from these events, with about 1,000 Palestinian children from the West Bank and another 1,000 from East Jerusalem taken every year, with some children taken from their beds [and detained].²⁴⁷ The treatment they suffer while in detention is very damaging, although prohibited under both Israeli law and the United Nations Convention on the Rights of the Child, which Israel has signed.²⁴⁸ "Forcible home invasions come amid already high levels of trauma, citing research that suggested the prevalence of Post-Traumatic Stress Disorder among children living in the occupied West Bank is between 34.1 percent to 50.4 percent, compared with an average of 6.8 percent to 12.2 percent worldwide."²⁴⁹

Administrative Detention

Administrative detention is a procedure under which no charges are laid against individuals, and the detainee is not intended to be tried. Palestinians' detention orders can be renewed indefinitely.²⁵⁰

"Israel routinely uses administrative detention and has, over the years, placed thousands of Palestinians behind bars for periods ranging from several months to several years or longer, without charging them, without telling them what they are accused of, and without disclosing the alleged evidence to their families or their lawyers."²⁵¹ Before October 7, Israel was holding over 1,200 detainees under administrative detention, 1,188 of which are Palestinian.²⁵² This included ten children held without charge in administrative detention for three months until the end of March 2023.²⁵³ Since October 7, the number of Palestinians being held under administrative detention is now more than 5,900.²⁵⁴

Jenin

One day, I arrived home from work, and my husband asked me whether I had heard about the latest events in the West Bank. I said, "No." After he told me, I searched the internet and social media on my phone. What I discovered was disturbing but not surprising since events like those in Jenin have occurred previously.

In a military operation just after 1am on Monday, 3 July 2023, the Israeli Defence Forces entered the Jenin refugee camp. Their weaponry included drones, which carried missiles, and armoured vehicles. Over 1000 ground troops were armed with their usual weapons, including guns and tear gas. They bombed targets, which primarily included the administration centre of several resistance groups. During this 'mission', approximately 12 people were killed, over 800 homes were damaged in varying degrees, as well as three hospitals.[255]

On April 3, 2002, in an operation called Operation Defensive Shield, Jenin was bombed as a part of the Second Intifada.[256] There was a 21-year gap to 19 June 2023 with the subsequent bombardment, followed by the 3 July attack, the worst attack since the 2002 attack.[257]

In light of what has happened in Jenin since the beginning of 2023, but especially since July 3, there have been international calls for Israel to stop its activities against Palestinians, but they have been ignored. Ongoing actions by the Israeli government provide no evidence of its desire to improve its relationship with the Palestinians. Furthermore, these increasing attacks by the Israeli Defence Forces will only bring reprisals from those being attacked.

The Israeli government will not stop their agenda of settlement building, appropriation of land from non-Jews, and conducting night raids of individual homes and towns. Their agenda is to make life so difficult for Palestinians that they will permanently leave the country in droves. If they refuse to go, they could eventually be forced to live in Gaza and be permanently locked away. Jeff Halper, who founded the Israeli Committee Against House Demolitions, calls it being 'warehoused'.[258]

Ethnic Cleansing in the West Bank

Further to blatant attacks on Palestinians in the West Bank, water scarcity is occurring. Palestinians are told they can have access to water if they prove land ownership or get a permit from the Israeli Civil Administration. In reality, supplies are diverted from Palestinian areas to the settlements, with water being restricted or stopped altogether.[259] Even wells have been plugged and sealed with concrete in raids around Hebron to prevent the watering of crops that support 25 Palestinian families.[260]

In May 2023, the Office for the Coordination of Humanitarian Affairs reported on water deprivation in the West Bank. They found that individuals in settlements use 247 litres of water daily, compared to Palestinians, who use 82.4 litres daily. It is worse for small Palestinian communities, which have 26 litres of water per day as they are not connected to the main water.[261] To help counter the water shortage, 92 percent of Palestinian homes have rooftop tanks to store water. Although the Jewish Israeli population in the West Bank is less than three times smaller than the Palestinians, they used ten times more water in 2022.[262]

THE GAZA STRIP

The 2023 population estimate of Gaza is 2,037,744, with the median age being 18.[263] A Labor Force Survey conducted in 2022 found that the unemployment rate of Palestinians living in Gaza was 45.3 percent.[264] Seventy percent of the population are registered as refugees, resulting from the expulsions of 1948 and 1967.[265] Tears came to my eyes as I just thought about my grandparents. If they were not born and raised in Nazareth but in another town and chose to stay rather than leave for Jordan in 1929, like so many others, would they have been displaced from their home and driven into Gaza, and what would have been their fate?

Out of the three areas where Palestinians live, those living in Gaza suffer the most. Like Palestinians living in the West Bank, they have the wall and border checkpoints with extreme restrictions on who can enter or leave Gaza. The citizens of Gaza have been locked away from the outside world for approximately 16 years. This means that few people can leave Gaza for any reason, and few people are permitted to visit Gaza. But more than that, Gaza is a place that looks like a war zone. A place where many homes have been bombed, making them uninhabitable. I used to have a wallpaper on my computer for years. The picture, taken during the 2014 bombing of Gaza by the Israeli Defence Forces, was of a bathtub with two young children sitting inside in the remains of their house, with their father standing nearby watching on.

Many of these homes have been in disrepair for many years. Materials for building construction, whether for entirely new projects or to repair those that have suffered damage due to the ongoing occupation, have been banned from Gaza since the election of Hamas, which has been the governing authority in Gaza since 2006. I was curious why such a ban would exist and who Hamas is.

WHO IS HAMAS?

Hamas was officially formed in 1987 during the First Intifada. I found two conflicting versions regarding the creation of Hamas. Some say that the group formed with Israeli support to counter Yasser Arafat's Palestinian Liberation Organisation.[266] One such person is Mr Cohen, a Tunisian-born Jew who worked in Gaza for over two decades, who said in a report in the Wall Street Journal in 2009, "Hamas, to my great regret, is Israel's creation."²⁶⁷ In addition, Brigadier General Yitzhak Segev, a military governor in Gaza in the early 1980s, states he financed Hamas in the early days.²⁶⁸ Former Prime Minister Ehud and former Director of Shin Bet Ami Ayalon confirmed that the Israeli policy under Prime Minister Benjamin Netanyahu is to prevent a Palestinian state from being established by keeping tension between the Palestinian Authority in the West Bank and Hamas in the Gaza Strip. Ayalon said, "So what we did with the permission of our prime minister is let Qatar transfer a huge amount of money in cash, probably more than 1.4 billion dollars, and to make sure that they will be able to send people to work in Israel and to achieve or to get intelligence if they need. By doing it, we increase the power of Hamas."²⁶⁹ Regarding Netanyahu, Barak said, "He deliberately and systematically and even told us on record that whoever wants to avoid the threat of a two-state solution has to support my policy of paying protection money to Hamas."²⁷⁰ This move ensured there would never be a Palestinian state because there would always be friction between the Palestinian Authority in the West Bank and Hamas in Gaza.

I was not surprised about learning such information because the United States was involved in 'creating' various organisations to benefit themselves, including the Taliban, to help prevent the Soviet Union from spreading their ideology and increasing their reach into other nations. The United States helped the Muslim Brotherhood in Egypt against Al Saddat and helped create ISIL to help eliminate Al Assad.²⁷¹

Conversely, Miko Peled spoke in Melbourne, Australia, on 14 December 2023. He expressed it was nonsense that the Israeli government had a part in the formation of Hamas. He inferred that adopting that stance demeans Palestinians' ability to do something themselves.²⁷² Also, Tareq Baconi, who has written extensively on Hamas, has yet to show that Israel was involved in its formation. Members of Hamas had their roots in the Palestine branch of the Muslim Brotherhood.[273] Its roots were established in 1928 as a "widespread Islamic political-religious organisation established in Egypt."[274] The Muslim Brotherhood began because Egyptians suffered under foreign occupation and foreign control of their resources. Then, they wanted to free the rest of the Middle East from colonial rule.[275]

The Muslim Brotherhood entered Palestine in 1946, but because of the division of Palestine after World War II by three states, Israel, Jordan and Egypt, it was not until 1967, when Israel gained control of all areas, that the Muslim Brotherhood seriously began its work there.[276] They built an infrastructure of social services, medical clinics, and schools, mainly in the impoverished Gaza Strip. These facilities were desperately needed because of Israel's grave failure to live up to its responsibilities as the Occupying Power, which is to care for those living under occupation.[277] The Muslim Brotherhood opened the first Islamic university in Gaza in 1978.[278]

During this time, Hamas focused on social rather than political and military activity.[279] However, between 1977 and 1987, when the Likud party came into power in Israel, restrictions on Palestinians in Gaza increased significantly, with the Gaza Strip becoming a giant prison.[280] It was during the early days of the First Intifada when the Palestinian population engaged in their popular struggle against their treatment by Israel, with the Israelis responding with force, that Palestinians began using small weapons such as knives, stones and Molotov cocktails and started shooting at Israeli military and civilian transportation.[281] Yitzchak Rabin ordered soldiers to break the arms and legs of those who were resisting being oppressed. This was predominantly against children who began throwing rocks at soldiers.[282]

Shortly after this, Hamas released its first charter in 1988, which called for the destruction of Israel. Because of the Charter's ideology, and because in early 1989, Hamas captured and killed two Israeli soldiers, which is acceptable under international law, Israel declared Hamas a terrorist organisation.[283] However, in 2009, Hamas leaders Musa Abu-Marzook and Khaled Mashaal denounced the 1988 Charter as being outdated and no longer applicable.[284]

According to the contents of Hamas' Charter of 1 May 2017,[285] I read that Hamas see Jerusalem as their capital, that the Al-Aqsa Mosque belongs to the Palestinian people, and that they do not recognise the ongoing settlement building for Jewish Israelis. They want the Palestinians to return to their land and homes (should their homes still exist) or to be given compensation, as under the United Nations General Assembly Resolution 194 (III) of 11 December 1948. Hamas sees Zionism as a racist and aggressive colonialist project that goes against the Palestinian people and is the foundation of the aggression. According to the 2017 charter, Hamas' issues are with Zionism and not with the Jews themselves because of their religion. They, therefore, class everything to do with Zionism as being illegitimate. The Charter states Hamas would accept a Palestinian State along the lines of 4 June 1967.

Hamas and the Palestinian Liberation Organisation

As Tareq Baconi states, after the State of Israel was declared in 1948, the Israeli government forced nearly 200,000 Palestinian refugees into the Gaza Strip, with conditions deteriorating rapidly. Being close to the armistice line, incursions into Israel began. The Muslim Brotherhood also started military training camps, with Yasser Arafat being trained in one of these camps. He had hoped to improve the conditions for the Palestinians, so he undertook small-scale armed operations, but these were met with harsh retaliation by Israel.

Arafat left Gaza for Kuwait before pressure was placed on the Muslim Brotherhood due to Egyptian President Nasser's determination to unite the Arab world through Arab identity and not by religion. This caused the

Muslim Brotherhood to be driven underground in Gaza. Arafat became inspired to seek liberation for Palestine from Zionism. He believed it would be achieved through armed struggle. Arafat and other students created Fatah, the Palestinian National Liberation Movement. They undertook insurgent activities in Syria, Lebanon, Jordan and the West Bank.

To bring the insurgencies under control, Arab leaders established the Palestinian Liberation Organisation in 1964, with Yasser Arafat becoming its leader in 1969. Their resistance activities increased with intensity, and the United States said they were becoming allied to the USSR, so they labelled them as a terrorist organisation, forcing them to leave Jordan for Lebanon.

Over time, and because of their isolation, Arafat decided to take the diplomatic route to gain freedom for Palestinians. Around then, the Muslim Brotherhood gained momentum and financial support from the Arab Gulf States, so it began investing in community services in Gaza.

A few months after Hamas released its first Charter in 1988, Arafat and his leaders in Algiers organised a convention. There he announced the independence of the State of Palestine and his willingness to accept twenty-two percent of the land of Palestine, including areas of the West Bank, East Jerusalem and the Gaza Strip. Along with this, he renounced terrorism. Hamas saw the concessions as unacceptable and unhelpful for the Palestinians.[286]

Consequently, from what I can see, although both Hamas and the Palestinian Liberation Organisation want freedom and independence for Palestinians, their methods towards achieving those goals are different. The Palestinian Liberation Organisation under Yasser Arafat started by using armed resistance against Israel; then, they moved to non-armed resistance, specifically diplomacy, which did not see their goals achieved. Conversely, Hamas initially began by using non-armed resistant methods. However, they found that from when the Likud Party came into power in Israel, the increased brutality of the Israeli Defence Forces between 1977 and 1987 against the Palestinians gave them no choice but to start using armed resistance.

Today, the Palestinian Liberation Organisation has been led by Mahmoud Abbas since 2004, and he has also been the elected leader of the Palestinian National Authority since 19 January 2005.[287] As leader, he prefers to negotiate with Israel on security issues and also inform Israel of any planned resistance, which is seen by some as collaboration with or subcontracting to the Israeli occupation.[288]

World View of Hamas

Living in Australia, I was keen to know the Australian government's view of Hamas. Hamas was declared a terrorist organisation on 04 March 2022. Previously, it was only the Izzy Al-Qassim Brigades which was listed as terrorists.[289] The United States listed Hamas as a terrorist organisation on October 8 1997.[290] The United States has also clarified that it would not involve itself in any 'peace process' until Hamas denounced any so-called terrorist activities and relinquished all of its weapons.

Because of a significant number of countries classifying Hamas as a terrorist organisation, official financial help to Gaza ended, apart from Israel allowing Qatar to provide for the Palestinian people through Hamas.[291]

National View of Hamas

Because the Israeli government declared Hamas a terrorist organisation in 1989, it continues its refusal to deal directly with them. Since Hamas won the 2006 elections in the Gaza Strip, Israel placed a general blockade on goods being able to enter and leave Gaza. This causes everyone to suffer.

However, basic food supplies were smuggled into the Gaza Strip through a network of tunnels constructed by Hamas, bypassing the Rafah Crossing on the Egyptian border.[292]

Hamas governs following the Sharia-based Palestinian Basic Law, and they appear to have some Palestinian public support because they defended the Al-Aqsa Mosque compound and the Jerusalem residents of Sheikh Jarrah who were facing eviction in 2021.[293] However, although most of the Palestinians living in Gaza support the resistance against Israel, the lack of unemployment and deep poverty frustrates them.[294]

Palestinian elections were to be held in May 2021. However, Abbas was concerned that internal rifts inside Fatah may have given Hamas a clear advantage, so he cancelled the election.[295] Two years later, a survey conducted in June 2023 found that Palestinians dislike the split of the West Bank and Gaza into two separate governing areas. The survey also revealed that more than half of Palestinians in Gaza and the West Bank would vote for Hamas's Haniyeh over PA President Mahmoud Abbas in a presidential election. At the same time, just one-third of Palestinians would choose Abbas.[296]

LIFE FOR PALESTINIANS IN GAZA

Life is the hardest for Palestinians in Gaza. The Israeli government restricts construction materials from entering Gaza because they say that Hamas can use some materials for their military purposes.[297] The materials needed to repair buildings and homes and even totally rebuild them are heavily restricted or stopped. Food including lentils, pasta, tomato paste and juice are prohibited. Batteries for hearing aids are banned. This means that many deaf children suffer even more than they are already suffering. The United Nations Relief and Works Agency, an organisation dedicated to helping Palestinian refugees in the Near East, provides help and support to Palestinians. Even though they provide basic food and oil, which prevents starvation, Palestinians in Gaza suffer from the worst anemia in the region, with children stunted in their growth because of malnutrition.[298] In a report issued in 2017, over one million Palestinians in Gaza are moderately to severely food insecure.[299]

Refugees may return to the homes they were driven from according to the *United Nations General Assembly Resolution 194 (III) of 11 December 1948,* 11: "Resolves that the refugees wishing to return to their homes and live at peace with their neighbours should be implemented at the earliest practicable date and compensation should be paid for the property of those choosing not to return and for loss of or property damage which, under principles of international law or in equity, should be made good by the Governments or authorities responsible."[300]

In reality, the Israeli government prevents Palestinians from ever returning to their homes. Expelling the Palestinians was always the Israeli government's plan, with Prime Minister Ben Gurion stating, "The Arabs will have to go, but one needs an opportune time to make it happen, such as a war."[301] The Israeli government refused to abide by GA Res.194 then, and it still does today. In 1954, there were reports of some refugees leaving Gaza and trying to return to their displaced homes. The Israeli government introduced a law, which in part relates specifically to Palestinians: *Prevention of Infiltration (Offences and Jurisdiction) Law 1954 (5714)* 1: "In this Law – 'infiltrator' means a person who has entered Israel knowingly and unlawfully and who at any time between the 16th Kislev, 3708 (29th November 1947) and his entry was… (3) a Palestinian citizen or a Palestinian resident without nationality or citizenship or whose nationality or citizenship was doubtful and who, during the said period, left his ordinary place of residence in an area which has become a part of Israel or for a place outside

Israel."³⁰² These refugees were considered infiltrators. After they were taken back to Gaza, their homes were demolished and burned, and mines were placed on the routes to block any attempt to return.³⁰³ Between 1967 and 2005, Israel built 21 settlements in Gaza, which were on 20 percent of Gaza's territory.³⁰⁴ Palestinians in Gaza were also under military rule. There were checkpoints and separate roads which only the Jewish Israelis were permitted to use. Palestinians were not allowed to undertake any form of political activity, such as handing out leaflets or raising a Palestinian flag.

Palestinians had their homes demolished for the building of new settlements. This situation, as well as the overall living conditions, led to the First and Second Intifadas. Any response to Palestinians' effort to resist what they had to endure was met with brutal retaliation by the Israeli Army. Stone-throwing began during this time as a form of resistance, just like the story of the battle between David and Goliath, with the Palestinians being David.³⁰⁵ It was also in 1967 that the Palestinians embraced the watermelon as their symbol because when it was cut, it had the same colours as their flag, which they were not permitted to fly for 26 years, so it was a quiet form of resistance.³⁰⁶ So, the use of pictures of watermelons on social media and in rallies and protests is not a recent phenomenon.

Within a year of Hamas winning the elections of 2006, and based on Major General Amos Yaldin's statement, "Israel would be happy if Hamas took over Gaza because the Israeli Defence Forces could then deal with Gaza as a hostile state", the Israeli government used collective punishment and locked up Gaza from the outside world.³⁰⁷ Prohibitions were introduced, which no longer allowed tourists, but only international aid workers, journalists and diplomats from entering Gaza.³⁰⁸

I cannot even find suitable words to describe the actions and behaviour of the Israeli government, which was shown to be increasing in its brutality towards all Palestinians, especially those in Gaza. The Israeli government *wanted* Hamas to be the government in Gaza, so the whole population there could be considered hostile. With Hamas winning the election, it gave the Israeli government the excuse they needed to lock up the people indefinitely. This was the situation before 7 October 2023.

'Mowing the Grass'

Every few years, the Israeli Defence Forces bomb Gaza, whether its actions are justified or not. 'Mowing the Grass' is a term that I have frequently heard when referring to what the Israeli Defence Forces have been doing in Gaza. That term was first used in 2006 when Israel attacked Lebanon and was initially called the 'Dahiya Doctrine'.

In 2006, the Israeli forces bombed the Dahiya quarter of Beirut with a tremendous amount of force because missiles had been fired into Israel from there. The disproportionate retaliation caused significant damage and destruction. The Israeli military no longer considered the villages in that area civilian villages but military bases.[309]

What happened in Beirut in 2006 is the same as what has been happening in Gaza ever since, with it being termed vis-à-vis Gaza: the 'Dahiya Doctrine'.[310] It is obvious to me that the Israeli Defence Forces deploy a disproportionate amount of weaponry against Palestinians in Gaza.

In August 2005, the Israeli forces and citizens left Gaza and moved back to Israel after 38 years. Prime Minister Ariel Sharon wanted to decrease the chance of further terrorist attacks, plus he realised that holding 3-1/2 million people under occupation was not sustainable for Israelis, Palestinians and the Israeli economy.[311]

During conversations I have had with others and interviews I have listened to, some point out that Israel pulled out of the Gaza Strip in 2005, so Hamas controls it now. Physically, yes, the Israeli forces and its citizens left in 2005. However, the Israeli government still has ultimate control, which is rarely acknowledged. This control is seen by the control they place on the food that enters Gaza, who enters and leaves Gaza through the borders and the overall health of the people living there.

Netanyahu has always been vocal about his dislike of Hamas, so he refuses to talk with them because of the group's designation as a terrorist organisation. In January 2006, Hamas won the general election and became the authority in Gaza. The United States blocked Palestinian access to finance to shift the ordinary Palestinian opinion against Hamas, which, it was hoped, would cause them to fail.[312] Instantly, the Israeli government tightened the conditions as a form of collective punishment which was felt by all the people living in Gaza. 140,000 workers were denied wages, causing Fatah and Hamas to begin engaging in fierce armed clashes, and life for the ordinary people became socially and economically harder. The Palestinian Authority also believed that it would benefit from its ties with Israeli officials.[313]

Since then, the Israeli Defence Forces have been sent into Gaza whenever it suits the Israeli government. The Israeli Defence Force appears to attack indiscriminately, which is prohibited. According to international law, "indiscriminate attacks are (a) those that are not directed at a specific military objective, (b) those that employ a method or means of combat that cannot be directed at a specific military objective, or (c) those that employ a method or means of combat the effects of which cannot be limited as required by this Protocol; and consequently, in each such case, are of a nature to strike military objectives and civilians or civilian objects without distinction."[314]

With the Israeli government's enforced blockade on Gaza and especially after particular violent or unjust actions from the Israeli Defence Force, such as home demolitions or evictions in East Jerusalem, Hamas and other Palestinian groups periodically fire missiles into Israeli towns and settlements. Since this action targets civilian areas, it is also against international humanitarian law.[315]

The primary attacks on Gaza have been:

1. *Operation Cast Lead (2008-2009).* The first significant attacks started on December 27, 2008, and lasted 21 days—ending on January 18, 2009. "Over three weeks, Israeli forces dropped around 1 million kilograms of explosives on the strip, causing the destruction of nearly 4,100 houses and damaging 17,500 others. Almost 1,500 (1,436) Palestinians were killed, and about 5,400 were wounded, including 300 children and women."[316]

   During this Operation, the Israeli Defence Forces fired a disproportionate amount of weaponry into Gaza. Although there were unfounded accusations that Hamas was using schools and, therefore, 'human shields' to fire their rockets, it was the Israeli Defence Forces that caused damage to schools and killed students and teachers. "At least 280 schools and kindergartens were damaged/severely damaged, including 18 destroyed schools (eight government, two private, and eight kindergartens). Six university buildings were destroyed, and 16 were damaged. 164 students and 12 teachers from its schools were killed during the Israeli military offensive; 98 of the students killed were from north Gaza. A further 454 students and five teachers were injured. A total of 86 children and three teachers who attend UNRWA schools were killed, and an additional 402 students and 14 teachers were injured."[317] A report by Human Rights Watch also revealed that the Israeli Defence Forces used Palestinians as human shields.[318]

2. *Operation Pillar of Defence (2012).* Israel killed Hamas's military chief of staff, Ahmad Jabari.[319] [The attack on Gaza] then started

on November 14, 2012, and lasted for eight days, ending on November 21, 2012. "Israeli warplanes killed 162 Palestinians, wounded nearly 1,300, and destroyed 200 houses. Another 1,500 homes were damaged."[320]

3. *Operation Protective Edge (2014).* Comparing the previous Operations undertaken by Israel since Hamas won the general election, this was the most prolonged and "most deadly Israeli attack on Gaza [up until that Operation], starting on July 8, 2014, and lasting 51 days—ending on August 26, 2014. Euro-Med Monitor's field team documented 60,664 Israeli land, sea and air raids, which killed 2,147 Palestinians (in many cases, involving whole families) and wounded 10,870 others. A recorded 17,123 homes were hit, of which 2,465 were destroyed. 73 Israelis, including 67 soldiers, were killed."[321]

Looking further, I discovered that just before Operation Protective Edge, Fatah and Hamas formed a unity government, which Minister Netanyahu refused to acknowledge. This is because of the Israeli government declaring Hamas to be a terrorist group.[322] Even though Netanyahu knew that a rogue cell and not Hamas leadership orchestrated a kidnapping and almost immediate killing of some Israeli teenagers, he used the situation to break up the unity government.[323] After a publicity campaign of a few weeks and getting the Israeli public on their side, he organised a pretend rescue mission to get the teenagers back. Instead, they killed five West Bank Palestinians, homes were demolished, and businesses ransacked. Also, 700 Palestinians were arrested, with the majority being Hamas members.[324] Even though Hamas initially resisted being involved, eventually they could no longer resist, and the war began. What I find disturbing is that the Israeli government were planning from late 2013 to start a war in Gaza. They intended to "deal a harsh blow to Gaza and to the organisations operating there, in a way that would damage their capabilities and exact a heavy toll."[325]

4. *Great March of Return (2018-2019).* Palestinian protests began at Gaza's fenced border with Israel. Israeli troops opened fire to keep them back. In 2018 alone, 183 Palestinians were killed in months of protests.[326]

5. *Operation Guardian of the Walls (2021).* "After weeks of tension during the Muslim holy month of Ramadan, hundreds of Palestinians were injured by Israeli security forces at the Al-Aqsa Mosque compound in Jerusalem. Hamas demanded Israel withdraw security forces from the compound."[327] "The attack started on 10 May 2021 and lasted 11 days, ending on 21 May 2021. The Israeli army focused its air and artillery attacks on the infrastructure of Gaza, especially streets, water wells, and public facilities, as well as the Strip's economic and productive capacities. As a result, these sectors sustained heavy losses. According to the Palestinian Ministry of Health, the attack resulted in the deaths of 254 Palestinians, including 66 children, 39 women, and 17 older adults. Additionally, about 1,948 others were injured."[328]

A medic working in Gaza, Mohammed Abu Mughaisib, worked during this Operation. Having also worked during previous 'wars', he could compare them. "The 2021 war was not like her siblings. The terrifying continuous bombing on a massive scale, the lack of safety anywhere at any time: we were petrified. There were no coordinated pauses to allow for humanitarian work."[329]

6. *August (2022).* "More than 30 Palestinians, including women and children, were killed in new air attacks carried out by Israeli planes.

Palestinian Islamic Jihad, whose two commanders were killed in the air strikes, fired dozens of rockets into Israel in response."[330]

7. *Operation Swords of Iron (8 October 2023-current).*

This latest operation by Israel on Gaza began after members of Hamas, as well as members of Islamic Jihad, broke out of the Gaza Strip on 7 October 2023, using a bulldozer, motorbikes, paragliders and even boats. The Palestinians also fired rockets into some of the southern towns of Israel. Due to the rockets and direct confrontation by the Palestinians, "695 Israeli civilians, as well as 373 security forces, were killed, along with 71 foreigners, totalling 1,139 people."[331] Also, 290 Israelis, which included civilians and military personnel, were taken back into Gaza on that October morning.

As of 1 June 2024, over 36,284 Palestinians have been killed by the Israeli Defence Force.[332]

Status Quo

This current structure of provocation by Israel, the response by Palestinians, and then disproportionate retaliation upon Gaza by the Israeli Defence Forces is unlikely to change. From my understanding, there seems to be an inability of the international community under the United Nations to stop the Israeli blockade of Gaza and its periodic disproportionate bombing. The Palestinians in Gaza appear to be on their own. If they remain quiet, it seems that the Israeli authorities will walk all over them, and if they show any form of resistance to the conditions under which they must live, then it is determined as being their fault if anyone gets killed. Whether Hamas or any other group undertake any other form of resistance to the blockade of Gaza or the overall occupation, they know that the retaliation by the Israeli army will be disproportionate to what they have done.

Ethnic Cleansing

The number of documents becoming declassified is increasing. The whole intent of the Israeli government's plan for Gaza is being revealed. Their goal is the ethnic cleansing of the Palestinian people from Gaza. In 1967, Prime Minister Levi Eschol wanted the Arabs to leave Gaza, and as a way of forcing them to go, he declared, "Perhaps if we don't give them enough water, they won't have a choice because the orchards will yellow and wither."[333]

Even before the current Swords of Iron Operation being undertaken by the Israeli government, the situation in Gaza was already critical, with "97 percent of freshwater being unsuitable for human consumption because of raw sewage that pours into the sea. Now, it is deadly. Also, the Israeli government controls the flow of fuel into the region."[334] On 28 July 2010, the United Nations General Assembly adopted Resolution 64/292 which gave humans water and sanitation rights, as they are both considered 'essential' in sustaining human life.[335] However, Palestinians in Gaza are denied the privilege of having clean drinking water and sanitation. A 2018 report by United Nations Special Rapporteur Michael Lynk said, "The Gaza economy is falling, and it is unknown when this decline will stop. There is 70 percent youth unemployment, the drinking water is contaminated, and the health care system has collapsed. Gaza is unlivable."[336]

Without enough food, the growth of upcoming youth will be stunted. Coupled with a lack of drinking water, the end for the people of Gaza will be a slow death. It may not happen in a generation, but it will happen.

7

REFUSING TO GIVE IN

Two areas I had to consider were terrorism and resistance. I had never considered either before September 2001 beyond just a cursory look. After September 2001, terrorism was something that people of the world, and especially governments, placed their priority on. For me, living in Australia, a safe country away from most global hostilities, terrorism was not an issue. Yes, we had the Hilton bombing in Sydney during the Commonwealth Heads of Government Regional Meeting on 13 February 1978 and the hostage siege at Lindt Café, Martin Place, on 15-16 December 2014, but that is all.[337] Although not labelled a terrorist attack by authorities, I have included the Port Arthur massacre on 28 April 1996 because 21 people were killed on the day, and 14 people later died because of their injuries.[338] Australia had not suffered with that many people being killed at one time through the use of a weapon outside of official war times. The Port Arthur massacre caused the Australian government to tighten the laws relating to gun ownership, making it harder for individuals to own a gun.

I knew even less about resistance within an occupation. I watched a few war movies while living at home during my teenage years. In these movies, the French Resistance was fighting to stop the German occupation of France. I did not know more than that. However, I have since learned that two significant forms of resistance often exist against any occupation. I first considered terrorism.

TERRORISM

During 2014, while I was reading 'The General's Son', the 2014 Gaza War began on 8 July 2014 and finished on 26 August 2014. "2,251 Palestinians, with 1,462 of them being civilians, including 551 children and 299 women. 66 Israeli soldiers and five civilians, including one child, were killed. Overall, 11,231 Palestinians were injured and almost 500,000 people internally displaced."[339] I found it hard to avoid what was happening in Gaza as it was all over the media. News broadcasters were showing pictures and footage of people being killed and buildings being blown up, which was confronting. Being engrossed in reading Miko's book and coming to terms with what I was reading, I did not know the reason for the Gaza War. I had heard enough news to know that the Gaza War was between the Israeli Defence Forces and Hamas. I did not know what either side stood for. Also, before this War and reading Miko's book, I had no reason to consider the news from Palestine. However, I knew that would quickly change, which it did.

My thinking and views were changing. I was no longer willing to accept any damaging accusations that were said about any Palestinians at face value. Overnight, I became highly suspicious of any reports that came out of Israel, especially from the Israeli government, Israeli Defence Forces and Israeli media. I decided I would always research and look behind an event to find potential reasons events particularly involving Palestinians were happening, including the reasons that brought about the Gaza War.

Five months later, another incident caught my attention, propelling me to investigate what happened. On 22 October 2014, a Palestinian man, Abd al-Rahman al-Shaludi, was shot dead by Israeli authorities after he rammed his car into a crowded Jerusalem train station, which killed a three-month-old Israeli American girl.[340] The event was immediately called a terrorist attack by the Israeli authorities.[341] The Western media also did not hesitate to call it a terrorist attack, but I was not ready to do that. Even in a few short months on this journey of discovery, it was easy for me to see that in any official Israeli governmental communication, as well as in some Israeli media, Palestinians were quickly called 'terrorists' at any possible opportunity. I believed then and still believe today that this automatic labelling and stereotyping, especially by the Israeli government, Israeli Defence Force and media, is not helpful due to their automatic bias. Also, I do not believe it allows room to understand the background and potential reason for such events.

I did some digging and found out that Abd al-Rahman al-Shaludi had been recently released from an Israeli jail after undergoing three weeks of interrogation by Shin Bet (Israel's secret police) in the Jerusalem Russian Compound. As a result of what he endured, he was suffering from mental health issues. That fateful morning, he was going to see a psychiatrist after being referred by a doctor.[342]

Since that incident, I have always tried to find independent reporting sources that are as unbiased as possible. Then, I make my conclusion or see if further information is forthcoming. One month later, on 19 November 2014, Israeli authorities, using collective punishment, destroyed the family home of Abd al-Rahman al-Shaludi, even though his parents were the owners of the house.[343] Also, I have found that the truth about events is usually disclosed in time, which can sometimes be different from the original story. Unfortunately, I have also observed that even if the truth has been revealed, it is not always broadly publicised. Hence, people still believe the original report, especially if it is sensational.

Even with these events, I found that articles, in many cases, were no longer reliable because they only sometimes present the background information that brought about the said event, as in the case I have just mentioned. Also, I did not have a definition of terrorism. I wanted to know because, from what I observed by looking at news reports on television and reading media, terrorism seems to have broad application. Four years later, in 2018, while studying in the Conflict, Security and Terrorism unit at Deakin University, I submitted an assignment on terrorism, including a definition of terrorism.

Defining Terrorism

While researching for that assignment, I discovered that a universally accepted definition did not exist, and it still does not, even today. This is because "the act of terrorism is very subjective, based on individual perceptions."[344] I also discovered that different contexts and environments can also provide other value judgments of what terrorism is, even for similar events.

When writing the assignment, I remembered a news report from Sydney a few years earlier. After finding it, I then went looking for a similar event in Palestine, which I found. Using these similar acts that teenagers undertook, I could show differences within different value judgements. "On 4 January 2011, three young teenagers were seen throwing rocks at a train near Macquarie Fields in Sydney, where a male passenger was injured in the chest and taken to hospital."[345] Within this event, at no point was the word terrorist used to describe the teenagers.

On March 14 2013, in a similar instance near the town of Ariel in the West Bank, Palestinian teenagers threw rocks at passing cars, injuring several people, including critically injuring a 2-year-old infant. In the documentary 'Stone Cold Justice', Lieutenant Colonel Maurice Hirsh, Israeli Army's head of prosecutions in the West Bank, described the act above as terrorism.[346]

The significant difference between these two episodes is that the Palestinians are considered an enemy of Israel by its government, so for the Israelis, it seems reasonable to attach the term 'terrorism' to the teenager's activity that day. It is apparent that any harmful activity undertaken by a presumed enemy [where people are injured or even killed, can easily be labelled as being an act of terrorism], yet when [similar acts are] undertaken by an accepted citizen, the activity is not considered terrorism. "The benefits to a government by labelling any group or individual as an enemy or terrorist is that the government can more easily uphold its power and control."[347]

The United States defines international and domestic terrorism slightly differently, with the Federal Bureau of Investigation defining International terrorism as "violent, criminal acts committed by individuals and groups who are inspired by, or associated with, designated foreign terrorist organisations or nations (state-sponsored)", and they define domestic terrorism as "violent, criminal acts committed by individuals and groups to further ideological goals stemming from domestic influences, such as those of a political, religious, social, racial, or environmental nature."[348]

In Australia, the Australian government does not have a working definition related to international terrorism, but it does within Australian Commonwealth Law, which states:

> An act or threat intended to advance a political, ideological, or religious cause; and coerce or intimidate an Australian or foreign government, the public or section of the public, including the foreign public. The conduct falls within the

definition if it causes serious physical harm to a person or serious property damage; causes death or endangers a person's life; creates a serious risk to the health and safety of the public, or section of the public, or seriously interferes, disrupts or destroys: electronic information, telecommunications or financial system; or an electronic system used for the delivery of essential government services, used for or by an essential public utility, or transport system.[349]

With these broad definitions in mind, we see that labelling an event an 'act of terrorism' can have far-reaching effects. Direct effects include deaths and sustained health issues due to physical and psychological injuries and trauma. Economically, businesses can be financially ruined, and depending on the scale of the event and which country it has occurred in, even national economies can suffer. Indirectly, individuals and people groups that are not even attached to the event in any way can also suffer. Racism through verbal and physical abuse can escalate towards individuals and people groups with the same ethnicity as the perpetrator just because the 'terrorist' label has been attached to the event.

An example occurred during and after the siege at the Lindt Café, Martin Place, Sydney, on 15-16 December 2014. Due to increased racist verbal and physical abuse directed towards a particular people group, an initiative started through a single social media hashtag: "If you reg take the #373 bus b/w Coogee/MartinPl, wear religious attire, & don't feel safe alone: I'll ride with you. @ me for schedule", and spread, with many others showing solidarity with Muslims feeling threatened, by using the hashtag, "#illridewithyou."[350]

I also learned that 'terrorism' can be the result of the action or inaction of the ruling government, where it refuses to improve conditions, especially for the minority groups and citizens living within its borders.

The events of September 2001, with the attacks on the United States Twin Towers in New York and the Pentagon in Washington DC undertaken by Al Qaeda, were considered the most devastating single terrorist attack in history, with approximately 3,000 deaths.[351] The war on terrorism moved into first gear from that date to prevent another event of such proportions. Before the September 2001 event, acts of terrorism occurred, but not on the same scale. One of the deadliest events was the bombing of Pan Am Flight 103 over Lockerbie on 21 December 1988, which killed 259 passengers and crew and 11 on the ground.[352] On 12 December 2022, the perpetrator of this bombing "Abu Agila Mohammad Mas'ud Kheir Al-Marimi (Mas'ud), 71, of Tunisia and Libya, made his initial appearance in the U.S. District Court for the District of Columbia on federal charges."[353] I have found no further information about the case at the time of writing.

It did not take long for my thinking to shift, to consider what was happening, particularly in Gaza, where in the Palestinian elections of 2006, Hamas was elected to be the Palestinian government to be based in Gaza after defeating Fatah.[354]

If anyone looks superficially, it may seem that Hamas undertake terrorist incursions into the State of Israel regularly. Through looking a little deeper, incursions predominantly occur because of Israeli provocation. Usually, members of the Israeli police or Israeli Defence Forces have attacked and even killed individual Palestinians without apparent reason, especially in Jerusalem and even at the site of the Al-Aqsa Mosque, which is the fourth most important site to Muslims. Also, as seen in the chapter on the West Bank, though applicable anywhere in Palestine where Palestinians live, Israeli authorities often undertake raids of Palestinian homes in the middle of the night with some of its occupants, which can include children, being dragged away and even placed in prison for unspecified periods, without conviction. The ongoing psychological abuse inflicted on Palestinian daily lives by the Israeli authorities must be excruciating. Eventually, this unwarranted and ongoing abuse may lead to retaliation by any individual Palestinian or resistance groups.

The Principle of Distinction

Because of these ongoing provocations and retaliations, I wanted to determine the official engagement rules between opposing sides. I remembered useful information from Amnesty International that Jeff Halper used.

Under international law, there must be a distinction between combatants and civilians during war. Also, there needs to be a distinction between civilian and military objects. Civilians who are not involved in the war are not to be targeted. It is known as The Principle of Distinction and codified in the four Geneva Conventions of 1949 and their two Additional Protocols of 1977. These are binding on all those involved in a war.[355]

Considering the parameters within The Principle of Distinction and applying it to Palestine, I find both Palestinian resistance groups and the Israeli Defence Forces could be guilty of targeting civilians. However, the situation between the Israeli Defence Forces and any Palestinian resistance is not a usual situation of war. Instead, one group of people is occupied by another, and rather than being protected by the occupier, the occupied people are suffering under a brutal, belligerent occupation. They are not two separate states, with both parties having statehood and full United Nations membership, as the Palestinian people are still seeking such. They are certainly not evenly matched in their access to weaponry available to them. I assert that others, individual or nation, do not have the right to suggest how a group of people resist their occupation. Sometimes, occupied people flaunt international law to get attention from the international community, especially if they have been ignored. I consider the Palestinians, and especially those in Gaza, to have been ignored for too many years, so they push the boundaries of international law. Certain resistance to an occupation, however, is catered for within international law.

Considering the ongoing 2023 Operation Swords of Iron, Israel, especially, has yet to be seen as abiding by international law. On 11 January 2024, the Republic of South Africa brought a case against Israel to the International Court of Justice on a Plausible Case for Genocide against Palestinian civilians. Enacting a plausible genocide against civilians goes against The Principle of Distinction. The Israeli government's decision to ignore the rulings of the International Court of Justice, which was handed down on 26 January 2024, shows its blatant disregard for international law. The judges made it clear that any activity causing harm to the Palestinians was to be stopped. And that humanitarian aid of all types was to be given to the Palestinians. Prior to the events of 7 October 2023 which instigated the 2023 Operation Swords of Iron, there were no cases brought against the Palestinians. However, in July 2024 the International Court of Justice brought charges against Hamas leaders and Benjamin Netanyahu.

When it seems easy to judge the behaviour of others, especially what is happening in Palestine, my husband often says something that infers that before anyone judges Palestinians, they should try and live the same way they have to. Most of us do not live in Palestine, and we do not have to endure living in an environment where a colonialist government and occupation control every part of one's life. Also, not everything is black and white; it also includes many shades of grey, so everything needs to be considered.

RESISTANCE

Historically, whenever there has been any form of occupation, there has always been some form of resistance by the citizens being occupied. The French resistance used armed resistance in 1940 against the Germans during World War II, as did the South Korean resistance in 1950 against North Korea. The West Papuans have been seeking their freedom from Indonesia from 1969 to the present day. They initially started with armed resistance and later moved to non-armed resistance. The current Ukraine resistance against Russia from 2014, which is still ongoing against Russia, is armed resistance.

Armed Resistance

Our heart races, and our adrenaline increases as self-preservation mechanisms kick in whenever our lives or the lives of our loved ones may be in danger. A home invasion could be one such scenario. We instinctively want to resist the intruder the best way we can, with some people resorting to using anything as a weapon. It is no different on a national level where a country has been occupied, and the people want to resist by any means possible.

There is provision for armed struggle based on the *United Nations General Assembly Resolution A/RES/33/24 of 29 November 1978*: "Point two reaffirms the legitimacy of peoples' struggle for independence, territorial integrity, national unity and liberation from colonial and foreign domination and foreign occupation by all available means, particularly armed struggle." This Resolution also explicitly names the Palestinian people. "Point three Reaffirms the inalienable right of the peoples of Namibia and Zimbabwe, of the Palestinian people and all peoples under alien and colonial domination to self-determination, national independence, territorial integrity, national unity and sovereignty without external interference."[356]

In point three, the General Assembly Resolution A/RES/3246 (XXIX) of 29 November 1974: "*reaffirms* the legitimacy of the people's struggle for liberation from colonial and foreign domination and alien subjugation by all available means, including armed struggle."[357] Furthermore, the resolution, in point seven, "strongly condemns all governments that do not recognise the right to self-determination and independence of peoples under colonial and foreign domination and alien subjugation, notably the peoples of Africa and the Palestinian people."[358]

Even though the Palestinian people have legitimacy and the right to use armed resistance, according to international law, I am still not one hundred percent comfortable with the idea of armed struggle due to my conservative upbringing and my Christian beliefs. However, the more I read about what has been happening under Zionism particularly since 1967 through to today in Palestine but especially in Gaza, the more I understand and accept the Palestinian people's need to resist Israel's belligerent occupation actively in the realm of armed resistance. For some, this means using hand weapons such as knives and guns. For others, it means using more sophisticated weapons.

When Palestinians refuse to accept their occupation and use armed resistance, the Israeli authorities always respond disproportionately, with the same results. Resistance to the occupation can mean instant death from a dropped bomb or missile, an accurately fired bullet from an Israeli Defence Forces sniper's gun, or a future completely shattered through the loss of limbs, which permanently alters individual lives and often excludes them from any future employment. There can be the destruction of homes, buildings and infrastructure. Individuals are imprisoned, which usually includes indescribable torture.

Even with these possible outcomes, the Palestinian community will continue to resist the occupation in any way possible.

Hamas is the local authority in Gaza, and they resist the occupation predominantly by using armed resistance. They also state in their charter that they use armed resistance according to international norms and laws.[359] So, who is this group? I wanted to know.

Is Hamas a terrorist group or freedom fighters?

When I started this project in January 2022 with some initial internet research on Hamas, a significant number of sites had the word 'terrorist' associated with them. As I have previously mentioned, I am no longer willing to accept the terrorist label without further investigation. With Palestinians, I have found that there is usually an underlying reason that drives individuals and groups to undertake actions that could label them as terrorists. I wanted to know whether Hamas is a terrorist group or a group of freedom fighters endeavouring to gain freedom and national statehood for all Palestinians.

According to Boaz Ganor, any organisation that is seeking liberty and statehood, which attacks civilians from the opposing side or any civilians anywhere to gain attention to that cause, is a terrorist organisation.[360] He also says that for any organisation not to be labelled as terrorist, they should engage in guerrilla warfare, which only targets military and security personnel.[361] This means that in no circumstances should civilians be targeted; otherwise, a war crime under the Rome Statute of the International Criminal Court Article 8 has been committed.[362]

I understand Ganor's stance in an ordinary situation. However, as previously stated, I consider that the situation in Gaza is far from ordinary as Palestinians within the Gaza Strip are all locked behind a high concrete wall and electrified barrier fence on the Israeli side. There is a 12 km border between Gaza and Egypt, with the Rafah Crossing on that border. In 2022, the Rafah Crossing was open for 245 days, with few Palestinians allowed through.[363] The remaining side is the Mediterranean Sea. In 2010, former British Prime Minister David Cameron called the Gaza Strip an "open-air prison."[364] As I have already shown, and according to the United Nations General Assembly Resolutions, arms struggle is permissible if against colonial and foreign domination, which I see is the ongoing situation in Palestine, which the Resolutions specifically named.

Once again, there is a new operation being undertaken by the Israeli Defence Forces in Gaza called Operation Swords of Iron. This operation began because members of Hamas and Islamic Jihad infiltrated Israel on 7 October 2023. Using a bulldozer, they broke through a section of the electronic barrier fence beyond the areas of the concrete wall that divide Israel and the Gaza Strip. They then entered Israel on foot and rode motorbikes. Some even entered using hang gliders. Israeli military personnel and citizens were killed as a part of the infiltration into several settlements. Over 200 hostages were taken back into Gaza. However, with the kidnapping of Israeli and foreign civilians, Hamas is liable to be charged with war crimes and brought before the International Criminal Court, as civilians are never to be the target of any operation, including against an occupying force. Palestinians in East Jerusalem, the West Bank, and Gaza have been suffering under 76 years of occupation and apartheid. Also, for the last sixteen years, Palestinians in Gaza have been suffering under an almost complete blockade. Even though many Palestinians have also been killed and are continuing to be killed by Israeli Defence Forces, police and Jewish settlers, with very few ever being charged, the kidnapping of civilians on 7 October 2023, according to international law, is not justified.

When considering again whether Hamas is a terrorist organisation, providing an answer is no longer critical when compared to the disproportionate response of the Israeli Defence Forces since 8 October 2023, who have purposely killed innocent civilians in Gaza, with nearly half of those killed being children. Suppose I am to call Hamas a terrorist organisation. In that case, I must also accuse the Israeli government and the Israeli Defence Forces of undertaking state-sanctioned terrorism. This is not only for what they are currently doing in Gaza during Operation Swords of Iron but also for what they have been doing to Palestinians in East Jerusalem, West Bank and Gaza for many years.

During October 2023, I heard a statement, "Israel cannot live in peace, cannot enjoy the freedom they desire, whilst at the same time having a boot of oppression on a Palestinian neck."[365] I do not live in Gaza, but based on what I have shared previously, the Palestinians living there were already suffering severely.

Now, especially during Swords of Iron Operation, Palestinians are being largely ignored by the governments of the Global North. Citizens of the world have been marching and protesting in increasing numbers, calling for a ceasefire, but their calls are being ignored. Historically, Hamas undertakes offensive activities to gain some traction within the international community to reconsider the grievances of the Palestinian people.[366] Although it is coming at a substantial civilian cost, the international community seems to be finally understanding the oppression of the Palestinian people.

The Israeli government is declaring this current operation as self-defence. There is an increasing number of Palestinian civilians being killed and little evidence that many from Hamas have been killed or captured. While at the National Press Club in Canberra, Australia in November 2023, United Nations Special Rapporteur Francesca Albanese stated:

> The right of self-defence can be invoked when a state is threatened by another state, which is not the case [with

Israel]. Israel has not claimed it has been threatened by another state. It's been threatened by an armed group. Qualify it as you want, but it's an armed group within occupied territory. Frankly, even saying the war between Gaza and Israel is wrong because Gaza is not a standalone entity, [it] is part of the Occupied Territory. Israel cannot claim the right of self-defence against a threat that emanates from the territory it occupies, from a territory that is kept under belligerent occupation.[367]

Furthermore, historian Caroline Elkins, writing about the idea that the British, who claimed the right to murder, terrorise and steal land under 'self-defence' during its occupation of Kenya, argues, "the British claim goes against the United Nations General Assembly Resolution 37/43 of 1982, which recognised the legitimacy of the struggle of peoples for independence, territorial integrity, national unity and liberation from colonial and foreign domination and foreign occupation by all available means, including armed struggle."[368] The situation in Israel relating to the occupation of the Palestinians is no different.

Hamas uses Human Shields

One thing I hear regularly is that Hamas uses its people as 'human shields'. Before determining whether or not Hamas used human shields, I needed to find out what conventions and laws say about their use. Civilians are to be protected unless they get involved in the conflict: The *Geneva Convention, Article 51 - Protection of the civilian population, 7*: "The presence or movements of the civilian population or individual civilians shall not be used to render specific points or areas immune from military operations, particularly in attempts to shield military objectives from attacks or to shield, favour or impede military operations. The parties to the conflict shall not direct the movement of the civilian population or individual civilians to attempt to shield military objectives from attacks or to shield military operations."[369]

During Operation Cast Lead in 2008-2009, Israel's media Channel 2 News accused Hamas of using United Nations Relief and Works Agency schools to fire their rockets. However, in a following report Channel 2 News admitted the information about the United Nations Relief and Works Agency school was incorrect, as the Israelis told the United Nations that the claims about Hamas were utterly false. Also, a report by Human Rights Watch said that they "found no evidence that the civilian victims were used by Palestinian fighters as human shields or were shot in the crossfire between opposing forces."[370]

During Operation Protective Edge in 2014, Amnesty International had found no evidence that civilians were used as human shields around areas where military equipment was being stored. However, Hamas did "encourage civilians to 'ignore Israeli warnings to evacuate', with their reason not to incite panic among its people." [371] Even if 'human shields' were being used, it was Israel's duty as an occupier to protect them.

Defence and Diplomat Correspondent Kim Sengupta was in Khan Younis at the time of the operation and also reported that there was no evidence that Hamas used any of the Palestinians as human shields. He said that the worst thing that Hamas "could be accused of [was] making people complacent, repeatedly stating in the media that the Israeli warnings were psychological games and asking the population to ignore them. Some mentioned this as a reason for staying behind, returning home having initially left."[372]

REFUSING TO GIVE IN

Non-armed Resistance

While reading about non-armed resistance, I found an interesting observation by Palestinian academic and theologian Mitri Raheb, who lives in Bethlehem, in the West Bank, and advocates for non-armed resistance. He said that Gandhi in India and Martin Luther King Jr. in the United States fought against the British Empire and racial discrimination and segregation, respectively. Both realised that violence could lead to further violence within communities, which "cannot be easily stopped and eliminated when the achieved goal is attained."[373]

Both movements were successful in using non-armed means. Gandhi's leadership success was achieved when the British moved out of India in 1947.[374] Martin Luther King Jr.'s success was achieved with the passage of the Civil Rights Act in 1964 and the Voting Rights Act in 1965.[375] The former Portuguese colony of East Timor was taken over by Indonesia in 1975 but eventually gained independence from Indonesia through non armed resistance.[376] The East Timorese population initially used guerrilla warfare, which failed due to Indonesia's brutality, which destroyed the armed resistance and killed one-third of the East Timorese population.[377] After restructuring and employing non-violent methods such as holding demonstrations, East Timorese youth seized on an opportunity by intruding on a Papal visit and having a demonstration then and there. The media covered the demonstration and released it to the outside world.[378] After further massacres by the Indonesian authorities, further demonstrations and intervention by the international community, including the United Nations Security Council, East Timor, now called Timor Leste, became a state in May 2002.[379]

West Papuans are another group currently fighting to gain their freedom and independence from Indonesia. In 1998, they saw the need to change how they operate to gain more support, as their guerrilla groups were poorly armed groups fighting in the mountains and jungles. They moved to "a popular non-armed civilian-based movement in the cities and towns."[380]

Comparing the examples of the East Timorese and West Papuans to Palestinians, the Palestinians are at a huge disadvantage because the Israeli government has divided the Palestinian population into two separate areas, the West Bank and Gaza, with one group being locked away. Three different parties govern these two areas. In the West Bank, Area A is governed by the Palestinian Authority. Area B is governed by the Palestinian Authority and the Israeli government, and the Israeli government entirely rules Area C. Gaza's authority is Hamas. Consequently, it would be tough for any activity to be organised, let alone be acted upon.

Bassem Tamimi is a Palestinian who believes in non-armed activism. He organises protests from the small town of Nabi Saleh, 20 kilometres northwest of Ramallah, in the West Bank. He endured a form of torture that was once used on him in 1993, which nearly ended his life. During the brutal interrogation session by the Israeli military, a method which they call 'Solution' was used on him. Bassem was prevented from moving his head. I did not know until I heard this testimony that the head needs to keep moving so that nutrition can reach the brain. With this form of interrogation, which is very dangerous and is used by the Israelis, confessions usually come quickly. After hours of being interrogated, Bassam felt weak and fell into a coma. Ten days later, he awoke in a hospital. After some time, he was released from the hospital.[381]

Other forms of non-armed resistance by Palestinians include open-ended prisoner hunger strikes. Some choose to risk their lives by sitting in front of bulldozers to delay the demolition of homes or additional extensions to the wall. National and international artists, including poets, visual artists, filmmakers, novelists, and memoirists, use their talent to express their struggle with living in an occupation. Where possible, clergy hold conferences in or beyond Palestine, providing opportunities for others to learn about what is happening in Palestine. Thanks to modern technology, mobile phones upload photos and videos of daily suffering to various social media platforms and news networks.

Internationally, the Boycott Divestment and Sanctions (BDS) is a movement with three strands. The boycott focus encourages individuals not to purchase goods from Israeli companies that are made in the Occupied Territories, as Israel or their profits support the Israeli occupation. It also lobbies businesses and governments to refrain from buying Israeli-made products and services based in the Occupied Territories. Different sectors within society put pressure on their peers to not hold events in Israel or invite Israel to be a part of any international event. It may also include pressuring performers to cancel concerts scheduled to be held in Israel. Within sports, competitors are increasingly refusing to compete against Israelis. Miko Peled believes that it is not up to individuals to potentially ruin their sporting career by refusing to compete against Israeli competitors, but rather it is up to sporting institutions to not allow Israel competitors to participate.[382]

Unfortunately, non-armed demonstrations are being put down by the Israeli Defence Force in the same brutal manner used as armed resistance, such as what happened in the Great March of Return.

The Great March of Return

When considering non-armed resistance, I immediately thought about the Great March of Return (GMR) in Gaza a few years ago, between 30 March 2018 and 31 December 2019.

The Israeli Defence Force Spokesman Brig.-Gen. Ronen Manelis said, "Hamas, who controls Gaza, was using the protests to undertake launch attacks against Israel and ignite the area."[383] The Israeli military also said "12,000-14,000 Palestinians in Gaza were participating in what it described as 'riots', and that some had tried to breach the border into Israel. It said troops 'had operated by the rules of engagement' to stop people crossing the border."[384]

However, the protest was undertaken purely by civilians, and although some members of the political parties were represented, the armed wings of these parties were not represented on the committee.[385] The leadership committee was diverse and led by academics, artists and journalists.[386] The idea for the Great March of Return came from a 34-year-old Palestinian poet and journalist, Ahmed Abu Artema.[387] He saw birds flying free in the sky over the border and thought about and placed on social media:

> What if 200,000 demonstrators marched peacefully and broke through the fence east of Gaza and entered a few kilometres into the lands that are ours, holding the flags of Palestine and the keys to return, accompanied by international media, and then set up tents inside and established a city there?[388]

Even before the start of the protest, those who planned to attend would have known they would be risking their lives. The Israeli Defence Forces intended to deploy 100 snipers to the Gaza border, who had orders to "use a lot of force", with their soldiers carrying out their orders with perfection.[389]

Due to the protest's casualties, an independent international commission of inquiry was held. A United Nations Human Rights Council report released the results, which found that amongst the Palestinians in just nine months, "from 30 March - 31 December 2018, there were 183 fatalities, which included 171 being shot in the head/neck or torso. 8,120 were wounded by live ammunition."[390] "Twenty-one were left paralysed, nine were left permanently blind, and 122 had to have limb amputations, which included 20 children."[391] Two days were evil. "On March 30, 2018, the first day - live ammunition was fired from 9 am, with 18 killed and 765 wounded."[392] "On May 14, 2018, 60 Palestinians, including seven children, were killed and 1162 wounded."[393]

Under international law, there is protection, especially for children, disabled people, journalists and medics. This protection, including the Fourth Geneva Convention, was to be applied during a war and in genuine armed conflict. This situation was so much worse, as there were armed personnel and unarmed civilians.

Children are protected under *The Fourth Geneva Convention, Article 77—Protection of children.* "Children shall be the object of special respect and shall be protected against any form of indecent assault. The Parties to the conflict shall provide them with the care and aid they require, whether because of their age or for any other reason."[394]

Again, based on the United Nations report, "Israeli snipers killed 35 children, with a further 940 injured by ammunition."[395] It also conveyed that several children were shot intentionally because they were children.[396]

The *Convention on the Rights of Persons with Disabilities protects the disabled under Article 11 – Situations of risk and humanitarian emergencies.* "State parties shall undertake their obligations under international law, including international humanitarian law and international human rights law, and all necessary measures to ensure the protection and safety of persons with disabilities in situations of risk, including situations of armed conflict, humanitarian emergencies and natural disasters."[397]

In the report, there were "several cases of direct targeting of disabled citizens despite having visible disabilities, during the 2018 marches."[398]

The *Fourth Geneva Convention protects journalists under Article 79 - Measures of protection for journalists.* "Journalists engaged in dangerous professional missions in areas of armed conflict are as civilians within the meaning of Article 50, paragraph 1."[399] Exploding bullets were used to target journalists, with their use prohibited according to *Declaration (IV,3) concerning Expanding Bullets: The Hague, 29 July 1899.* "Like the Declaration of Saint Petersburg of 1868, the Hague Declaration (IV,3) of 1899 gives expression regarding a particular bullet, prohibiting the use of weapons that inflict unnecessarily cruel wounds. The Dum-Dum bullet, which is so called after the arsenal near Calcutta, where the bullet was first made, was the reason for the Declaration."[400]

"As well as using exploding bullets against journalists, an unidentifiable toxic gas was also used against them, which was first thought to be tear gas, but the gas used makes you lose consciousness, have seizures, and is lethal."[401] Lethal gas is prohibited under the Chemical Weapons Convention.[402] The United Nations found that the Israeli Defence Forces "killed two journalists marked 'Press' and wounded 39 others covering the demonstrations."[403]

Medics were also targeted, although they are also protected under the *Fourth Geneva Convention under Article 15 - Protection of civilian medical and religious personnel.* "Civilian medical personnel shall be respected and protected. All available help shall be afforded to civilian medical personnel in an area where combat activity disrupts civilian medical services. The Occupying Power shall afford civilian medical personnel in occupied territories every assistance to enable them to perform their humanitarian functions to the best of their ability. The Occupying Power may not require that, in performing those functions, such personnel shall prioritise the treatment of any person except on medical grounds. They shall not be compelled to carry out tasks incompatible with their humanitarian mission."[404] During the Great March of Return, "although their uniform identified them, three paramedics were killed."[405]

As for any direct part that any members of Hamas played in the Great March of Return, a United Nations report found that Hamas "encouraged or defended demonstrators' use of incendiary kites and balloons, causing fear and significant damage in southern Israel. The de facto authorities in Gaza failed in their due diligence obligations to prevent and stop the use of these indiscriminate devices."[406]

So, the only accusation railed against Hamas by the United Nations report was that they did not stop the incendiary kites from being launched, which caused damage to some Israeli crops. Such a minor misdemeanour compared to the death and destruction caused by the Israeli Defence Forces.

Even though this peaceful and non-violent demonstration was brutally put down, Defence Minister Avigdor Lieberman said, "there would be no Israeli investigation of the killings and that the government would not cooperate with any investigation inquiry as called for by the United Nations Secretary-General and the European Union."[407] Consequently, "there have been no prosecutions brought against any of the commanders and soldiers for crimes and violations committed against Palestinians or to provide reparation to victims in accordance with international norms."[408]

A survey conducted by Tel Aviv University revealed that "83 percent of Jewish Israelis not only supported an open-fire policy against the Gaza protestors but believed that purposely killing Palestinians at the Great March of Return was justified."[409]

After looking into the Great March of Return and seeing how much death and injury the Israeli Defence Forces inflicted on the Palestinians, I was struck by how many times Israel has bombed Gaza disproportionately and with impunity if any Hamas members or any other Palestinian in any part of Palestine reacted negatively to any form of unjustified Israeli authority.

ISRAELI DEFENCE FORCES

The Israeli Defence Force appears quick to state that they are the most moral army in the world.[371] I previously mentioned that Miko Peled's father was a general in the Israeli military and that he resigned to become an advocate for the Palestinians. His defining moment was an event that occurred no more than a week after the 1967 war.

An Israeli army officer went to Rafah Refugee Camp in Gaza with between 100 and 225 soldiers and a bulldozer. The officer called everyone out of their homes. He told the women and the children who were under 13 years of age to return to their homes. The remaining men and boys were then taken to another part of the camp where they could not be seen. The officer proceeded to shoot each one in the head. The dead bodies were then placed in a row, and the bulldozer was driven back and forth over the bodies so that they were only recognisable by the clothes they wore. That day, over 30 were killed, which included a 13-year-old boy and an 86-year-old man.[410]

Miko's father heard about what had happened in Rafah Camp and went and visited the families who had their loved ones killed on that day. Within a month of the visit, he resigned from the army.

The Israeli government and the Israeli Defence Forces rightly say that the State of Israel may defend itself from any attack. I agree that nation-states have the right to protect themselves. However, within the United Nations, in both political and academic environments, what is happening in Palestine is being called apartheid. As it is by B'tselem, an Israeli human rights organisation in Palestine.[411] Consequently, I refrain from using the word 'normal' to describe what is happening there. The Israeli government's actions have never been 'normal' self-defence.

I delved further back to October 29, 1948. The official military of a sovereign state, the 89th Battalion, massacred the Palestinians of Al-Dawayima.[412] I have included the account that I read while crying. While acting under orders:

> The soldiers forced many of the people into houses and then blew them up. Of those who escaped, some took refuge in the mosque. The next day, the bodies of men, women, and children littered the streets. Sixty men, women, and children who hid in the cave were butchered. The hundreds murdered included 175 women and children. A soldier who took part in the attack testified that "the children they [the soldiers] killed by breaking their heads with sticks. There was not one house without dead… One soldier boasted he had raped a woman and then shot her. One woman, with a newborn baby in her arms, worked to clean the courtyard where the soldiers ate. [Then] they shot her and her baby.

In another case:

> An Arab woman [was] perched high on a pile of rubble. Here and there, between the rocks, you could see a tiny hand or foot protruding… the lifeless bodies of her six children. The bullet riddled body of the husband lay face down in the dusty road behind her.[413]

Occasionally, some members of the different units refused to take part in the murderous raids of Palestinian towns and villages. One member of Ariel

Sharon's Unit 101 asked him why there was so much murder of women. He just said they were "Arab whores."[414] Qibya was another West Bank village where half of the Palestinians were women. Palestinians were forced to stay in their homes, which were then bombed. The virtual demolishing and the blatant murder of the inhabitants of this village involved approximately 400 men who used demolition bombs, Bangalore torpedoes, hand grenades, automatic weapons and incendiary bombs, with anyone trying to escape being machine-gunned.[415] Soldiers also killed Palestinians, raising white flags.[416]

I could share many more similar cases, but I have given enough examples to show the slaughtering undertaken by Israel. Yes, many armies from other countries throughout history have undertaken similar activities. However, I have never once heard these armies claim they were the most moral army in the world.

By looking back just a little into history, I soon saw that from the time that Israel won the 1967 war, the Palestinians resisted the Israeli occupation in any way they could. Eventually, they had to resort to armed struggle.[417] After 1967, under Ariel Sharon, there came "24-hour curfews." After all the men were taken from their homes, "house-to-house searches" were done. Some men were "forced to stand waist-deep in the Mediterranean Sea for hours."… "Twelve thousand members of families of suspected guerrillas were expelled to detention camps in Sinai." It was easy to see that the situation was deteriorating, as the "Israeli press was criticising the soldiers" for "beating people, shooting into crowds, smashing belongings in houses, and imposing extreme restrictions during curfews". In just one month from "July 1971… the military also uprooted over 13,000 residents… bulldozed wide roads through camps and some citrus groves" so that the military could "easily bring in mechanised units and infantry". These ruthless measures "broke the back of the resistance."[418]

I wanted to know how many people had been killed on both sides even since 2000. I have found that the total number of Israelis that Palestinians killed between 2000-2021 was "1,369 plus 12,007 injured, while the number of Palestinians killed by Israelis was 10,809 plus 31 wounded."[419] Looking at these figures, I instantly noticed the vast difference between the deaths and casualties caused by Israel compared to the Palestinians.

Today, with advances in phone technology, the ability to post instantly to the internet reveals the ongoing brutality of the methods used by Israel. In Operation Swords of Iron, the Israeli Defence Forces is brazenly using bulldozers. Unlike in the above account, when a bulldozer was used after the Palestinians were killed, a bulldozer was used to kill civilians in tents within a hospital compound while they were still alive.[420]

I have known for quite a while that the Israeli Defence Forces sell weaponry to other nations. Sometime within the last six months, I heard that the Israeli Defence Forces use Gaza as a testing ground for some of the new weaponry that they are developing. I want to say that I was stunned to hear that, but sadly, I was not. The depths that the Israeli Defence Forces sink to appear to have no end.

The Testing Ground of New Weapons

For a small country, in 2022, "Israel spent 4.5 percent of its national income on weaponry. It also has a booming weapon export industry that produced $12.5 billion, increasing by 50 percent in three years."[421] In 2023, "sales increased to $13 billion, again breaking the record. Weapons manufacturers were working 24/7 to provide weapons for foreign orders, as well as keeping the Israeli Defence Force equipped."[422]

With all of the direct shoot-to-kill and the wounding of thousands of Palestinians taking place in the Great March of Return demonstration, I did not realise that the drones that were used to drop tear gas canisters over the demonstrators were a new technology that was being tested during the demonstration. Although they were not 100 percent accurate, a load of canisters was dropped on a tent full of women and children.[423] The event was the perfect opportunity to tell the world, "Look and see our latest new weapon you can purchase." They were aptly named the 'Sea of Tears'.[424]

The turning point for the Israeli arms industry was the Operation Protective Edge attack in 2014. "New battle-tested Israeli weapons that were developed and tested operationally for the first time - such as drones, bombs and land surveillance equipment - were sold globally in deals worth hundreds of millions of dollars."[425] In the aftermath of the Guardian of the Walls Operation in 2021, "Israeli weapons sales reached a record $11.3 billion, with the primary purchasers being Europe, Asia-Pacific and North America."[426] "During 2017-2021, Israel ranked tenth on the global arms exporter sales list, with 2.4 percent of international sales, behind countries including the United States, Russia, France and China."[427] Human rights investigator Iyad Haddad, who has spent over thirty years documenting Israel's violence against the Palestinians, disapproves of peaceful demonstrations. "Palestinians holding these kinds of activities have allowed Israel to grow a commercial industry through the testing and selling of weapons to other countries. These weapons tested in the West Bank and Gaza have been 'battle proven' before they are sold."[428] Shlomo Brom, a retired brigadier general who works for one of the three primary weapons manufacturing companies in Israel, confirms that "testing weapons on Palestinians is good marketing."[429]

Israeli weapon innovation was happening successfully between 1947 and 1949, with "the Israelis [being] the first to weaponise the car successfully", with "cars or trucks becoming the favoured weapons of Zionist guerrillas." These weapons were used initially against the British, and then

"The Jews were the first to use explosives for the purpose of killing Arabs indiscriminately."[430]

I suddenly find myself thinking back to Boaz Ganor's understanding of a terrorist organisation, where he said, "If any organisation is seeking liberty and statehood, and they attack civilians from the opposing side, or any civilians anywhere to gain attention, they are then considered a terrorist organisation."

In 1947, the State of Israel had not been declared. Its military was attacking the British and the Palestinian Arabs to hasten establishing their state. Today, the Israeli Defence Forces continue to expand their territory through land confiscations, house demolitions, night raids, administration detention, targeted bombing and 'mowing the grass'. In my thinking, they could easily be defined as operating as state-sanctioned terrorists. So, according to Ganor's definition of what makes an organisation terrorist, the Israeli military operating under whatever name it chooses fits his definition.

As for gaining attention, the Israeli government tries to prevent the full extent of their activities from getting to the international community. This is done by threatening journalists in any way possible, including through the activities of Israeli lobby groups within countries. Australian Journalist John Lyons recognises that he has dealt with some intelligent and powerful lobby groups in his forty years in journalism. He says that "none compares to the pro-Israel lobby in Australia. It is formidable, well-funded and effective. Too effective, in my view. The material the lobby opposes being published in Australia is routinely published in Israel… The pressure that the lobby places on journalists is well known, but it is something which only tends to be discussed in hushed tones for fear of reprisals."[431] Conversely, if journalists only print what the Israeli lobby wants, then they are extravagantly wined and dined both here and in Israel with first-class flights and top accommodation.[432] Sad, but for some, there seems to be a price they are willing to pay.

CROSSING OVER

JEWISH SETTLERS

The number of settlements approved and built by the Israeli government, as well as the number of settlers moving into the West Bank and East Jerusalem, is increasing. According to a report in March 2023 by a spokesperson for the High Commissioner for Human Rights, Christian Salazar Volkmann, the number of settlers currently living in the West Bank, East Jerusalem, and Golan Heights sits at approximately 700,000.[433] With settlers continuing to move into these areas, violence against the Palestinians is increasing. "In 2020 alone, settlers carried out 127 incursions into Palestinian villages and towns where they wrote racist slogans against Arabs on some 137 Palestinian vehicles. About 75 attacks by settlers on Palestinian agricultural lands were recorded, resulting in the uprooting and damage of 6,507 olive trees and vines."[434] Since the start of 2022, 400 people have been driven from their homes, and more than 100 incidents a month have been reported to the United Nations.[435] On top of those figures, from 7 October 2023 until 7 January 2024, 1,208 people have been pushed out of their homes by settlers.[436]

Settlers decide that they want to move into an area that Palestinians currently occupy. One such area is Al-Baqa'a, which has a Bedouin community. "After three weeks of harassment, intimidation and physical assaults, thirty-six people in total, including 20 children, had but to leave."[437] Once these areas are cleared, outposts are set up, eventually becoming a new settlement (see Land Confiscations and Settlements in Chapter 6: Beyond Occupation). In the West Bank, settler violence has pushed out nearly 500 Palestinians from seven communities over the last twelve months.[438]

Parliamentarian and settler Itamar Ben-Gvir, a member of the ultranationalist Otzma Yehudit party, has been inciting other settlers to "head to hilltops and expand outposts."[439] Furthermore, he wants a military offensive to be launched in the West Bank to "blow up buildings and eliminate not just one or two, but dozens and hundreds and if needed, thousands of Palestinians."[440]

Settlers have undertaken riots with numerous towns being under attack in one night in late June 2023, which has resulted in the burning of homes, cars and general property belonging to Palestinians in the towns of Huwarah, a-Lubban a-Sharqiyah, Burqah, Yasuf and numerous other towns. Settlers are allowed to carry weapons, which makes it easy for them to attack and harm Palestinians. Often, the police and soldiers are just watching on or, as in this night of violence, soldiers also shot at Palestinians who tried to protect their property.[441]

8

FEATHERING THEIR OWN NEST

While I have been observing from afar over several years, I see there is an inability, or an unwillingness, by any nation-state within the international community to call out and bring the Israeli government to account for its actions against the Palestinian people. All the significant nation-states behave like an ambush of toothless tigers, as they do not even have any real political power to start with, let alone make the Israeli government change their actions and treatment towards the Palestinians.

It makes me angry, so I vent my frustrations on my husband and mum, but neither can quench my frustrations. I still get angry and frustrated at what is still happening in Palestine, and yes, I still vent just a little, but not as often.

I do understand the Israeli government and people appear untouchable out of a sense of guilt for their suffering during the Holocaust, but I still do not have to like it. Because they suffered, I do not believe it gives them the right to treat others similarly.

I see the reason is more significant than just Hamas being designated a terrorist group by the United States and other nation-states, as previously discussed. Even with that designation, Hamas is the governing body with limited authority in Gaza, and by August 2024 there have been 145 countries that have already recognised Palestine as a state. Not that the Palestinian people have been granted statehood, but rather recognition involves a formal statement that there should be a Palestinian state.

Stopping Israel's treatment of the Palestinians is more than just the United Nations Security Council's inability to pass any resolutions calling for sanctions against the Israeli government, as it has placed sanctions on other nation-states, including Russia and Iran, in recent years.

I see that the United States is the reason there have never been sanctions placed on Israel for its treatment of the Palestinians.

THE UNITED STATES AND THE MIDDLE EAST

As part of my Middle East studies, a lecture in 2017 was the most insightful I listened to. It allowed me to see the potential reason for the Palestinians' inability to obtain significant help and justice from the international community.

My conclusion is that the United States is responsible for the lack of change and improved conditions for Palestinians in Palestine. The United States does everything to benefit itself, including its meddling in the Middle East. I will share what I gleaned from the first half of that lecture.[442] Also, since the lecture was six and a half years ago at the time of writing this, the principal objectives of the United States remain the same, with only some figures having changed.

At the end of World War II, the United States was economically the strongest nation due primarily to its late entry into the war. Therefore, it became the global hegemon, taking over from Britain. As with any nation-state, the United States wanted to thrive. Thus, foreign and domestic policies are in place to best feed that goal. The United States has been planning policy centred in the Middle East since around 1795, when it formed its navy to deal with pirates in the Middle East. The United States is still involved in the Middle East two hundred years later. Today, their objectives for the Middle East are three-fold: security, oil, and Israel. These three areas do not operate independently but rely on the others.

Security

After World War II, particularly from the 1950s and onwards during the Cold War, the focus of security in the Middle East was preventing the possible infiltration and spread of Russian communism.[443] Russia intended "to drive toward the oil-bearing areas of the Near and Middle East, and strengthen Communist gains in the Far East."[444] After the State of Israel became a reality in 1948, there was concern by the United States that Israel could become the breeding ground for communism, which could quickly spread throughout the Middle East, which was because of the socialist ideology of the Jews who were moving there from the Soviet Union.

With the Cold War officially ending at the end of 1989, security became focused on containing rogue states, including Iran and Iraq, which the United States considered a threat to the region. From there, there has been a move to 'countering violent extremism' like the Islamic State. If the region is not secure, then oil cannot flow out.

Oil

Until fairly recently, the United States relied on the importation of oil. Unlike what many believe, the oil-producing countries within the Middle East are not the principal oil suppliers to the United States, but Canada supplied 52 percent of its needs in 2022.[445] Today, the United States supplies its own needs, with 18.4 million barrels of oil being produced daily in 2020, and they consumed 18.12 million. Although the United States is self-sufficient in oil, the oil that comes out of Russia and the Middle East is heavier than the lighter grade of oil that the United States produces which requires a unique process to make the oil usable. So, until the United States encourages changes within their refining plants, the imported oil fills a gap in the market. But I suspect that the United States will continue 'needing' Middle Eastern-based oil just so it can have a reason to pressure oil supplier countries, should they see a need to do so.

Israel

The fostering of the relationship between the United States and Israel began with sympathy for the Jews because of what they endured during World War II. The United States was the first to congratulate them when their new state became a reality, and their relationship grew from there.

The United States' interest in Israel is because Israel is a "Democratic and pro-US country in a sea of hostility."[446] As a close ally, Israel must be the most potent military power in the region. If Israel falls, some security and power balance will evaporate. If the region is insecure, then Israel is under more threat than expected, so all these things are mutually supporting. These objectives are nowhere else except in the Middle East power politics.

Israel has been the largest cumulative recipient of United States foreign assistance since World War II. Between 1946 and 2023, $260 billion was estimated to have been given to Israel.[447] In the early days, economic assistance was given, but most of the aid since has been military assistance and packages. The assistance is provided as credit, only used to buy military equipment, training, and software from the United States.

For thirty-five years until the Obama presidency, the United States has always permitted Israel to use one-quarter of the funding it received to develop and grow its domestic capabilities, which would not have been possible without the aid. Although Obama ended this, he set up a $38 billion aid package for ten years, the most significant aid package ever given to Israel. With military assistance, Israel is being kept the most powerful military in the region to ensure stability and to ensure that the United States gets whatever it wants from the Middle East.

The Israeli government's plan to have all of Palestine as a Jewish-only State means the elimination of all Palestinians by any means possible, whether it is achieved quickly through military means or slowly over many years. I expect the United States would be aware of this and is very calculated in formulating both its foreign and domestic policies and its dealings with Israel so that it helps itself and Israel. Due to the United States domestic policy, the government ensures that factories related to supplying Israel with what it needs remain open and that workers are employed. This takes priority over protecting 5,399,803 vulnerable people (at the time of writing) whose end will be their total demise if nothing changes.[448]

If that is not bad enough, the more that the government looks after Israel and the needs of the Jewish lobby, the more votes the incumbent will receive at election time, which is just another reason to ignore the Palestinian people. It is such a vicious cycle.

The formation of the State of Israel was the perfect way for the United States foreign policy to inject life into its domestic policy to ensure it remained strong. Therefore, Israel knows that the United States needs them, so Israel can do anything it wants, and the United States remains silent. This has included increasing its supply of weaponry to Israel during Operation Swords of Iron, which has been ongoing since October 8 2023.

THE WORLD CAN ONLY WATCH

Before the State of Israel was created, according to my mum and Palestinian friends, there was relative peace between the Jews and the Arabs throughout the Middle East. Yes, there were occasional general skirmishes when different people lived close to each other, but that was all. Although Jews were immigrating to Palestine from the early 1880s, once the European Jews left the horrors of World War II behind them and moved to their own state, they became more emboldened in revealing their true agenda, which was to have a state only for themselves and to push out the Palestinians.

From the mid-1800s and because of the long history of war, several meetings and conferences were held to work out mechanisms for settling a crisis before war broke out and to work out rules of engagement within a war situation. Representatives of various nations attended these gatherings. At the close of World War 1, change was needed because there was so much death and destruction. After the relatively short-lived League of Nations, what resulted was the establishment of the United Nations around the close of World War II. Any nation could join, as membership was and is always voluntary. The objective of the United Nations as an organisation is to reduce the violent tendencies within anarchical nation-states.

To do this, the United Nations operates with an Ethical benchmark, which states a regard for human rights, environmental agreements, resettlement of refugees, aid to the developing world as binding. Stabilising agreements preserve order and limit violence, including arms control and disarmament treaties, seabed boundary agreements, and the diplomatic system.

Sanctity of contracts and agreements such as international law, respect for the sovereignty of all states, and equality of states.[449]

The United Nations has two central bodies, the General Assembly and the Security Council, where members vote on resolutions. The General Assembly is the largest voting body in the United Nations, and every nation-state represented is allowed one vote. The General Assembly votes on resolutions relating to international peace and security, admitting new members, and addressing the United Nations budget. For a resolution to be passed, it must receive a two-thirds majority. Resolutions that the General Assembly passes are not legally binding.

The Security Council is a different matter. Its current structure has fifteen members. Five members are permanent members, including the United States, the United Kingdom, China, France, and Russia. These permanent members also have veto powers. Resolutions are brought to the Security Council from any Security Council members, the General Assembly, the Economic and Social Council, and the Human Rights Council. Resolutions voted on by the Security Council often include military intervention, establishing international courts to try those convicted of serious international crimes, approving peacekeeping forces, and approving bans and sanctions on nation-states. For these resolutions to be passed, nine out of the fifteen Security Council members must pass the resolution, including all five permanent members. If even one permanent member used their veto power or abstained, the resolution would not be passed to be enacted. Generally, the resolutions passed by the Security Council are legally binding.

South Africa, a nation that has been through occupation brought a case against Israel for genocide against the Palestinians in Gaza to the International Court of Justice in January 2024. Other nations have since joined the case. Also, on 19 July 2024, the International Criminal Court planned to issue arrest warrants against the leaders of Hamas and Israel for their targeting of civilians from and including 7 October 2023. At the time of writing, 4 weeks have passed, and the International Criminal Court is yet to issue the arrest warrants. Israel has chosen to ignore the rulings of the Courts and continues to act with impunity against the Palestinians in Gaza. The International Courts do not have the power to enforce its rulings, so it is up to the United Nations Security Council to enact resolutions.

Historically, in cases where resolutions have been brought against Israel, the United States has used its veto power most of the time. Consequently, Israel is given free rein to continue doing whatever it wants to do. The United States' use of its veto power has never been more apparent than during Operation Swords of Iron, when it has vetoed every resolution brought to the Security Council from 8 October 2023.

9

7 OCTOBER 2023

While we were driving home from my mum's house on Saturday evening, 7 October 2023, I was looking at social media on my phone while in the car and saw a disturbing post from a friend: "Prayers for all my friends in Israel/Palestine." Looking further, I found news reports that the sound of sirens awakened those living in southern Israeli towns nearing the Gaza border and of rockets exploding. The rest of the world heard of the incursion as further news emerged.

At least 5000 rockets were fired into southern Israeli towns. Members of Hamas, Islamic Jihad, other groups, and civilians were involved in the highly coordinated attack on southern Israeli military bases and settlements. A section of the barrier fence on the Gaza Strip border was cut and broken through with a bulldozer. Some drove into southern Israel on motorcycles and flew in on hang gliders in a carefully orchestrated military attack that was undertaken against the Israeli Army.[450]

Separate figures from Human Rights Council and Israeli social security data have indicated that between 1,139 and 1,200 civilians of Israel, Israeli security forces, and foreign nationals were killed directly by members of the Palestinian groups or by rockets and mortars, and between 252 and 290 civilians and military personnel were taken back into Gaza on that October morning.[451]

According to Osama Hamden, a member of the Political Bureau of Hamas, Hamas undertook "a military operation to target the Israeli Army for political reasons and to bring back the Palestinian cause for liberation against the occupation."[452]

A document released by Hamas on 21 January 2024 confirmed Hamas' intent to target "Israeli military sites. They sought to arrest the enemy's soldiers, to pressure the Israeli authorities to release the thousands of Palestinians held in Israeli jails through a prisoner's exchange deal… [They also intended] to destroy the Israeli army's Gaza Division, the Israeli military sites stationed near the Israeli settlements around Gaza."[453]

I looked at the kidnapping of Corporal Gilad Shilat in June 2006 and his release in 2011 in exchange for 1,027 Palestinian prisoners.[454] Journalist Max Blumenthal also affirms Hamas' aim was an exchange of Palestinian political prisoners, including individuals held under administrative detention.[455]

I concluded that based on the outcome of the Shilat kidnapping and the work of Blumenthal, Hamas' goal was to capture Israeli military personnel on 7 October 2023 and use them for future prisoner exchanges. However, the Islamic Jihad presence seemed to escalate the planned intent.

As well as the ongoing 75-year occupation, the multiple reasons given by Hamas for undertaking their operation included the ongoing appropriation of Palestinian land in the West Bank.[456] There have been increasing numbers of attacks on Palestinians, their towns and villages in the West Bank by both Jewish settlers and also by the Israeli military, especially since the start of 2023.[457] There have also been ongoing incursions into the grounds of the Al-Aqsa Mosque by Jewish settlers.[458] The Israeli government is Judaizing Jerusalem and talking about demolishing the Palestinian cause and not recognising Palestinian rights.[459]

Israel, whether it is the military, police or Jewish settlers, undertakes unprovoked action against Palestinians and their property, whether in East Jerusalem, the West Bank or in Gaza. Before 7 October 2023, there had already been an increase in attacks against Palestinians in the West Bank, with 234 killed by Israeli forces and nine killed by Jewish settlers.[460] Also in 2023, Israeli police allowed increased Jewish settlers onto the Al-Aqsa Mosque site, with an official in the Islamic Waqf Department in Jerusalem, who looks after the site, saying "48,223 settlers stormed the Al-Aqsa Mosque complex."[461] Consequently, the military attack was considered a retaliatory measure for the injustices and to bring back the cause for liberation of the Palestinian people against the occupation.[462]

Looking on from the comfort of my home in Australia, I do not have the right to judge the Palestinians in Gaza because there is no way that I can ever understand how they live and what they are forced to endure. Furthermore, I do not think that they had any other option other than to give up, lie down and die. The Global North, in particular, has ignored the Palestinians' calls for help over many years. Also, based on their previous experiences, whether resistance to the occupation was non-violent or violent, they were still ignored even though the same brutal response was always forthcoming from the Israeli government and military.

Even Palestinian Pastor Munther Isaac said, "I never ever want to hear you lecture us on human rights or international law again, and I mean this. We are not white, so I guess it does not apply to us according to your own logic."[463] Through the numerous interviews that I have watched since October 7 2023, it quickly became clear to me that human rights are only to be afforded to white people. In my introduction, I mentioned that sanctions were placed promptly on Russia for their invasion of Ukraine, but not so on Israel. So, it appears to me that Palestinians do not have the same status as Ukrainians, who are white and European. To be clear, I do not hold anything against the Ukrainians for being white.

Regarding Hamas' military operation, Nasser Mashni, president of Australia Palestine Advocacy Network, has said several times since 7 October 2023, "Some people would rather die on their feet than live on their knees." Nazareth-based journalist Jonathan Cook noted, "This is the first time that there has been a breakout by the Palestinians from their "caged in coastal enclave", with there being significant injury brought against Israel since they were entombed in a cage in 2007 when Israel began its blockade by land, sea and air."[464] He also called out the West for its hypocrisy "because Palestinian civilians in Gaza have faced repeated rampages from Israel decade after decade, producing far more suffering, but have never elicited a fraction of the concern currently being expressed by Western politicians or publics."[465]

ISRAEL'S RESPONSE

On 8 October 2023, the Israeli government and the Israeli Defence Force began their retaliatory Swords of Iron Operation by bombing Gaza. There was a mixed response by governments within the international community. Some governments were against Hamas' attack on Israeli civilians. Most countries were calling for a stop to the violence. Some said that the response by the Israeli government was disproportionate. Some governments that supported the Palestinian people's quest for freedom were on the side of Hamas. Governments, particularly from the West, were condemning the actions of Hamas, while others said that Israel was to blame.[466]

The retaliation by the Israeli government and military was disproportionate from the start. Nasser Mashni stated on The Project, Monday 9 October 2023, "We've got to get to a point when the world says to

Benjamin Netanyahu that you can't bomb your way to peace. There is a solution here, and it's a shared humanity. There is enough time for the world to say enough. International law needs to be applied."[467] Mashni also stated that there is no care for Palestinians. During the night, 12-year-old children are taken from their homes and are questioned and accused of many things, but they do not understand the language. Five thousand Palestinians are being held in Israeli jails under administrative detention, and nobody cares. He railed accusations that the world seems to accept the apartheid situation. He closed the interview by saying, "When is somebody going to speak up for us?"[468]

As early as 10 October 2023, according to Euro-Med Monitor, "Israelis bombed and killed 880 Palestinians, with approximately 59% of them being civilians, including 185 children and 120 women… They destroyed industrial buildings and 970 residential units and caused significant damage to 7,920 more. Fourteen sanitation stations, 40 media organisations, 56 schools and 30 kindergartens were also destroyed." Even by then, the toll was enough to consider that war crimes were already being committed and that a humanitarian catastrophe could happen at any time.[469]

Rimal was bombed in its central business area, which includes offices, universities, mosques, residential buildings, Gaza's main telecommunications centre and Bar Association. No warning missiles were being fired, just bombing. "These sounds are different," 30-year-old Saman Ashour in Gaza City texted as she lay awake in a neighbourhood north of Rimal, listening to the roar of explosions. "It's the sound of revenge."[470]

GENOCIDE

Individuals within the international community who hold authoritative positions are no longer calling what has been happening in Gaza ethnic cleansing but genocide. Craig Mokhiber, a top United Nations human rights official, resigned on 28 October 2023. He alluded that "using the term genocide should occur where there is firm evidence, including what we are witnessing in Gaza."[471] On 2 November 2023, experts reported to the United Nations, "[We]remain convinced that the Palestinian people are at grave risk of genocide."[472] On 15 November 2023, United Nations Special Rapporteur Francesca Albanese addressed the National Press Club of Australia. She said that three weeks before the address, she and other special rapporteurs were forewarned that there might be a genocide being committed against the Palestinians by the Israeli politicians and military based on their intent.[473]

Intent to commit genocide

In an interview on 21 November 2023, Raz Segal, an Israeli associate professor of Holocaust and Genocide Studies at Stockton University in the United States, said that the Palestinians are undergoing genocide.

Note the following United Nations Convention: *December 1948: Convention on the Prevention and Punishment of the Crime of Genocide Article II:* "In the present Convention, genocide means any of the following acts committed with intent to destroy, in whole or in part, a national, ethnical, racial or religious group. Their actions include killing members of the group. Causing serious bodily or mental harm to members of the group. Deliberately inflicting on the group conditions of life calculated to bring about its physical destruction in whole or part. Imposing measures intended to prevent births within the group. Forcibly transferring children of the group to another group."[474]

As expressed through their language and within the context of Israel and Gaza, Raz Segal says, "the intent of Israel to eliminate the Palestinians from Gaza is extremely strong and is verbalised within every part of Israeli society. There are calls to annihilate Gaza, to flatten Gaza, to kill everyone."[475] He further said "state leaders such as war cabinet members and senior army officers use the same language."[476] "Explicit, dehumanising language was being used. This includes talk about deporting all the Palestinians to the desert."[477] He also referred to the Armenians who were subjected to dehumanising language in the 20th century.[478]

There are so many quotes showing genocidal intent. The following are just a few of them, including one from Israeli President Isaac Herzog, who said, "It's an entire nation out there that is responsible. It's not true this rhetoric about civilians not aware and not involved. It's absolutely not true…. and we will fight until we break their backbone."[479] I could not believe what I was reading. In 2022, 47.3 per cent of the population, which is nearly half of the population of Gaza, were children.[480] Such talk portrays and makes all of the 2.3 million people, with half of them under 18 years of age, enemy targets, which is considered genocidal language.[481]

Before the ground invasion on 28 October 2023, Israeli Prime Minister Netanyahu invoked the Biblical story of Amalek, where all men, women, children and livestock were to be killed, stating, "You must remember what Amalek has done to you, says our Holy Bible. And we do remember."[482]

Minister Yoav Gallant called the Palestinians human animals, "We are fighting human animals, and we are acting accordingly."[483] "Gaza won't return to what it was before. We will eliminate everything. If it doesn't take one day, it will take a week. It will take weeks or even months. We will reach all places."[484]

The Minister for Energy and Infrastructure, Israel Katz, said, "All the civilian population in Gaza is ordered to leave immediately. We will win. They will not receive a drop of water or a single battery until they leave the world."[485]

7 OCTOBER 2023

It is one thing for someone to say they are going to harm you intentionally. It is another thing to carry out those threats. For the citizens of Gaza, Israeli threats have become a reality. Thousands of photos and videos have been uploaded month after month by Palestinians themselves, showing the Israeli Defence Force's genocidal acts.

Actions of Genocide

On 9 October 2023, Defence Minister Yoav Gallant ordered a 'complete siege' of the Gaza Strip, "I have ordered a complete siege … There will be no electricity, no food, no fuel. Everything is closed…We are fighting human animals, and we are acting accordingly."[486] The United Nations condemned this move as collective punishment.[487] Troops were also being gathered for a full-on ground invasion. Defence Minister Yoav Gallant told soldiers in the south, "We have taken control of the situation and are transitioning to a full scale offensive."[488]

On the same day, 2.2 million Palestinian civilians were given 24 hours to move to the southern part of Gaza or suffer the consequences of more significant destruction and death in the north. The ones who remain would be killed as they would be considered a supporter of Hamas. Israel knew that such a move was impossible, as most were women and children. There were many sick and in critical condition in hospitals that could not be moved.

Even within the time frame provided, there were reports of people in cars and trucks being targeted and killed as they headed to the south on a road that they were told would not be bombed. There were numerous reported instances of shelling along the routes and of other violence by Israeli forces against evacuating Palestinian civilians, including inhuman and degrading treatment, arbitrary arrests, unlawful detention, and killings. A convoy of vehicles carrying fleeing civilians was hit by a deadly airstrike... which killed a reported 70 people, including children."[489]

I heard a testimony from a friend who has numerous relatives in Gaza. A niece and her family were forced to walk to the south on a road that took them at least 3 hours. The road was flanked by armed soldiers and tanks (which was not shown in any Western news reports). They were not allowed to look back or even look around. If they did, they would be shot. They could not even pick up anything they dropped but had to keep walking. The soldiers could even take personal possessions from you, and you could not do anything about it.

While they were walking, they saw some of the men being beaten. Armed soldiers were also beating the young men and demanded that they undress until they were fully naked in the street in front of everyone, including women and children. They had to stay naked and be humiliated as other people walked by.

She also saw one family walking. The wife was nine months pregnant. The wife started having labour pains but was told by the soldiers to keep walking, or else she would be shot. They forced her to walk. She walked for as long as possible, then had to stop. Her husband stopped to be with his wife, but he was told that if he stayed, he would be shot. The couple made a hard decision, with the husband taking the children and walking away. He could not look back at his wife, or else he would be shot. Nobody knows what happened to the pregnant woman and her unborn baby.

Overnight between the 17th and 18th of October, Israel bombed the courtyard of the Ahli Hospital, where over 1,000 Palestinians were sheltering. At least 500 civilians were killed, and many were unaccounted for, still trapped under the rubble. Many reports were saying that it was undertaken by the misfiring of a rocket by Hamas, but these reports have been debunked.[490] A hall on the site of Gaza's Saint Porphyrius Church, the third

7 OCTOBER 2023

oldest church in the world where people were taking shelter, was hit by an Israeli bomb on 19 October, killing 16 people.[491]

Meanwhile, Palestinian Pastors were focusing on what was happening. Part of a sermon from 22 October 2023:

> Then, they talk about international law and human rights. "Go away with your laws and human rights." They lecture us about human rights and look down upon us as if they are superior to everyone else in terms of values and morals. You Europeans and Americans have been stripped naked in front of the whole world today, and your racism and hypocrisy have been exposed... but in reality, "those who were ashamed died." I personally do not want to hear about peace and reconciliation. The people of Gaza today want life... They want a night without bombing... They want medicines... Surgical operations with anaesthesia... They want the simplest necessities of life... They want food... Clean water... Electricity... They want freedom... Life with dignity... The person under bombardment, beatings and persecution does not want to hear about reconciliation and peace... He wants the end of aggression and aggression![492]

With the ground forces entering Gaza on 27 October 2023, the coming days, weeks and even months were going to be extremely hard on Palestinians in Gaza. The morning of Saturday 28 October 2023, revealed two changes overnight. In the United Nations General Assembly, Jordan put forward a resolution calling for an "immediate, durable and sustained humanitarian truce" between Israeli forces and Hamas militants in Gaza. It also demands "continuous, sufficient and unhindered" provision of life-saving supplies and services for civilians trapped inside the enclave.[493] The resolution passed with 120 votes in favour, 14 against and 45 abstentions. Australia abstained from voting for the resolution because the resolution did not mention the reason for this round of bombing on Gaza that started earlier this month.

Seeing those results, I felt angry and on the verge of tears, which was my reality up to the time of writing this, and beyond. I believe that providing a reason for this round of bombing in Gaza was unnecessary when innocent civilians were being killed in an outburst of revenge.

So much information was being circulated that I found it hard to keep up with who said what. Many commentators continued to say that someone must be blamed for what happened. Many continued to point to the events of 7 October 2023 in isolation without even looking beyond that date. So, for those who want to play the blame game, then I blame the Israeli Zionist Government for what is currently happening in Gaza. It is the Israeli government that started pushing Palestinians out of Palestine over 75 years ago. They slaughtered innocent men, women, and children from over 500 villages without reason. They continue with their ethnic cleansing of the West Bank. That is without even considering the periodic bombing or 'mowing the grass' in Gaza before 7 October 2023 which I have preciously discussed.

Although this resolution passed, it was not legally binding, so there was going to be no change for the Palestinians in Gaza. Going through the motions of submitting resolutions at the United Nations, only to have them rejected, took time and effort. I eventually conceded that what it did was provide an official environment where nation-state representatives could express their government's stance on what is currently happening in Gaza within a safe environment. So, I thought it was probably a good thing after all, even though I was still somewhat skeptical.

7 OCTOBER 2023

The other development overnight was that the Israeli Defence Forces expanded their ground invasion of Gaza and intensified the bombing. The bombing had turned off any communication facilities, which means that the Palestinians are unable to communicate with family, both inside of Gaza or with their families living in other countries. Ambulances did not know where the injured were, and they could only find out any information when the wounded were somehow brought to any of the hospitals that were still operational.

By 20 November 2023, after the aerial bombardment, which was at the time equivalent to 1.5 times the amount that was dropped on Hiroshima, there were 16,413 Palestinians killed and nearly 34,000 injured, according to United Nations Special Rapporteur on Palestine, Richard Falk. This figure included those dead buried under the rubble.[494]

Throughout this campaign, the Israeli Defence Forces have bombed most, if not all, hospitals, schools, universities, mosques and churches. Israa University in Gaza City appears to have undergone a controlled demolition, much like what is undertaken to demolish old residential blocks.[495] A significant amount of the infrastructure that allows people to live within a society has been destroyed or damaged through Israeli bombing.

Doctors have conducted operations without anesthesia, including limb amputations. Pregnant women are having C-sections without anesthesia. Most of the hospitals in Gaza are no longer functioning as hospitals due to the lack of fuel, electricity and medical supplies.

According to Euro-Med Human Rights Monitor, by 15 January 2024, "31,497 Palestinian citizens had been killed, which included 12,345 children, 6,471 women, 295 health personnel, 41 civil defence personnel and 113 journalists."[496]

Apart from the ongoing bombing, sniping and killing of civilians by using drones, tanks and missiles, there has been the targeting of specific individuals. Journalists and their families and other highly respected members of the Palestinian community have been the primary targets. The killing of Professor Refaat al-Areer was deliberate, as the third-floor apartment where he and his family were sheltering was 'surgically bombed' out of an entire building, according to Euro-Med Monitor.[497] Al Jazeera journalist Wael al-Dahdouh "lost his wife, two children and a grandson as a result of Israeli bombing on 25 October 2023, endured a drone attack himself that killed his cameraman in late December and lost another son, also an Al-Jazeera journalist, along with another journalist, killed by Israeli drone strike targeting their car on 7 January 2024."[498]

According to a World Health Organisation Report released on 21 December 2023, famine and disease will contribute to the overall casualties of the Israeli bombing of Gazan civilians. Ninety-three percent of the Gazan population is not getting sufficient food and is suffering from malnutrition. Infectious disease is running rife with "over 100,000 cases of diarrhea… half of these are among young children under the age of 5 years."[499] Over 150,000 cases of upper respiratory infection and numerous cases of meningitis, skin rashes, scabies, lice, and chickenpox have been reported. Hepatitis is also suspected, as many people present with the telltale signs of jaundice. Over 1.9 million people have been displaced, of whom over 1.4 million stay in overcrowded shelters. These conditions are ripe for a continued rise in infectious diseases. In Gaza today, on average, there is only one shower for every 4500 people and one toilet for every 220. Clean water remains scarce, and there are rising levels of outdoor defecation. These conditions make the spread of infectious diseases inevitable."[500] In August 2024, the first case of Polio was contracted by an 11 month old boy in Gaza after 25 years.[501] This comes after the virus was detected in sewage water in July 2024.[502]

7 OCTOBER 2023

I was shocked to hear that out of all the people that are currently suffering starvation throughout the world, eighty percent of them are in Gaza.[503] United Nations expert Husain said the situation "across the entire region is unprecedented in its severity."[504]

KIDNAPPINGS, IMPRISONMENT, AND TORTURE OF PALESTINIANS

The deliberate killing of Palestinian civilians by Israel was more than enough for individuals of the world to see and bear. But hearing and reading reports and seeing pictures of Palestinians being kidnapped, imprisoned and tortured was beyond words. Early in December 2023, images were seen over mainstream media and social media of groups of men being stripped down to their underpants, blindfolded and with their hands tied behind their backs. They were paraded through the streets of Gaza City after being taken from their families. They were then herded into trucks and taken out to an unknown destination.[505] From the pictures, numerous family members and work colleagues were recognised by others. The action was seen as a way of humiliating the Palestinian people, which was considered psychological warfare designed to break the Palestinian people.[506]

Within the first two weeks of February 2024, there was a picture of a naked man sitting and strapped in a chair who appeared to be defiantly gazing at an Israeli Defence Forces soldier who was standing in front of him. The Palestinian was Hamza Abu Halima. Soldiers had randomly shot him. He was then stripped entirely naked and dragged with others to the Palestine Stadium, west of the city. It is from this stadium that Israeli soldiers have taken many photos. A soldier uploaded the picture of Hamza in an attempt to humiliate him. However, the image showed "pride and bravery."[507]

Apart from over 300 medical staff who have been killed in Gaza, doctors have been kidnapped and tortured. Doctor Said Abdulrahman Maarouf was held captive for seven weeks with "his hands cuffed, his legs shackled and his eyes masked." He was also made to "sleep in places covered with pebbles without a mattress, pillow or cover and with loud music blaring." He lost 25 kilograms in 45 days, and his balance, focus and feeling.[508]

In another case, Doctor Mohamed Abu Salmi was arrested when the Israeli Defence Forces stormed Al-Shifa Hospital. They broke both of his arms and tied a chain around his neck. He was made to crawl like an animal, and they dragged him in front of everyone. When given food on a plate, he was forced to eat it off the floor like a dog in front of everyone.[509]

There are so many testimonies coming out of Gaza of atrocities being committed, particularly in and around hospitals, including Nasser Medical Complex in Khan Younis, al-Shifa Hospital in Gaza City and Kamal Adwan Hospital in Beit Lahiya, where over 500 bodies have been found in mass burial sites. Testimonies from those working at the sites say that there is evidence that could amount to war crimes being committed, including torture and unauthorised killings of civilians. Bodies were found with their hands bound and medical tubes still attached. Even bodies without heads have been found.[510] Civilians were giving the medical staff regular clothing to change into when they left the hospital because wearing scrubs made them a target of the Israeli snipers.

In June 2024, a report revealed reports of rape which included a Palestinian man being forced onto a metal rod and held there for five seconds, causing bleeding and immense pain in his rectum.[511]

I find all of these accounts extremely heart-wrenching to read and view. I am concerned that I will become emotionally hardened due to the oversaturation of images and many other real-life accounts coming out of Gaza. If I am feeling like this, how many others feel the same? Is it our self-preservation mechanism kicking in? I do not know.

MAINSTREAM MEDIA

I have learned to be careful about what media I watch and read, especially how the reports are portrayed. I now follow the news from independent sources or those based in the Middle East, with the media owners associated with the Middle East. Whether those who run any media organisations are driven by money or by their sense of humanity is also something that I also consider. I have discovered that time and patience are ways of revealing the truth rather than jumping to conclusions. Much damage can be done when news stories are disseminated prematurely.

In the section Terrorism in Chapter 7: Refusing to Give Up, I mentioned that on 22 October 2014, Israeli authorities shot dead a Palestinian man, Abd al-Rahman al-Shaludi, after he rammed his car into a crowded Jerusalem train station, which killed a three-month-old Israeli American girl. I did some research and found out that Abd al-Rahman al-Shaludi was suffering from mental issues after undergoing three weeks of interrogation by Shin Bet (Israel's secret police) in the Jerusalem Russian Compound Jail and had been recently released. That fateful morning, he was going to see a psychiatrist after being referred by a doctor. Because he was Palestinian and what he did was termed a 'terrorist' attack, he was instantly labelled a terrorist.

During 2023, there was an increase in the number of Jewish settler attacks on Palestinians and their towns. On 4 August 2023, a Jewish settler killed Qusai Mattan from a Burqa east of Ramallah in the West Bank.[512] The United States described it as a "terror attack", with the word choice "not an accident." However, Agriculture Minister Avi Dichter rebuffed the accusation because the United States only went by media reports.[513]

Reports were quickly disseminated throughout world media outlets of Hamas' orchestrated military operation on 7 October 2023 and about the thousands of Israelis that were killed. There were also stories of decapitated babies' heads, mass rapes and mass killings undertaken by the infiltrating Palestinians.

The report of the decapitated babies' heads quickly made it through to United States' President Biden, who expressed immediate outrage over the reported act.[514] I found it interesting that there was no caution from any member of the Israeli government to question the media reports regarding that allegation. Yet, caution was applied regarding the killing of Mattan from Burqa by a Jewish settler.

Decapitated babies' heads

An extreme settler, Ben-Zion, who had previously called for the destruction of a Palestinian town, initially started the story of the decapitated babies' heads.[515] Israeli independent reporter Nicole Zedek was with the Israeli Defence Forces. After initially reporting the beheadings, she later clarified and stated, "Soldiers told me they believe 40 babies/children were killed."[516] Israeli reporter Oren Ziv, attached to the Israeli Defence Forces, said, "During the tour, we didn't see any evidence of this, and the army spokesperson or commanders also didn't mention any such incidents."[517] Max Blumenthal revealed the lie about the decapitated babies' heads. According to Anadolu, the Israeli army has "no information confirming the allegations." Jonathan Cook questions why the media is also ignoring evidence, and Haaretz journalist Muhammad Shehada said, "Haaretz debunks… 40 beheaded babies, baby burned in the oven, a pregnant woman's stomach opened and her fetus removed. Children bound together and burned, pregnant hostage giving birth."⁵¹⁸

Mass rapes

Two elderly Israeli women who were held hostage by Hamas were released. Before the Israeli authorities could intercept them, they did a media interview and stated that they were treated well by members of Hamas. At the interview, the older lady was asked why she shook hands with one of the Hamas members during her release. She said, "They treated us well and took care of all our needs."⁵¹⁹

Hamas held an Israeli mother and daughter for five weeks. During their interview, they reported that they were treated very well and their needs were addressed. They even arm-wrestled with one of the guards for fun, but before they did, the guard placed a towel over the women's arms because they were not to touch a woman.⁵²⁰

Again, considering the veracity of allegations against the Palestinians, I found that time and these two separate interviews of released women provided me with enough information to at least wonder if the Israeli women were not subject to rape. To strengthen my position, I found a report from CNN that investigators "do not have first-hand testimonies" of any rape victims even though there have been "more than 1,000 statements and more than 600,000 video clips" relating to the Hamas operation.⁵²¹ The Times of Israel said that "physical evidence of sexual assault was not collected from corpses… many of whose bodies were mutilated and burned."⁵²² An article published by Max Blumenthal has found that a New York Times article of 28 December 2023 claiming Gal Abduah was raped during the October operation is lacking in evidence, with the rape being denied by her family.⁵²³ Journalist Sulaiman Ahmed further states that the New York Times manipulated the family, saying they were writing a story about Gal Abduah's memory.[524] Furthermore, the New York Times was due to air a 'Daily' podcast on the Hamas rape story, but they pulled it due to its lacking validity.[525]

The Israeli military created a video of the events of 7 October 2023. Journalist Owen Jones attended an Israeli Defence Forces screening. According to Jones, there was no video footage of beheaded people, torture of any kind or footage of rape and sexual violence.[526]

Lastly, Volker Turk, the United Nations high commissioner for human rights, has called on Israel repeatedly to allow access to an independent investigation of the allegations of rape. The request has been ignored.[527] For any government to ignore the request of the United Nations to have an independent inquiry into such allegations seems suspicious to me.

Mass killings

Reports of brutal killings of innocent civilians quickly hit the media following the infiltration of Palestinians on 7 October 2023, with initial figures being 1,400 dead, according to the Israeli Prime Minister's office.[528] However, over time, the number of those killed on that day has been revised down several times. It is now thought to be 695 Israeli civilians, including 36 children, as well as 373 security forces and 71 foreigners, giving a total of 1,139.[529]

In a report correlated from Israel's media, Max Blumenthal provides information revealing that the Israeli Defence Forces caused a lot of the deaths.[530] The Electronic Intifada also showed similar findings, with a retired Israeli army major admitting, "Israeli detainees in Palestinian custody were 'possibly killed' by Israeli airstrikes when the Israeli Air Force attacked vehicles that were returning into Gaza."[531] Furthermore, the Israeli government has not allowed an independent investigation, and "appears to be covering up the evidence, burying some bodies before they have been identified."[532]

In a report released on Israel's own Ynet, pilots of two Apache helicopters fired "two missiles and dozens of shells from the helicopter cannon, indiscriminately…with the helicopter duo evacuating to re-arm."[533] The individuals who were killed around the Nova Festival from the actions of these pilots included both Israeli citizens and Palestinians. The pilots also fired at vehicles containing Palestinians and Israeli hostages as they were fleeing the area. Israeli reserve pilot Col. Nof Erez said that the "Hannibal Directive was probably deployed because once you detect a hostage situation, this is Hannibal."[534] Under this directive, Israel opens fire on its people, whether military personnel or civilians, in preference to them being taken hostage.[535]

During the Hamas military operation, homes within the settlements sustained severe damage, which was initially attributed to the Palestinians. However, "video from a police helicopter shows that an Israeli tank opened fire on a house where 13 Israeli captives were killed."[536] Israeli settler Yasmin Porat claimed that it was the Israeli forces that killed Israeli civilians and not Hamas. She also said that she and others were treated 'humanely'.[537] The same police helicopter video also provides "evidence that Israeli forces killed many of the 1,200 Israeli soldiers and civilians who died…. during the attack."[538]

Even away from the immediate events happening in Palestine, media outlets appeared to be quick to publish related stories without really confirming the facts, including the Australian media.

Australian Media

On 9 October 2023, the first pro-Palestinian protest and rally in Australia was held in Sydney. During the rally, there were reports of some of the Palestinian supporters chanting "Gas the Jews", which was reported by various media outlets, including CBN News.[539] However, a February 1 2024 report was released by New South Wales Police, which forensically analysed the presented video. They found that such phrases were not used at the rally but rather "Where's the Jews?" This official finding vindicated the initial report.[540] Unfortunately, as with other claims surrounding 7 October 2023, which have since been debunked, the damage was already done, with individuals still claiming it happened.

Regarding Australia's national broadcaster, 200 staff from ABC in November 2023 expressed their concerns about what they perceive as biased coverage of the Gaza conflict in favour of Israel due to its overreliance on Israeli sources and their distrust of Palestinian sources. They do not use words such as "war crimes, genocide, ethnic cleansing, apartheid, and occupation to describe various aspects of Israeli practices in Gaza and the West Bank, even when the words are attributed to respectable organisations and sources."[541]

Furthermore, there appears to be a bias against non-white reporters, such as Antoinette Lattouf, who was sacked by ABC over a private post on social media, where she mentioned a Human Rights Watch report, even though white reporters have said worse than she did, without consequences. Jewish lobbyists were also unhappy with Lattouf because she "publicly criticised Israel." Fair Work has since found that the ABC unlawfully sacked her.[542]

I believe the ABC has forgone opportunities to correct narratives. An ABC Four Corners report by John Lyons aired in March 2024 could have revealed that much of the destruction caused to settlements on 7 October 2023 was caused by Israeli Defence Forces tanks and Apache helicopters rather than by the Palestinians. Israel's own Ynet had already released a report stating that their Defence Forces caused the damage. The ABC chose not to disclose any information in the report, although there was ample opportunity. In other ways, however, the John Lyons program was refreshingly honest.

AUSTRALIAN NATIONAL RACISM

Being a predominantly white colonial outpost of the United Kingdom meant that until 1945, Australia wanted to attract people from the United Kingdom. Since then, economic migration has been the priority.[543] This has allowed people from many different nations to come to Australia, which is considered multicultural.

Before proceeding further, I say that racism of any kind should not exist anywhere. This includes any form of genuine antisemitism against the Jewish people. Again, I repeat that I am not against the Jewish people, and neither are other Palestinians and supporters. What we are against is the Zionist project and the apartheid system that is currently used to oppress Palestinians. There are increasing numbers of those from the Jewish community who are standing with Palestinians at rallies and marches here in Brisbane and globally, declaring, "Not in our name." In other words, they do not support what the Israeli government is doing to the Palestinian people in Palestine.

Unfortunately, when people need to be treated equally, Australia, as a nation, can be seen failing the test. Palestinians are currently suffering backlash because of what is happening in Gaza. They are being ill-treated and dehumanised within the political sphere and broader society.

Political Sphere

Before the last federal government election of May 2022, the Labor Party platform of 2021 confirmed that it would "Support the recognition and right of Israel and Palestine to exist as two states within secure and recognised borders; calls on the next Labor Government to recognise Palestine as a state; and expects that this issue will be an important priority for the next Labor Government."[544] With significant numbers of Australian citizens voting for the Labor Party, their success on the May 21, 2022, election day was assured. It seemed the government would stand for justice and liberty for the Palestinian people within the international community.

However, at the National Labor Conference held in Brisbane in August 2023, although on their agenda, the members failed to vote on the government taking definitive action relating to the ongoing building of settlements, which is illegal under international law.

Furthermore, and more widely, it quickly became clear that Palestinians were blamed for the events of 7 October 2023 and, from then on, basically ignored. When Palestinians and supporters needed government support on all levels, federal, state and local, they had backflipped in their support of Palestinians.

The capital cities of the individual states were lighting up prominent landmarks in the colours of the Israeli flag, honouring the Israelis killed on 7 October 2023.[545] These do not exclusively include the Sydney Opera House in New South Wales, the Parliament House in Canberra, and the Story Bridge in Brisbane. Palestinians are still waiting to see a similar gesture.

On a local level here in Brisbane, Queensland, the Brisbane City Council refused to light the Story Bridge or any bridge in the colours of the Palestinian flag, even though letters were written to the Mayor from members of the Palestinian community; the words of reply show there is no support for the Palestinians living here. The response of many to the Lord Mayor's letter echoed the sentiments that if the Brisbane City Council wants "to maintain the harmony we have always enjoyed here in Brisbane", then in this situation, they need to treat the communities of both sides the same. As it is now, and contrary to the reply, the Brisbane City Council does not support all members of our community.

Furthermore, an Australian Indigenous flag is permanently painted on the road in the suburb of West End. With the approval of the local indigenous population, the Palestinian flag has been painted next to the Australian Indigenous flag. Since the Brisbane City Council has made it a priority to remove any painted signage relating to the Palestinians, the Palestinian flag on the road keeps being removed by Brisbane City Council workers. By ordering the flag's removal, this action again proves the Brisbane City Council do not care about Palestinians in their community.

In May 2024, a member of the Australian Senate brought a motion to ban the chant "From the river to the sea, Palestine will be free", which was backed by the government and opposition, passing 56 for the ban and 12 against.[546] The false understanding of the phrase is that Palestinians are calling for the destruction of the State of Israel when it is just calling for all people of the land to live with liberty, equity and peace, no matter their race or belief system. On the contrary, as previously mentioned in Chapter 4: Palestine and Palestinians, it is the Israeli Likud Party who, in their charter, will not allow any other group to own any of the land between the river and the sea.

Broader society

Within the broader society, there have been too many instances of racism against Palestinians to list them all.

These include comments to individuals, graffiti messages on buildings and roads, hate spewed on social media, degrading comments at social gatherings, attacks on students at various university campuses, and comments from Christians. The list is not exhaustive.

Local weekend markets are held where stalls sell fresh produce and other items, which do not exclusively include second-hand goods, new clothing, jewelry and other items sold by individuals and businesses. At one of these markets, Palestinian Fair Trade Australia Shop ran a stall selling products made by artisans living in the West Bank, with the proceeds returning to them. In October 2023, the market owners forced the Palestinian stall to shut down in the interest of not upsetting some of the residents of the local community. There was little consideration given to the Palestinians in the community who were also suffering. Their suffering seemed irrelevant. In August 2024, the stall returned to the market by agreeing to not display a 'disappearing Palestine' map, and the previous manager had to have no part in the stall.

The daughter of a friend, a young Palestinian woman with an incredible passion for her people, was asked not to wear her Palestinian t-shirt to church. Little did they know she had personally lost family members in Gaza, and she needed their support rather than condemnation.

Someone I know from outside the Palestinian community recently said, "I have had some pretty nasty things said to me from Christians for me not wanting the slaughter of the precious Palestinian people so their precious rapture can happen."

The last example I will give is from another friend:

> Woman: "Palestinian women are oppressed by Palestinian men as much as they are by Israelis"?
>
> Friend: "That's racist, and that's incorrect."
>
> All eyes on this angry Arab woman who God forbid got offended by that comment.
>
> [Response to the woman at close of event].

7 OCTOBER 2023

Friend: "Why do you people think you can humiliate us in public and then apologise in private? My husband is Palestinian, my father is Palestinian, my brothers are Palestinians. Do I look like an oppressed woman?

That's exactly the kind of statements that are used to justify killing Palestinian men."

Indeed, as a nation, we can do much better.

WORLD PROTESTS

From the initial days of Israel's retaliation upon the Palestinians in Gaza, citizens of many nations began protesting because the number of those that they saw as being brutally killed by the Israeli Defence Forces was quickly climbing.

Rallies and protests have been held in every capital city in Australia. They will be ongoing until the Palestinians receive justice. As early as Saturday, 21 October, 30,000 people joined the protest in Melbourne, essentially closing down the city. Here in Brisbane, on that same day, 4,500 of us joined together. Up to that date, it was the most significant number of people protesting at one gathering, about the 75 years of occupation by Israel. Likewise, throughout many capitals and cities of the world, as it became clear that the bombardment of Gaza by the Israeli Defence Force was not going to end soon, protests became a weekly event.

As the weeks have turned into months, the number of people attending these worldwide protests has increased to millions as people are calling for an end to the genocide. Even with the large numbers of people mobilising, many leaders of the Global North remain silent. During the first weeks, there were a few feeble calls on Israel to pause the bombing on Palestinians so they could receive much-needed food, water and medical aid supplies, including from our Foreign Minister Penny Wong, "We call for humanitarian pauses on hostilities, so food, water, medicine and other essential help can reach people in desperate need, and so civilians can get to safety."[547] I consider the statement of Foreign Minister Penny Wong far too inadequate. To me, a pause in this situation means stopping the killing of Palestinians, giving them some food, water and medical supplies, and then resuming the killing and destruction. How cruel. How thoughtless and uncaring can people be?

Israel has continued to act with impunity. First, the Israeli government and the Israeli Defence Force told Palestinians to move to the south, where they would be safe. A significant number of Palestinians made the move. Then Israel continues to bomb the south and killed Palestinians there. The people are told to move continually to designated areas, which became smaller and smaller, making it impossible for increasing numbers of people to have the basic requirements for life. There is now no adequate shelter apart from make-shift tents. Sourcing food, water, medical supplies and basic essential needs just for survival is getting harder and harder. Life for Palestinians as they knew it no longer exists.

Yet the citizens of the world keep protesting. In Washington in the United States alone, the number of those gathered outside the White House was over one million during the early months of this genocide. They hoped the international community would stop the genocide against the Palestinians. Eight months later, the number of people gathering in different cities worldwide has increased and will continue to grow.

I have attended most rallies and marches in Brisbane and listened to many speakers sharing their experiences. Some are those who have been directly affected by the deliberate ethnic cleansing and slaughter of family members. Others have been professionals who have given up their time and have spent from weeks to months in Gaza trying to help the Palestinians survive somehow. These individuals will never be able to forget what they have seen or have personally experienced. Even though they have gone through so much, I have not heard one of them say that they want to physically eliminate the Israeli people, whether they are Jewish or Zionist. All they want to see is a permanent ceasefire, and see the Zionist apartheid system dismantled and allow all the people, whether they are Palestinian or Israeli, to be able to live in genuine liberty, equity and peace.

UNIVERSITY STUDENT PROTESTS

Historically, where there has been a need for changes within society, activism has helped to bring about that change, including student activism. Student activism was involved in bringing anti-war ideas into the public sphere, especially during the war in Vietnam.[548] In 1985, led by the Coalition for a Free South Africa, "United States Columbia University students encamped for three weeks. Five months later, the university cut ties with the apartheid regime in South Africa."[549]

The students at Columbia University again helping the global movement to stop the genocide happening in Gaza by calling for the university to divest from supporting the Israeli government or any organisations attached to the State of Israel. On 17 April 2024, students set up camp with an initial 50 tents joining the encampment. Since then, many students from universities worldwide have joined in solidarity with the students of Columbia University, including seven universities here in Australia.[550]

The Columbia University administration has threatened students with disciplinary action if they do not cease their encampments. They also called police, who came dressed in riot gear, to break up the students' encampments. Administrations from other universities have also called in the police to try to break up the student encampments. Under the Constitution of the United States, where freedom of speech is a right, it seems that in this case, where students are trying to stop a genocide, they are not free to express their views.[551] Over 2,000 student and faculty arrests occurred throughout United States universities up until 3 May 2024.[552]

Furthermore, other groups who are aligned with the agenda of the Israeli government have entered some of these encampments in an attempt also to break up the students, including one group entering Monash University in Victoria, Australia, several times. They have threatened students, destroyed food and cooking facilities, and stolen students' possessions.[553]

It is too early to know whether the actions of these students will again change what is happening in the immediate future, but I suspect that the next generation of leaders will come from their ranks. I recently saw a statement somewhere that heralded that thought:

> Future Job Interviews:
> I got kicked out of college for protesting genocide.
> Future Bosses:
> You're hired.

THE WEST BANK

With everything happening in Gaza, life for Palestinians living in the West Bank has become increasingly challenging, with increasing settler attacks, which now sit at more than 700, up until 3 April 2024, according to the United Nations.[554] Killings and growing numbers of Palestinians are being dragged off to prison by the Israeli Defence Force under administrative detention.[555] Children are being killed.[556]

Even King Abdullah III of Jordan said, "We must not ignore the situation in the West Bank and the holy sites in Jerusalem. Continued escalations have killed nearly 400 Palestinians in the West Bank from 7 October 2023 to early February 2024, including almost 100 children, and over 4,000 had been injured."[557] Approximately six weeks later, the number of those killed in the West Bank had increased to 460, according to the Palestinian Health Ministry.[558] By June 2024, nearly 9,000 people were arrested, with many detained in administrative detention.[559]

While the eyes of a significant number of people are on Gaza, we need to remember the West Bank, where Palestinians are being pushed out of their homes, especially in Area C.[560]

On 8 May 2024, 300 people were made homeless overnight at Wadi al-Khalil, a Bedouin village, to make way for the continuation of a major highway. There are 35 Bedouin villages under constant threat of demolition because the Israeli authorities do not recognise them, even though some of these villages existed before there was an Israeli state in 1948. These villages do not have access to water, electricity and other facilities.[561]

Even United States President Biden has placed sanctions on four settlers for their violence in the West Bank by freezing the bank accounts of dual citizens. He did not rule out further sanctions either.[562]

I have a sinking feeling that once the Israeli government has finished in Gaza, then they will start doing similar in the West Bank. I hope I am wrong.

INTERNATIONAL COURT OF JUSTICE

On 29 December 2023, South Africa submitted to the International Court of Justice its application against Israel for its alleged actions against the Palestinian people in Gaza, which could be considered as potential acts of genocide under the Convention on the Prevention and Punishment of the Crime of Genocide.[563] On 11 January 2024, the South African team representing Palestine presented its case for genocide against Israel. They asked for provisional measures to seek relief for the Palestinians because they knew that it could take many years for cases to be brought to the International Court of Justice to receive an ultimate judgment of genocide.[564] Seventeen judges presided over the South African submission. The following day, the team representing Israel presented their submission. After the submission of both sides, it was time for the judges to decide the fate of Palestine and the Palestinian people.

After waiting what appeared to be a long time, the International Court of Justice judges finally presented their decision two weeks later, on Friday, 26 January 2024. The International Court of Justice ruled in favour of the South African case against Israel. Israel was to "take all measures in its power" to prevent killing, prevent serious harm, and stop activities to bring about the destruction of the people. They were to stop the military forces from undertaking such acts. Israel must prevent the incitement to commit genocide. Israel must allow humanitarian aid and relief into Gaza. They must also be fervent in preventing the destruction of evidence relating to potential genocidal acts. Lastly, they were to submit a report within one month with proof that it is honouring these measures.[565]

I was disappointed in the judgement because it did not use the word 'ceasefire', which is what Palestinians were seeking and expecting. However, it quickly became clear to me that for the handed-down measures to be enacted, there had to be a ceasefire, as stated by the South African Foreign Minister in a press conference following the judges' decision.[566] Also, if the Court had ordered a ceasefire, the authority to enforce it is lacking. Consequently, implementing the truce would be up to the United Nations Security Council.[567] Knowing the voting history of the United States, it would be probable that they would again use their veto power within the Security Council to protect Israel.

Consequently, I concluded the fate of the Palestinians had been put back into the hands of the citizens of the world to keep protesting, marching, lobbying governments, and voting against governments who are continuing to support the Israeli state.[568] Therefore, the decision of the International Court of Justice was not the end of the matter but rather the starting point.

Furthermore, and based on the current bombardment of Rafah, and with Israel's disregard for the judges' rulings of 26 January, on 13 February 2024, the South African government made an urgent request to the International Court of Justice to move on the Palestinians' behalf to prevent further breaches against them.[569]

WILL ISRAEL ACHIEVE ITS GOAL?

On 24 October 2023, I read a news journal article that a friend posted on social media that arrested my heart. I have included it here so that the strength of what was conveyed in the article is not lost:

> Children have often been a marker for whether one has gone too far. Once children are explicitly framed as "not innocent," you know that all-out genocidal warfare is possible. It is not for nothing that Netanyahu cited Haim Nachman Bialik's poem from 1904, saying, "Revenge for the blood of a little child has yet been devised by Satan" when he vowed to "destroy [Hamas]" and "forcefully avenge this dark day." That poem, "On the Slaughter," is often cited in Israeli culture and is often quoted by Netanyahu.

> It was written in the wake of the 1903 Kishiniev pogrom. The outcry is always about the death of Israeli children. But interestingly, the line that comes just before the one cited says: "And cursed be the man who says: Avenge!"[570]

I immediately did some research and discovered that in 1903, many Jewish people were brutally killed in the Kishinev Pogrom in Russia. Passover was being celebrated, and on the seventh day, one-third of the 50,000 Jewish population was attacked. A boy who was two years old had his tongue cut out. A shop owner who tried to help, who was blind in one eye from when he was a youth, had his other eye gouged out. Jews were killed brutally, including having nails driven through their heads. Bodies were hacked in half, including bellies being split open and filled with feathers. Women and girls were raped, with some of them having their breasts cut off.[571] Upon reading this account, I was reminded of the initial accounts that were reported about the events of 7 October 2023, which, in time, were shown to be false accusations. Accusations included women's breasts being cut off and a report that a pregnant woman's belly was cut open.

Although I have never studied psychology, by reading about the poem and the Kishinev pogrom, I have possibly started to understand just a little bit about why the Israeli government is potentially harsh in its stance against Palestinians in Gaza. As a people group, they appear to me to be still looking for revenge, even 120 years after they suffered horrendous atrocities. They also seem unwilling to put aside the historical suffering, change their societal psyche and embrace a future full of life. Instead, they appear fixated on keeping the hurt alive generationally and seeking revenge at any cost. Consequently, they do not seem to care about the deaths of people who, under international law, are supposed to be protected, including the next generation of children.

# 7 OCTOBER 2023

In Gaza, so much killing has been undertaken in what the Israeli government is calling a war. The Palestinians in Gaza have been constantly forced to move from one area to another. The areas they were told to move to were supposed to be safe, but they were not. These areas are full of people who were also bombed, fired at by tanks and missiles, and targeted by Israeli snipers. Added to that, virtually all forms of humanitarian aid have been prevented from reaching the people by the Israeli government. Official assistance from the United Nations Relief and Works Agency had almost stopped because of allegations by the Israeli government that several workers were involved in the attack on 7 October 2023. The commissioner general did not substantiate these allegations.[572] Several countries that pulled their funding, including Australia, have now reinstated their funding. after investigation.[573]

The last area that the Palestinians were pushed to was Rafah, where currently 1.4 million people were mainly sheltering in tents. Before the case was due to be brought to the International Court of Justice, the Israel Defence Force was already undertaking bombing in Rafah. While waiting for the judges' ruling to be passed down at the International Court of Justice, the Israeli Defence Forces did not waste their time. They increased their voracious bombing, which saw increases in the number of Palestinians who were killed. They continued to bomb infrastructure, including hospitals, schools, homes, universities, mosques, and churches which were destroyed or severely damaged.

During the middle of February 2024, Israel continued to prevent humanitarian aid from entering Gaza. Although some trucks carrying food and other supplies were then allowed in, there was great danger for the convoys and the aid workers and the supplies were vastly inadequate.

Israel keeps bombing the Palestinians in Rafah, including the tents where thousands had been displaced. The Rafah Crossing into Egypt was also closed by Israel so that nobody could get out. I suspect that if the international community does not stop the Israeli government, they will continue killing Palestinians. With the ongoing bombing, one thing that seems apparent to me is that Israel cannot eliminate Hamas. For all of the killing of civilians, there appears to be minimal casualties amongst those of Hamas.

At the six-month mark of the genocide, I typed my thoughts in a piece called 'Six Months'.

> Six months too long of killing, slaughtering, intentionally starving civilians, making children orphans, and traumatising children so they suffer for the rest of their lives. Too much sniping of medical staff and journalists, bombing men, women, and whole families, and demolishing homes, universities, and schools. The list goes on. The atrocities that have been committed, most of which are too horrific to photograph and share.
>
> Where is humanity? Does it even exist? Why can the people of a tiny country wield such power over nearly every other country in the world? What do they know that the rest of us do not?
>
> Yes, they have suffered through a Holocaust, and yes, they have had to flee pogroms before then. But why be so vicious? Usually, people who suffer have compassion and understanding for others, but not these people.
>
> They have beguiled many by quoting sacred texts they do not believe in. They have made the international law

7 OCTOBER 2023

institutions that protect all people null and void. They have made the United Nations a laughing stock.

The people that are being slaughtered will not give in. These people are strong, resilient and determined. They are more highly educated than others in the region in which they live. They are gentle and kind. They will continue until their last breath. They will not be defeated. Once the deliberate killing of them is over, those remaining will rise again from the rubble. They will rebuild.

They are the Palestinians.

In a report released on 5 July 2024 by the Lancet, there is a suggestion that a conservative figure of 186,000 Palestinians could be killed as a result of the current genocide in Gaza.[574] According to humanitarian activist Susan Abulhawa, based on those killed from direct fire, lack of medication for chronic illness and conditions, those dying from starvation, those missing, presumed dead, kidnapped and from disease, she estimates that a more accurate figure of those dead could "be closer to 194,768 to 511,824 people, with 221,760 injured."[575] And counting.

I envisage that if the international community continues to let the Israeli government act with impunity that government will then move into the West Bank and give it the same treatment as they did to Gaza. If then the Israeli government succeeds in its cleansing of both the West Bank and Gaza, their original Zionist goal of a Jewish-only state would have taken just over 140 years from when the first Zionist Jewish immigrants arrived in Palestine because of an increase in European and, in particular, Russian persecution.[576]

ISRAELI OCCUPATION IS ILLEGAL

On July 19 2024, the International Court of Justice ruled that the Israeli occupation of Palestinian areas is illegal under international law and that it must desist from its actions. Within its ruling, the judges conveyed that the settlers must leave the Palestinian areas, and the settlements have to be dismantled, with the wall being brought down. This also means that the apartheid system has to be dismantled in its entirety. Furthermore, reparations have to be paid to the Palestinians for the suffering they have endured since 1967. [577]

Little response to the ruling has been forthcoming from governments within the international community and the media seems to have placed no pressure on governments. However, the ruling has once again placed pressure on the citizens of the international community to continue to pressure their own governments to place sanctions and boycotts on the Israeli government in an attempt to make it comply with the demands of the International Court of Justice ruling.

10

FINAL THOUGHTS

Since discovering that I am Palestinian and Irish and also learning about the treatment of Palestinians in Palestine over the last nine years, I have wanted to share what I have learned. Through this writing, I have aimed to show the foundation that undergirds what has been happening over the last one hundred years in Palestine. I have spent most of my exploration highlighting the conditions that Palestinians have had to live under, especially since the significant expulsions of indigenous Palestinians, first around 1948 and then in 1967. What is currently happening is an entirely new level of brutality and erasure against Palestinians.

THE BIBLE, THE STATE OF ISRAEL, AND CHRISTIAN ZIONISM

Palestine is a patch of land on which two groups say they have a right to live. Some of the claims are based on God's promise to Abraham. When Abram came into the land from what would be modern Iran, he lived a nomadic life. He did not own any land until he bought a cave in the hill region of Hebron to bury his wife, Sarah. He insisted on buying the land and having a legal contract rather than accepting it as a gift or just taking it.[578] I believe there is no sense of morality in the actions of the Israeli government, which are based on the belief that they have been promised the whole of the land of Palestine, and they see it as their right to take it.

Furthermore, according to Christian Zionism, the whole land must belong to the Jews only, before Jesus can return. This is why these groups lobby governments, especially in the United States, to ensure they continue supporting Israel in their ventures. However, one should look beyond those few carefully selected verses. It is easy to see that possession of the land by the children of Israel was always based on ongoing obedience, which was never able to be sustained.

Ownership of the land was only meant to be a temporary situation and to be treated as if they were only caretakers because according to my understanding, the children of Israel were to disperse themselves into the world and tell others through words and deeds that the Messiah was coming and that humankind's relationship with God was going to be restored. While they did live on the land, they were to treat others living there the same way they would treat themselves. But the Bible passages that relate to these things are forgotten by some Christians, who hold fast that the land is only for the Jewish people.

As with what happened alongside conquests for land throughout the centuries, some of the people from the children of Israel's ten northern tribes were dispersed out of the land by the Assyrians. The leaders of the remaining two tribes were taken captive by the Babylonians approximately 1500 years later, with some returning. While under Roman occupation, there was a Jewish revolt in 70 CE, which was put down after four and a half years. Although some Jews left, the majority remained in the land. Jews were expelled, however, in 135 CE as a result of the Bar Kokhba Revolt.

FINAL THOUGHTS

From the late 1800s, European Zionist Jews fleeing persecution were determined to make the whole of historical Palestine their homeland. They were encouraged to do so by Christian Zionists, as it correlated with their theological belief that the whole land of Palestine must belong only to the Jewish people.

ISRAELI GOVERNANCE

The Israeli government has been officially governing Palestine since the State of Israel was proclaimed in 1948. The account of Abraham is different to how the previous and current governments of the State of Israel operate with their appropriation of Palestinian land, especially in the West Bank. From the time of the Oslo Accords, it has been becoming more apparent by the day that the Israeli government does not want to see any form of a State of Palestine established. The ongoing confiscation of Palestinian land for the building of settlements is evidence for this. Dividing the West Bank into smaller and smaller pockets is making a Palestinian State untenable.

Also, there has been an almost complete blockade of the Gaza Strip for the last 17 years, since 2006, which has stifled their economy. Added to this is the random and disproportionate bombing by the Israeli military, termed as 'mowing the grass', ensuring Palestinians live impoverished lives with no genuine hope for the future. This is seen especially now with the complete razing to the ground of the whole of Gaza. More than that, eradicating a whole people group appears to be their agenda. But from what I see, Palestinians are resilient, and those who manage to survive will rise and somehow rebuild.

In 2019, Prime Minister Benjamin Netanyahu clarified that he had no intention of seeing the Palestinian people have a state of their own when he unequivocally stated, "A Palestinian state won't be created."[579] He also said, "The hopes of establishing a state must be eliminated."[580]

Benjamin Netanyahu has continued to make such statements. I see that for this to become a reality, all that the Israeli government would need to do is to continue doing what it is already doing. To displace the Palestinians, it continues to refuse to issue building permits so that when Palestinians build a home, there is a risk to building, knowing that at any time, it can be demolished. The Israeli government is continuing to confiscate Palestinian land for settlements.

To implement the agenda of eradicating Palestinians from their land, there is a formula that is being followed. Continue to employ and even increase the shoot-to-kill policy on more Palestinians. Continue to bomb Gaza disproportionately, using any excuse to do so, even if it is not justified. Continue to deny Palestinian prisoners access to medical facilities. Restrict Palestinian access to water and continue to steal their farming land. Continue to refuse Palestinians permission to access medical services for chronic health conditions. Continue refusing to allow Palestinian pregnant mothers in labour permission to pass through checkpoints to access clinics and hospitals. Continue to limit the amount of food permitted into Gaza.

Continue placing Palestinians in prison under administrative detention for a maximum of six months and then continually renew the administrative detention order every six months so that they are never released. For the prisoners that have been charged and serve their time and are released, continue rearresting them the day after they are released and imprison them again.

When I was considering undertaking this project in January 2022, there were some topics that I wanted to include and others I had yet to consider. However, when I was approximately three-quarters of the way to finishing the first draft, I decided to add a small section on Israeli weapons develop-

FINAL THOUGHTS

ment, which I included under Israeli Armed Forces in Chapter 7: Refusing to Give In.

I discovered that the Israeli government spends a considerable amount of money developing new weapons, which the Israeli Defence Forces then test on the Palestinian people before they are sold to interested parties within the international community. Even with just scratching the surface of that topic, as I have done with every topic covered within these pages, it would have to be the topic that messed with my mind more than any other topic I have covered. For any government to be willing to manufacture new weapons and then purposely test them on anyone who is supposed to be under their care shows the utter depth of their moral depravity.

After considering the activities of the Palestinians, the Israeli Defence Forces and the Jewish settlers, I have concluded that much of the activities of these three groups are interrelated. The Palestinian people are an occupied people who are doing all they can to survive under the Zionist Israeli occupying government who wants to eradicate them from Palestine, even though many have been living there for more generations than the Jews who moved there from Europe. The Jewish settlers are continuing to move into areas of the West Bank, breaking up the Palestinian areas into even smaller areas and making a proper state no longer viable. Added to this, settlers often destroy crops, uproot olive trees, pollute wells and even kill Palestinians, as they are permitted to have whatever weapons they want.

The Israeli Defence Force not only protects the settlers in the West Bank but also acts to cause harm to the Palestinian people overall. Remember that the Israeli government wanted a reason to attack Gaza and had been planning to do so since 2013, with it finally bombing Gaza in 2014.

OPERATION SWORDS OF IRON

Operation Swords of Iron has escalated the agenda of the Israeli government from ethnic cleansing to genocide. Upon waking every morning since 8 October 2023, I have looked through the overnight news within my social media feeds to see what was happening in Gaza and the West Bank. I know that there is going to be more news of the death, destruction and senseless killing of Palestinian people, the people I belong to. I consider that what Israel is doing is beyond immoral. Governments of the international community have not intervened to stop the current genocide being conducted by Israel. Some of these same governments are also providing the Israeli government with weapons, which is making them complicit in what the Israeli government is doing to the indigenous Palestinians. It also makes these governments and their leaders liable to potential prosecution at the International Criminal Court. The actions of Israel are no different to any other form of colonialism from early modern and late modern history.[581] Nations such as France, Spain, Britain, and others displaced and killed many people groups to gain possession of land and its resources.

As with so many others looking from afar, my heart has been heavy since that October day. I do not have any family living there, so I cannot comprehend what those who have family in Gaza must be going through. Attending a rally that was held on 13 January 2024, I heard of one Palestinian man who lives on the Gold Coast in Queensland, who, until that day, had 200 family members killed by the Israeli Defence Forces during this genocide. I cannot even fathom what this man must be going through.

I probably spend too much time looking at what is happening to the Palestinians both in Gaza and the West Bank. The deliberate killing and the displacement are ongoing. There is the intentional use of starvation as

FINAL THOUGHTS

a weapon against the Palestinians by banning aid trucks into Gaza. This is causing the people to resort to eating animal food that is usually fed to donkeys, bird seed, grass, and leaves from trees. They are also resorting to eating stray cats and dogs. The number of children without families is increasing. The number of children without parents is rising. Increasing numbers of children have had limbs removed through bombing, being shot, or having their bodies mangled in their demolished homes. Gaza now contains the most children in the world who have had limbs amputated because of a conflict, with an estimated ten children a day needing amputations, which are undertaken without anesthetic.[582]

Whenever we visit my mum, Gaza is on my mind. I say little to my mum as she is concerned that I am obsessive about following what is happening. Maybe I am. I find it impossible to stop following what happens because I feel strongly connected. Mum does not follow what is happening in Gaza as it saddens her too much. She gave up hope a long time ago that there would be a change to what has been happening in Palestine since 1948.

THE PALESTINIAN COMMUNITY IN AUSTRALIA

A common question that is currently being asked of Palestinians is, "Are you ok?" For many who do not live in Gaza but have family in Gaza, they are certainly not ok. Many are going through the daily motions as if on automatic pilot as they wait for subsequent communication from their family, whether it is news that they have lived for another day or someone has been killed. Within the Palestinian communities in Brisbane and the

Gold Coast alone, there have been many who have had multiple family members killed by the ongoing genocide in Gaza.

During Ramadan, the most important time on the Muslim calendar, members of their community do not consume food and drink (including water) throughout the day and eat a modest evening meal. During this month, prayer is prioritised, and charity works are undertaken. During the 2024 Ramadan, I heard some Muslims share their thoughts. They wondered how they would get through the month, knowing their families did not have food. Many even feel guilty because they sleep at night in a bed.

Many have been trying to get family members out of Gaza but have found that the Australian government needs to be more helpful. The successful ones granted a temporary visa to enter Australia for twelve months need to guarantee they will return at the end of the twelve months. Where are they to return to? They have no home to return to. They need infrastructure, and the place is unlivable. Restoring Gaza to a level where one can adequately live, will take many years. That is, of course, if Israel has finished its current Operation in twelve months. [Author's note: In August 2024, the Australian government has announced that humanitarian visas for people from Gaza will become possible.]

AS A PALESTINIAN CHRISTIAN

I had heard for years that because of God's covenant with Abraham, historical Palestine and today's Palestine was to be Israel's land and only Israel's land. The Israeli government uses specific passages from the Old Testament in the Bible, the Hebrew Scriptures, to show their apparent entitlement. This entitlement transcends time and justifies their action in oppressing the indigenous Palestinian people through their European Zionist agenda in Palestine today. I realised that that teaching was based on literal Biblical

FINAL THOUGHTS

interpretation within my Christian context. Since then, I have considered some teachings unsound and even toxic because all Palestinians, whether Christian, Muslim, secular or having another belief, are to be pushed out of their homes and off their land.

I believe that Palestine does not belong to the Jewish or Palestinian people any more than you and I own the land that we are living on. When Palestinians and Middle Eastern Jews living in Palestine say the land belongs to them, they infer their family's longevity in caring for and farming the land over many generations and even over many centuries. European Jews, however, have limited generations living in Palestine, as most have emigrated to Palestine since the early 1880s. What the State of Israel is doing to Palestinians is wrong and against the nature of God and the Scriptures, and is certainly not Christian and not how we should be treating others.

Everyone must have an open mind and heart when looking at this situation. Lecturer of Islamic Studies Colin Chapman suggests that stories within the Bible need to be considered as a Jewish only interpretation of their history or even accept that such behaviour today is not acceptable under international law.[583]

In early January 2024, I realised it had been a few months shy of 40 years from when I had come under such literal interpretation and teaching and had believed it to some extent. I was feeling quite emotional, and I wrote the following:

'A Time of Reflection'

> I am angry, I am sad, I feel cheated, I feel lied to.
> I wasted so many years believing lies.
> No, I did not fully believe what I heard, as I read other parts of the Bible that told a different story from what I heard preached.

But I never questioned these preachers.
I never asked those who should know better, those who taught a different interpretation to what I now know and believe.

I have walked away; I have turned my back. I can't stand to be anywhere near those places anymore, especially now. I still believe the essential parts, that Jesus is Saviour and that my relationship with God is restored through belief in His work on the cross.
I do not know how the world will end, as I now question everything I was taught.
All I know is that those who endure to the end will be saved and go to heaven.
That is clearly stated and cannot be twisted.
There is no pre-tribulation rapture, no secret escape.

As for the belief that Jesus cannot return until the whole land belongs to the current Jews in Israel.
That has caused the last 76+ years of pain for Palestinians.
That has caused displacement and death to many.
The Western church even ignores the Palestinian Christians, as highlighted by Palestinian Pastors in Bethlehem.
They are a problem that needs to go away.
These Pastors speak their minds and express their anger that the Western church ignores them.
They are accused of not condemning the events of 7 October 2023.

FINAL THOUGHTS

Cannot Christians in the West see they are causing the damage?
Are they so blind? Can't they see they are complicit in the genocide?
Of course, they can. They are excited because once the Palestinians are gone, they say that Jesus will return.
The modern Western Evangelical Church, with its Zionist leanings, is to blame.
If it were not for their support, the State of Israel would not be getting away with committing genocide…

The silence is deafening.

Where are the Christian voices? Why can I not hear them speaking out against what is happening in Gaza? People go on with their lives as if nothing is happening.

In July 2024, as a Palestinian and Christian in Australia, I am feeling so alone. I do not have anyone that I can regularly talk to about what is happening to the Palestinians. I have mentioned some aspects to former lecturers. I have connections on social media. These people truly apologise for what is happening but do not fully understand the situation in the Occupied Territories. Still new to the Palestinian community, I do not know anyone well enough to encroach on their time, especially now, as my issues are insignificant compared to what many others are enduring.

A few months ago, I was asked to participate in the World Day of Prayer, which focused on Palestinian women. I was asked which church I attend during a conversation with one of the congregants after the service. I said I was between churches. I was instantly judged, as there was an awkward silence and a quick ending to the conversation.

Presently, I would not be comfortable being involved in church communities as congregations are either fully supportive of Israel or are split, with some supporting the Israeli belief that the whole land only belongs to the Jewish people and others supporting the Palestinians. Even still, there is silence from the leaders of these congregations. Where is their outrage over the thousands of civilians killed in Gaza?

I am in no hurry to do anything. I must also reconsider Biblical Scripture and determine how best to understand what is recorded on those pages. My next exploration will be focused on how Palestinian Christian theologians have interpreted these same Scriptures.

FUTURE HOPE

If you are Palestinian and living in Palestine and are somehow holding a copy of this in your hands, know that although I am not there with you in person, my heart is with you because I am one of you.

Even with the toxic words from the Israeli Prime Minister that there will never be a Palestinian State and the ongoing conditions under which the Palestinians live, the Palestinians hope that the international community will come to their aid and help them gain their freedom from the Zionist Israeli apartheid system. The younger generation must keep the momentum to work to see genuine equity and justice for their people. Seventy-six years is a long time to hang on, and from my observation, some older Palestinians are losing hope in their dream. I hope that someday, in the not-too-distant future, life will improve for Palestinians.

Even with governments of nation-states calling on the United Nations to help the Palestinians gain their freedom from apartheid, it is virtually impossible to stop Israel. The United States is a close ally and fully supports Israel by using its veto power in the United Nations Security Council to prevent

FINAL THOUGHTS

any resolutions from being passed that would stop Israel. Also, nations are continuing to arm Israel with weaponry, as it benefits their economies.

I pray that one day, the current veto system in the United Nations Security Council will undergo reforms and restructuring so that you in Palestine will receive freedom and justice after the years of oppression that you have been living under. I pray that the United States will get a conscience and become a true hegemon who genuinely looks after the interests of all nations and peoples groups, not just their interests; that they will reconsider their foreign and domestic policies and decide to support the Israeli government no longer in its endeavours to eradicate all Palestinians from Palestine.

Since starting this journey, I have heard and read of two main futures for Palestinians. The first option is for the Palestinians to have a state of their own alongside the Israeli State with a genuine redistribution of the land with a border genuinely-placed along the 1967 Green Line. The Jewish settlers would decide whether to stay in the West Bank and East Jerusalem or move to the State of Israel.

Also, since the Gaza Strip and the West Bank are separated by the State of Israel, land would have to be redistributed to connect them. Currently, two separate states are not a workable option. Also, reaching a place where both sides will be happy could take many more years and continue to perpetuate the current situation, which is untenable.

With the ongoing building of settlements and confiscation of land, the second option, which some see as the better option, is to have the current apartheid system dismantled. This would mean pulling down the wall, eliminating the checkpoints, and introducing civil law throughout all areas of Palestine, ensuring that genuine equity and justice would be afforded to all people. People would live where they want. Then, and only then, will peace occur for all those living between the river and the sea, whether Jew or Palestinian. This option is often labelled a one state solution.

For those who may not have known what has been happening to the indigenous Palestinians, I hope that you now understand just a little more about what they have had to endure as a people group in the past and what they have to continue to survive in their daily lives now, with land confiscations, house demolitions, the wall, checkpoints, restrictions of movement, night raids and administrative detention and, in certain places being bombed at any time.

The current genocidal operation by the Israeli government in Gaza, which is still ongoing ten months after 7 October 2023, has helped many people around the world to see that Palestinians, not only in Gaza but also in the West Bank and East Jerusalem, are living under belligerent occupation. I hope you will continue to look for truth, not only when considering the plight of the Palestinians but also the plight of *all* indigenous peoples who are living under colonialist occupation. Indigenous people in every country need support and help to gain freedom and justice.

In the meantime, it is up to all of us to consider all individuals important, no matter the colour of their skin or their belief system. We are to "Give justice to the weak and the fatherless; maintain the right of the afflicted and the destitute. Rescue the weak and the needy; deliver them from the hand of the wicked."[584]

RECOMMENDED SOURCES

Isaac M (2020) The Other Side of The Wall, InterVarsity Press, Downers Grove.
Lyons J (2017) Balcony Over Jerusalem, Harper Collins Publishers, Sydney.
Martin A (2019) *"Gaza Fights For Freedom"* [video], YouTube, uploaded by *Empire Files*.
Masalha N (2018) Palestine A Four Thousand Year History, Zed Books London.
Pappe I (2010) The Ethnic Cleansing of Palestine, Oneworld Publications, London.
Peled M (2016) The General's Son Journey of an Israel in Palestine (second edition), Just World Books, Charlottesville, Virginia.
Qumsiyeh M B (2004) Sharing the Land of Canaan, Human Rights and the Israeli-Palestinian Struggle, University of Michigan Press, Ann Arbor.
Sizer S (2007) Zion's Christian Soldiers, Inter-Varsity Press, Downers Grove, Illinois.
Sizer S (2004) Christian Zionism, Inter-Varsity Press, Nottingham, England.

BIBLIOGRAPHY

ABC News (2024) "Israel-Gaza updates: US government imposes sanctions on Israeli settlers accused of West Bank violence." https://www.abc.net.au/news/2024-02-02/us-sanctions-on-israeli-settlers-accused-of-west-bank-violence/103418146

_____ (2023) "Australian among expanding Jewish Settlements in West Bank" [video], YouTube, uploaded by *ABC News*. https://www.youtube.com/watch?v=Ah49Es2z5Fk&ab_channel=ABCNews%28Australia%29

_____ (2023) "Government to harden stance against Israel's illegal settlements in occupied West Bank." https://www.abc.net.au/news/2023-08-08/government-hardens-against-israel-palestine-settlements/102702558

_____ (2011) "Train Passenger hurt by thrown rock." https://www.abc.net.au/news/2011-01-05/train-passenger-hurt-by-thrown-rock/1894724

Abdullah D (2020) Engaging the World: The Making of Hamas's Foreign Policy, Afro-Middle East Centre, Johannesburg.

Abulhawa S (2024) "Math proves that Israel's stated goals are an epic lie", *Electronic Intifada*. https://electronicintifada.net/content/math-proves-israels-stated-goals-are-epic-lie/47371

Abu T K (2021) "Why is Hamas popular in Jerusalem? –analysis", *The Jerusalem Post*.
https://www.jpost.com/arab-israeli-conflict/why-is-hamas-popular-in-jerusalem-analysis-685596

Adalah (2017) "The Discriminatory Laws Database."
https://www.adalah.org/en/content/view/7771

Addameer (2016) "Administrative Detention in the Occupied Palestinian Territory."
https://www.addameer.org/sites/default/files/publications/administrative_detention_analysis_report_2016.pdf

Aderet O (2017) "Israeli Prime Minister After Six-Day War: 'We'll Deprive Gaza of Water, and the Arabs Will Leave'", *Haaretz*.
https://www.haaretz.com/israel-news/2017-11-17/ty-article/.premium/israeli-pm-in-67-well-deprive-gaza-of-water-and-the-arabs-will-leave/0000017f-e8df-da9b-a1ff-ecff5b720000

Adwin I (2023) "Unprecedented Israeli bombardment lays waste to upscale Rimal, the beating heart of Gaza City", *AP News*.
https://apnews.com/article/gaza-rimal-israel-hamas-incursion-war-0411aa82d51fc801c117213e508a1a1d

AFP Agence France Presse (2023) "Over 1,400 Killed In Hamas Attacks On Israel: PM Office", *Barron's*.
https://www.barrons.com/news/over-1-400-killed-in-hamas-attacks-on-israel-pm-office-787d2b0f

Ahmed A (2024) "Gaza death toll from Israeli attacks since Oct. 7 surges to 36,284", *Anadolu Ajansi*.
https://www.aa.com.tr/en/middle-east/gaza-death-toll-from-israeli-attacks-since-oct-7-surges-to-36-284/3236603

_____ (2024) "Over 48,000 Israeli settlers stormed Al-Aqsa Mosque in 2023", *Anadolu Ajansi*.

BIBLIOGRAPHY

https://www.aa.com.tr/en/middle-east/over-48-000-israeli-settlers-stormed-al-aqsa-mosque-in-2023/3097644

_____ (2023) "Released Israeli woman says she was treated well in Hamas captivity", *Anadolu Ajansi*.
https://www.aa.com.tr/en/middle-east/released-israeli-woman-says-she-was-treated-well-in-hamas-captivity/3030944

Ahmed S (12:31 am January 3, 2024) Breaking: Gal Abduah's sister denies rape claims in NYT article and says NYT manipulated the family" [Tweet], @ShaykhSulaiman.
https://twitter.com/ShaykhSulaiman/status/1742191943243764084?ref_src=twsrc%5Etfw%7Ctwcamp%5Etweetembed%7Ctwterm%5E1742191943243764084%7Ctwgr%5Ee16bc9f06ab0808d04c1c4906e1df428624fd7bc%7Ctwcon%5Es1_&ref_url=https%3A%2F%2Fthegrayzone.com%2F2024%2F01%2F10%2Fquestions-nyt-hamas-rape-report%2F

Aidone D and Tomevska S (2024) "Senate condemns 'from the river to the sea' chant after Labor MP broke ranks." *SBS News*.
https://www.sbs.com.au/news/article/senate-condemns-from-the-river-to-the-sea-chant-after-labor-mp-broke-ranks/tfl1qh0u9

Albanese F (2023) "Address to the National Press Club of Australia" [video], YouTube, uploaded by *National Press Club of Australia*.
https://www.youtube.com/watch?v=XAnn07kilFk

Alexander R H (1986) "Ezekiel", in Gaebelein F E (ed.) The Expositor's Bible Commentary: Isaiah, Jeremiah, Lamentations, Ezekiel, Zondervan Publishing House, Grand Rapids, Michigan.
https://ref.ly/logosres/ebc06?ref=Bible.Eze33.21-22&off=317&ctx=is+in+these+verses.+~The+siege+of+Jerusal

Alia A, Arden F, Gianluca M and Nadir M (2023) "The intersection of economic conditions, trauma and mental health in the West Bank and Gaza", *World Bank.*
https://blogs.worldbank.org/arabvoices/intersection-economic-conditions-trauma-and-mental-health-west-bank-and-gaza

Al Jazeera (2024) "'Ticking time bomb': Poliovirus found in Gaza sewage."
https://www.aljazeera.com/news/2024/7/19/ticking-time-bomb-poliovirus-found-in-gaza-sewage

_____ (2023) "'Accusing Israel of apartheid is not anti-Semitic': Holocaust historian."
https://www.aljazeera.com/news/2023/8/27/accusing-israel-of-apartheid-is-not-anti-semitic-holocaust-historian

_____ (2023) "Israeli minister dismisses US 'terror' label after deadly settler attack."
https://www.aljazeera.com/news/2023/8/8/israeli-minister-dismisses-us-terror-label-after-deadly-settler-attack

_____ (2023) "Is 'total' Gaza blockade a collective punishment against Palestinians?"
https://www.aljazeera.com/news/2023/10/9/is-total-gaza-blockade-a-collective-punishment-against-palestinians

_____ (2023) "Jenin updates: Israel hits Gaza after 12 killed in Jenin raid."
https://www.aljazeera.com/news/liveblog/2023/7/4/jenin-attack-live-10-killed-as-israeli-raid-enters-second-day

_____ (2023) "PA health minister seeks probe into deadly Israeli raid on Gaza hospital."
https://www.aljazeera.com/news/2023/12/17/pa-health-minister-seeks-probe-into-deadly-israeli-raid-on-gaza-hospital

BIBLIOGRAPHY

_____ (2023) "Palestinians detained by Israel in Gaza blindfolded, stripped to underwear."
https://www.aljazeera.com/news/2023/12/8/video-photos-appear-to-show-detainees-stripped-to-underwear-in-gaza

_____ (2023) "Physicians for Human Rights say Israeli forces attacked Jenin hospitals."
https://www.aljazeera.com/news/liveblog/2023/7/4/jenin-attack-live-10-killed-as-israeli-raid-enters-second-day

_____ (2023) "Q&A: Former UN official Craig Mokhiber on Gaza, Israel and genocide."
https://www.aljazeera.com/news/2023/11/2/qa-former-un-official-craig-mokhiber-on-gaza-and-genocide

_____ (2023) "Timeline: Israel's attacks on Gaza since 2005."
https://www.aljazeera.com/news/2022/8/7/timeline-israels-attacks-on-gaza-since-2005

_____ (2023) "Why the Palestinian group Hamas launched an attack on Israel? All to know."
https://www.aljazeera.com/news/2023/10/7/palestinian-group-hamas-launches-surprise-attack-on-israel-what-to-know

_____ (2021) "Palestinian children traumatised by Israeli home invasions."
https://www.aljazeera.com/news/2021/9/23/palestinian-children-left-traumtised-by-israeli-home-invasions

_____ (2019) "What are areas A, B, and C of the occupied West Bank?"
https://www.aljazeera.com/news/2019/9/11/what-are-areas-a-b-and-c-of-the-occupied-west-bank

_____ (2014) "#illridewithyou goes viral after Sydney siege."
https://www.aljazeera.com/news/2014/12/15/illridewithyou-goes-viral-after-sydney-siege/

Al-Kassim M (2023) "Palestinians furious over Netanyahu claims that Israel must 'crush' statehood ambitions", *The Jerusalem Post*.
https://www.jpost.com/arab-israeli-conflict/article-748435

Allen-Ebrahimian, Bethany (2016) "Evangelical's side with Israel. That's hurting Palestinian Christians", *The Washington Post*.
https://www.washingtonpost.com/posteverything/wp/2016/12/23/evangelicals-side-with-israel-thats-hurting-palestinian-christians/

Al-Mughrabi N (2018) "Israeli forces kill three Gaza border protesters, wound 600: medics", *Reuters*.
https://www.reuters.com/article/idUSKBN1HY1Z9/

Alsaafin L and Siddiqui U (2024) "Israel's war on Gaza updates: 'No homes, no hope' in Rafah – UN chief", *Al Jazeera*.
https://www.aljazeera.com/news/liveblog/2024/2/10/israels-war-on-gaza-live-death-toll-nears-28000-as-rafah-assault-looms

Al Tahhan Z (2023) "Israel doubles number of Palestinian prisoners to 10,000 in two weeks", *Al Jazeera*.
https://www.aljazeera.com/features/2023/10/21/number-of-palestinian-prisoners-in-israel-doubles-to-10000-in-two-weeks

_____ (2017) "Hamas and Fatah: How are the two groups different?" *Al Jazeera*.
https://www.aljazeera.com/features/2017/10/12/hamas-and-fatah-how-are-the-two-groups-different

Al-Warra A (2020) "Palestinians say Israel is using power cuts to apply pressure in the West Bank", *Middle East Eye*.
https://www.middleeasteye.net/news/palestine-israel-west-bank-power-cuts-accusing

Amer A A (2021) "Hamas' Inability to Capitalize on the War in Gaza", *Carnegie Endowment for International Peace*.

https://carnegieendowment.org/sada/2021/07/hamas-inability-to-capitalize-on-the-war-in-gaza?lang=en

———— (2021) "Postponed Palestinian Elections: Causes and Repercussions", *Carnegie Endowment for International Peace.*
https://carnegieendowment.org/sada/84509

Amnesty International (2014) "Israel/Gaza conflict: Questions And Answers."
https://www.amnesty.org/en/latest/news/2014/07/israelgaza-conflict-questions-and-answers/

———— (2009) "Israel/Gaza: Operation 'Cast Lead'– 22 Days of Death and Destruction."
https://www.amnesty.org/en/wp-content/uploads/2021/07/mde150212009eng.pdf

Anadolu staff (2023) "Israel allegedly enforces 'Hannibal Protocol' on Oct. 7, killing festival-goers to prevent their captivity."
https://www.aa.com.tr/en/middle-east/israel-allegedly-enforces-hannibal-protocol-on-oct-7-killing-festival-goers-to-prevent-their-captivity/3060949

Andrews K (2022) "Hamas listed as terrorist organisation", *Australian Government.*
https://minister.homeaffairs.gov.au/KarenAndrews/Pages/hamas-listed-as-terrorist-organisation.aspx

Anera (n.d.) "What are Area A, Area B, and Area C in the West Bank?"
https://www.anera.org/what-are-area-a-area-b-and-area-c-in-the-west-bank/

Arab News (2024) **"**Australia's ABC staff raise concerns over alleged Israeli bias in Gaza reporting."
https://www.arabnews.com/node/2483786/media

Ashraf A (2021) "How US, Israel Birthed the Suicide Car Bomber', *News Click*.
https://www.newsclick.in/How-US-Israel-Birthed-Suicide-Car-Bomber

Assaf K (2022) "The Israeli arms companies that will profit from the latest assault on Gaza", *+972 Magazine*.
https://www.972mag.com/israeli-arms-companies-surveillance-gaza/

Associated Press in Jerusalem (2014) "Israeli-Palestinian violence in 2014-timeline", *The Guardian*.
https://www.theguardian.com/world/2014/nov/18/israel-palestinian-violence-timeline

Ateek N S (2014) A Concluding Theological Postscript in Wagner, Donald E and Davis W T (Eds), *Zionism and the Quest for Justice in the Holy Land*, Kindle Edition, Wipf and Stock, Eugene, p.217-221.

Australia Palestine Advocacy Network (2022) "Poll: Government out of Touch with Australians on Palestine."
https://apan.org.au/media_release/poll-government-out-of-touch-with-australians-on-palestine/

Awad A (2012) 'A Palestinian Theology of the Land', in Munayer S J and Loden L (eds) (2012) *The Land Cries Out*, Cascade Books, Oregon, USA.

Ayalon A (2024, March 11) "Self-defence or genocide? Asking Israel's powerful voices about Gaza|Four Corners" [video], YouTube, uploaded by *ABC News In-Depth*.
https://www.youtube.com/watch?v=BHlFLsf7ot0&ab_channel=ABCNewsIn-depth

Bachega H (2024) "Deadly West Bank settler attacks on Palestinians follow Israeli boy's killing." *BBC*.
https://www.bbc.com/news/world-middle-east-68830552

BIBLIOGRAPHY

Baconi T (2023, October 26) "On the Origins, Goals and Future of Hamas (interview by Michelle Martin)" [video], YouTube, uploaded by *Amanpour and Company*.
https://www.youtube.com/watch?v=OwckjA_DJW0&ab_channel=AmanpourandCompany

_____ (2018) *Hamas Contained: The Rise and Pacification of Palestinian Resistance*, Stanford University Press, Stanford.

Baker A (2011) "Addressing the Components of the Delegitimisation of Israel", (Fall 2011) *Jewish Political Studies Review*, Fall 2011, Vol. 23, No. 3/4, pp. 32-39.
https://www.jstor.org/stable/pdf/41575858.pdf?refreqid=excelsior%3Ae5b8e906f1c6126fa96a77343738a19a&ab_segments=&origin=&initiator=&acceptTC=1

Bakhos C (2019) 'What's in a name? The implications of 'Abrahamic' for Jewish, Christian and Muslim relations', in Asian, E and Rausch, Margaret (eds) *Jewish-Muslim Relations: Historical and Contemporary Interactions and Exchanges*, Springer Nature, Germany.

_____ (2014) *The Family of Abraham: Jewish, Christian and Muslim Interpretations*, Harvard University Press, Cambridge.

Balility O (2022) "AP PHOTOS: Israel's separation barrier, 20 years on", *Associated Press*.
https://apnews.com/article/politics-middle-east-jerusalem-israel-west-bank-2ce5d9956b729ad6169c880d00068977

Baltzer A (2007) *Witness in Palestine*, Paradigm Publishers, Boulder.

Barak E (2024, March 11) "Self-defence or genocide? Asking Israel's powerful voices about Gaza|Four Corners" [video], YouTube, uploaded by *ABC News In-Depth*.
https://www.youtube.com/watch?v=BHlFLsf7ot0&ab_channel=ABCNewsIn-depth

Barak J (2018) "Reality Check: The most moral army in the world. Really?" *The Jerusalem Post.*
https://www.jpost.com/opinion/reality-check-the-most-moral-army-in-the-world-really-549906

Barghouti O, Jones T and Ransby B (2024) "Let us remember the last time students occupied Columbia University", *The Guardian.*
https://www.theguardian.com/commentisfree/article/2024/may/03/columbia-pro-palestinian-protest-south-africa-divestment

BBC News (2010) "David Cameron describes blockaded Gaza as a 'prison'."
https://www.bbc.com/news/world-middle-east-10778110

Beaumont P (2024) "Why ICJ ruling against Israel's settlement policies will be hard to ignore", *The Guardian.*
https://www.theguardian.com/law/article/2024/jul/19/why-icj-ruling-against-israel-settlement-policies-hard-to-ignore-occupation-palestinian-territories

_____ (2023) "Footage shows IDF parading scores of Palestinian men around in underwear", *The Guardian.*
https://www.theguardian.com/world/2023/dec/08/footage-idf-israel-military-parading-palestinian-men-around-in-underwear

Benoist C (2016) "Fear of the dark: The crushing impact of Israeli night raids on Palestinians", *Equal Times.*
https://www.equaltimes.org/fear-of-the-dark-the-crushing

Bloomberg (2023) "Israeli Defence Minister Warns Hamas 'Will Regret' Deadly Attacks" [video], YouTube, uploaded by *Bloomberg.*
https://www.youtube.com/watch?v=vtjHcnNB0E8&ab_channel=BloombergQuicktake

Blumenthal M and Maté A (2024) "Screams without proof: questions for NYT about shoddy 'Hamas mass rape' report", *The Grayzone.*

BIBLIOGRAPHY

https://thegrayzone.com/2024/01/10/questions-nyt-hamas-rape-report/

Blumenthal M and Rubinstein A (2023) "Source of dubious 'beheaded babies' claim is Israeli settler leader who incited riots to 'wipe out' Palestinian village", *The Grayzone*.
https://thegrayzone.com/2023/10/11/beheaded-israeli-babies-settler-wipe-out-palestinian/

Blumenthal M (2024, January 5) "Mass Rape By Hamas on Oct 7th? NYT Coverage Questioned by Blumenthal: Rising Debates (interview)" [video], YouTube, uploaded by *The Hill*.
https://www.youtube.com/watch?v=bN9Rh3XOeo8

_____ (2023) "October 7 testimonies reveal Israel's military 'shelling' Israeli citizens with tanks, missiles."
https://thegrayzone.com/2023/10/27/israels-military-shelled-burning-tanks-helicopters/

_____ (2015) *Ruin and Resistance in Gaza: The 51 Day War*, Verso, London.

Boyraz T A (2023) "Israeli army says it does not have 'confirmation' about allegations that 'Hamas beheaded babies'", *Anadolu*.
https://www.aa.com.tr/en/middle-east/israeli-army-says-it-does-not-have-confirmation-about-allegations-that-hamas-beheaded-babies-/3014787

B'Tselem (n.d.) "Administrative Detention."
https://www.btselem.org/administrative_detention

_____ (2023) "Under cover of Gaza war, settlers working to fulfil state goal of Judaizing Area C."
https://www.btselem.org/press_releases/20231019_under_cover_of_gaza_fighting_settlers_working_to_fulfil_state_goal_of_judaizing_area_c

_____ (2021) "A regime of Jewish supremacy from the Jordan River to the Mediterranean Sea: This is apartheid."
https://www.btselem.org/publications/fulltext/202101_this_is_apartheid

_____ (2021) "This Is Ours – And This, Too: Israel's Settlement Policy In the West Bank."
https://www.btselem.org/publications/202103_this_is_ours_and_this_too

_____ (2017) "Home demolition as collective punishment."
https://www.btselem.org/punitive_demolitions

_____ (2017) "Restrictions on Movement."
https://www.btselem.org/freedom_of_movement

_____ (2017) "The Separation Barrier."
https://www.btselem.org/separation_barrier

Bullock T (2007) "The Palestinian Faction Fatah: A Primer", *NPR*.
https://www.npr.org/2007/01/13/6659712/the-palestinian-faction-fatah-a-primer

Burchill S (21 September 2021) "Lecture 8: The English School" [lecture notes], Key Concepts in International Relations, AIR242, *Deakin University*.

Burge G M (2013) *Whose Land? Whose Promise?* Pilgrim Press, Cleveland, Ohio.

Buzaid R (n.d.) "Jerusalem Hitting Home", *Remix Al Jazeera*.
https://remix.aljazeera.com/aje/PalestineRemix/jerusalem-hitting-home.html#/26

Cahill K M (2009) "Gaza Destruction and Hope", *Fordham*.
https://www.fordham.edu/media/review/content-assets/migrated/pdfs/jadu-single-folder-pdfs/Gaza_Destruction_and_Hope.pdf

BIBLIOGRAPHY

Cameron E (2012) *The European Reformation*, Oxford University Press, Oxford.

Canadians for Justice and Peace in the Middle East (2023) "Who is talking about Israeli Apartheid?"
https://www.cjpme.org/apartheid_list

Casebook (2024) "Indiscriminate Attacks", *ICRC*.
https://casebook.icrc.org/a_to_z/glossary/indiscriminate-attacks

Cassidy C (2024) "Monash University: police investigate alleged attack on pro-Palestine camp", *The Guardian*.
https://www.theguardian.com/australia-news/article/2024/may/08/monash-university-pro-palestine-camp-police-investigation-gaza-solidarity-ntwnfb

CBN News (2023) "Hamas Supporters Shout 'Gas' and 'F the Jews' in Sydney."
https://www.youtube.com/watch?v=Nu0fZNl5S9Q&ab_channel=CBNNews

Census (2023) "76th India Independence Day (1947): August 15, 2023", *United States Government*.
https://www.census.gov/newsroom/stories/india-independence-day.html

Central Bureau of Statistics (2022) "The Muslim Population in Israel 2022."
https://www.cbs.gov.il/en/mediarelease/Pages/2022/The-Muslim-Population-in-Israel-2022.aspx

Chapman C (2015) *Whose Promised Land?* Lion Hudson, Oxford, England.

Chomsky N and Pappe I (2010) *Gaza in Crisis Reflections on Israel's war against the Palestinians*, Hamish Hamilton, London.

Chrysanthos N (2023) "Wong steps up calls for humanitarian pause' to hostilities in Gaza", *The Age*.
https://www.theage.com.au/politics/federal/wong-joins-allies-asking-for-humanitarian-pause-to-hostilities-in-gaza-20231025-p5eetz.html

CIA World Factbook (2023) "Gaza Strip: Median Age."
https://www.cia.gov/the-world-factbook/countries/gaza-strip/#people-and-society

_____ (2023) "Gaza Strip: Population."
https://www.cia.gov/the-world-factbook/countries/gaza-strip/#people-and-society

Citino N, Martín G A and Norman K P (2023) "Generations of Palestinian Refugees Face Protracted Displacement and Dispossession", *Migration Policy Institute*.
https://www.migrationpolicy.org/article/palestinian-refugees-dispossession

Colonization & Wall Resistance Commission (CWRC) (2012) "CWRC: 4073 occupation violations in the first half of 2023."
https://www.cwrc.ps/page-1223-en.html

Congressional Research Service (2023) "U.S. Foreign Aid to Israel", *Federation of American Scientists*.
https://sgp.fas.org/crs/mideast/RL33222.pdf

Cook J (2023) "Israel's long-held plan to drive Gaza's people into Sinai is now within reach."
https://jonathancook.substack.com/p/israels-long-held-plan-to-drive-gazas?utm_source=post-email-title&publication_id=476450&post_id=138328326&utm_campaign=email-post-title&isFreemail=true&r=2hatbr&utm_medium=email

_____ (2023) "The West's hypocrisy towards Gaza's breakout is stomach-turning", *Jonathan Cook*.

https://www.jonathan-cook.net/2023-10-08/west-hypocrisy-gaza-breakout/

_____ (2023) Why is the media ignoring evidence of Israel's own actions on 7 October? https://jonathancook.substack.com/p/why-is-the-media-ignoring-evidence

_____ (2022) "Social media giants allow hate speech against Russia but silence Israel's critics", *Middle East Eye*. https://www.middleeasteye.net/opinion/russia-ukraine-war-israel-facebook-hate-speech-silence-critics

Dallasheh L (2016) "Persevering through Colonial Transition: Nazareth's Palestinian Residents after 1948", *Journal of Palestine Studies*, Vol. 45, No. 2 (178) (Winter 2016), pp. 8-23. https://www.jstor.org/stable/pdf/26378571.pdf?refreqid=excelsior%3Afba9d8e30197dcc02102d12b61a998cf&ab_segments=&origin=&initiator=&acceptTC=1

David A (2017) "Ancient Egyptian Records Indicate Philistines Weren't Aegean Pirates After All", *Haaretz*. https://www.haaretz.com/archaeology/2017-07-23/ty-article-magazine/ancient-records-indicate-philistines-werent-aegean-pirates/0000017f-eef9-ddba-a37f-eeff03cd0000

Davis U (2003) *Apartheid Israel: Possibilities for the Struggle Within*, Zed Books, London.

Defence For Children International (2023) "Israeli forces kill six Palestinian children in the occupied West Bank." https://www.dci-palestine.org/israeli_forces_kill_six_palestinian_children_in_the_occupied_west_bank

Department of Economic and Social Affairs (n.d.) "Article 11 – Situations of risk and humanitarian emergencies", *UN*.

https://www.un.org/development/desa/disabilities/convention-on-the-rights-of-persons-with-disabilities/article-11-situations-of-risk-and-humanitarian-emergencies.html

Doherty B, Jabour B, Delaney B, Wahlquist C, Davidson H, Safi M, Milman O and Farrell P (2014) "Sydney siege: how a day and night of terror unfolded at the Lindt café", *The Guardian*.
https://www.theguardian.com/australia-news/2014/dec/20/sydney-siege-timeline-how-a-day-and-night-of-terror-unfolded-at-the-lindt-cafe

Energy Information Administration (2023) "How much Petroleum does the United States import and export?"
https://www.eia.gov/tools/faqs/faq.php?id=727&t=6

Erakat N (2024) "Quick thoughts on the ICJ decision this morning", *Instagram*.
https://www.instagram.com/p/C2keNSaAO5A/?img_index=7

_____ (2019) *Justice for Some Law and the Question of Palestine*, Stanford University Press, Stanford.

Erickson P (2021) "ALP National Party Platform as adopted at the 2021 Special Platform Conference", *ALP*.
https://alp.org.au/media/2594/2021-alp-national-platform-final-endorsed-platform.pdf

Estrin D and Bashir AB (2019) "Here's What Tourists Might See If They Were Allowed To Visit Gaza", *NP*.
https://www.npr.org/2019/08/08/748661511/heres-what-tourists-might-see-if-they-were-allowed-to-visit-gaza

European-Mediterranean Human Rights Monitor (n.d.) "Suffocation and Isolation: 15 Years of Israeli Blockade on Gaza."
https://euromedmonitor.org/en/article/4116/New-report:-Gaza-is-almost-unlivable-after-15-years-of-blockade

BIBLIOGRAPHY

_____ (n.d.) "Suffocation: 17 Years of Israeli Blockade on Gaza." https://euromedmonitor.org/en/gaza

_____ (2024) "Euro-Med:100,000 Palestinians killed, wounded, missing in Gaza", *The Palestinian Information Centre*. https://english.palinfo.com/news/2024/01/15/312797/

_____ (2023) "Israel commits widespread war crimes in Gaza, Humanitarian catastrophe is imminent." https://euromedmonitor.org/en/article/5846/Israel-commits-widespread-war-crimes-in-Gaza,-humanitarian-catastrophe-is-imminent

_____ (2023) "Israeli Strike on Refaat al-Areer Apparently Deliberate." https://euromedmonitor.org/en/article/6014/Israeli-Strike-on-Refaat-al-Areer-Apparently-Deliberate

Fabian E (2024) "Israeli arms sales break record for 3rd year in row, reaching $13 billion in 2023", *The Times Of Israel*. https://www.timesofisrael.com/israeli-arms-sales-break-record-for-3rd-year-in-row-reaching-13-billion-in-2023/

_____ (2023) "Defence minister announces 'complete siege' of Gaza: No power, food or fuel", *The Times of Israel*. https://www.timesofisrael.com/liveblog_entry/defense-minister-announces-complete-siege-of-gaza-no-power-food-or-fuel/

_____ (2022) "Israeli arms sales hit new record of $11.3 billion in 2021 — with 7% to Gulf", *The Times of Israel*. https://www.timesofisrael.com/israeli-arms-sales-hit-new-record-of-11-3-billion-in-2021/

Federal Bureau of Investigation (a) (n.d.) "Pan Am 103 Bombing." https://www.fbi.gov/history/famous-cases/pan-am-103-bombing

_____ (b) (n.d.) "What We Investigate." https://www.fbi.gov/investigate/terrorism

Fernández B (2023) "Israel wants to turn Jenin into another Gaza, siege by siege", *Al Jazeera*.
https://www.aljazeera.com/opinions/2023/7/13/israel-wants-to-turn-jenin-into-another-gaza-siege-by-siege

Finkelstein N G (2018) *Gaza an Inquest into its Martyrdom*, University of California Press, Oakland.

Fisher M (2014) "Everything you need to know about the 2014 Ukraine crisis", *Vox*.
https://www.vox.com/2014/9/3/18088560/ukraine-everything-you-need-to-know

Flavius J (1987) *The Works of Josephus: Complete and unabridged*, translated by William Whiston, Hendrickson Publishers, Peabody.

Forensic Architecture (2024) "Israeli Disinformation: Al-Ahli Hospital."
https://forensic-architecture.org/investigation/israeli-disinformation-al-ahli-hospital

France24 (2023) "Israel social security data reveals true picture of Oct 7 deaths."
https://www.france24.com/en/live-news/20231215-israel-social-security-data-reveals-true-picture-of-oct-7-deaths

―――― (2023) "UN seeks Israel access for Hamas sexual violence investigation."
https://www.france24.com/en/live-news/20231206-un-seeks-israel-access-for-hamas-sexual-violence-investigation

Frankel J (2023) "Israel holds over 1,200 detainees without charge. That's the most in 3 decades, a rights group says", *ABC News*.
https://www.independent.co.uk/news/ap-palestinians-jerusalem-israelis-jews-b2385800.html

Fruchtman M (2023) "Who Will Protect the Thousands of Palestinian Children Israel Detains?" *Haaretz*.

BIBLIOGRAPHY

https://www.haaretz.com/israel-news/2023-05-28/ty-article/.premium/imagine-being-one-of-the-2-000-palestinian-children-israel-detains-every-year/00000188-4e24-dde3-abf9-fe2dde2c0000

Gadzo M (2024) "Israel's war on Gaza live: Wave of attacks as Israel told to end occupation", *Al Jazeera*.
https://www.aljazeera.com/news/liveblog/2024/7/20/israels-war-on-gaza-live-calls-grow-on-israel-to-end-palestine-occupation

Ganor B (2002) "'Defining Terrorism: Is One Man's Terrorist Another Man's Freedom Fighter?'", Media Asia, 29:3, *State Library of Queensland*.
https://www.proquest.com/docview/211523623?accountid=13378&parentSessionId=h%2Fa5PHQENYgBHdc5XF9MaraI8s-rIcTQJOYSLub3pTfo%3D&pq-origsite=primo

Gathara P (2021) "The fallacy of the colonial 'right to self-defence'", *Al Jazeera*.
https://www.aljazeera.com/opinions/2021/5/16/the-fallacy-of-the-colonial-right-to-defense

Gordon N (2009) "Boycott Israel", *Los Angeles Times*.
https://www.latimes.com/archives/la-xpm-2009-aug-20-oe-gordon20-story.html

Government Press Office (2023) "Ministry of Defense Spokesperson's Statement: Israel Sets New Record in Defense Exports: Over $12.5 Billion in 2022", *gov.il*.
https://www.gov.il/en/pages/esibat

Graham-Harrison E (2023) "'Destruction chased them': funeral held for those killed in Gaza church airstrike", *The Guardian*.
https://www.theguardian.com/world/2023/oct/20/destruction-chased-them-funeral-held-for-those-killed-in-gaza-church-airstrike

Grantee M K (2016) "The Cruel Experiments of Israel's Arms Industry", *Pulitzer Center*.

https://pulitzercenter.org/stories/cruel-experiments-israels-arms-industry

Greenwald D B (n.d.) "Military Rule in the West Bank", *Middle East Political Science*.
https://pomeps.org/military-rule-in-the-west-bank

Hagee J (2020) "Who owns the land of Israel?" *Israel Hayom*.
https://www.israelhayom.com/2020/05/31/who-owns-the-land-of-israel/

Haj-Yahya N H, Khalaily M, Rudnitzky A and Fargeon B (2022) "Statistical Report on Arab Society in Israel: 2021", *Israel Democracy Institute*.
https://en.idi.org.il/articles/38540

Halper J (2010) *An Israeli in Palestine*. Pluto Books, New York.

Halpern O (n.d.) "Deadly Pattern: 20 journalists died by Israeli military fire In 22 years. No one has been held accountable", *Committee to Protect Journalists*.
https://cpj.org/reports/2023/05/deadly-pattern-20-journalists-died-by-israeli-military-fire-in-22-years-no-one-has-been-held-accountable/

Halsell G (1996) *Prophecy and Politics: Militant Evangelists on The Road to Nuclear War*, Lawrence Hill & Co, Chicago.

Hamas (2024) "Our Narrative… Operation Al-Aqsa Flood", *Palestine Chronicle*.
https://www.palestinechronicle.com/wp-content/uploads/2024/01/PDF.pdf

Hamden O (2023 December 25) "Why did Hamas attack Israel on October 7?" [video], YouTube, uploaded by *TRT World Now*.
https://www.youtube.com/watch?v=Kth_d8mboIk&t=12s&ab_channel=TRTWorldNow

BIBLIOGRAPHY

Hamdy I A (2008) "The Druze in Israel", *JSTOR*, University of California Press.
https://www-jstor-org.ezproxy-f.deakin.edu.au/stable/48599551?searchText=Reshaping+Druze+Particularism+in+Israel&searchUri=%2Faction%2FdoBasicSearch%3FQuery%3DReshaping%2BDruze%2BParticularism%2Bin%2BIsrael%26so%3Drel&ab_segments=0%2FSYC-6490%2Ftest_segment_3&refreqid=fastly-default%3Aed46a4dcb0dd9efff13bcfcf63a5eea5&seq=4

Hamouda L and Hamouda H (2023) *The Shape of Dust*, Pantera Press, Neutral Bay.

Hardy M (21 March 2017) "The United States and the Middle East" [lecture], Issues and Themes in Middle East Politics AIE255, *Deakin University*.

Hasan M and Sayedahmed D (2018) "Blowback: How Israel Went From Helping Create Hamas to Bombing It", *The Intercept*.
https://theintercept.com/2018/02/19/hamas-israel-palestine-conflict/

Hass A (2005) "Broken Bones and Broken Hopes", *Haaretz*.
https://www.haaretz.com/2005-11-04/ty-article/broken-bones-and-broken-hopes/0000017f-f6e1-d47e-a37f-fffda3b20000

Haydar N (2023) "Greens say Israel is 'practising crime of apartheid' and call for boycotts of far-right figures", *ABC News*.
https://www.abc.net.au/news/2023-06-05/greens-change-part-platform-on-palestine-israel-bandt/102440458

Henry E (2023) Modern Age History, Timeline & Facts | What Is the Modern Era?", *study.com*.
https://study.com/academy/lesson/modern-age-history-timeline-facts-era.html

Hermann T and Yarr E (2018) "The Majority of the Israeli Public Believes Moving the US Embassy to Jerusalem is in Israel's Best Interests", *The Israel Democracy Institute*.
https://en.idi.org.il/articles/23407

Herzl T (1960) "The Complete Diaries of Theodore Herzl Volume 1", *Internet Archive*.
https://archive.org/details/TheCompleteDiariesOfTheodorHerzl_201606/TheCompleteDiariesOfTheodorHerzlEngVolume1_OCR/page/n51/mode/2up

Howeidy H (2023) "Jewish personalities accuse Israel of apartheid", *Ahram*.
https://english.ahram.org.eg/News/507055.aspx

Horn A, Jones H and Halpern O (2023) "Israel is Rapidly Expanding Jewish settlements in the West Bank. This Australian man is among them", *ABC News*.
https://www.abc.net.au/news/2023-07-30/australian-settlers-in-israel-west-bank/102642486

Human Rights Council (2024) "Detailed findings on attacks carried out on and after 7 October 2023 in Israel", *Office for the Coordination of Humanitarian Affairs*.
https://www.ohchr.org/sites/default/files/documents/hrbodies/hrcouncil/sessions-regular/session56/a-hrc-56-crp-3.pdf?__cf_chl_tk=2z8z5elYDOMa0Q3h0cjrFGJU.BUhvDqEMsaDGLsLFOU-1723582859-0.0.1.1-4756

―――― (2019) "Report of the independent international commission of inquiry on the protests in the Occupied Palestinian Territory", *OHCHR*.
https://www.ohchr.org/sites/default/files/Documents/HRBodies/HRCouncil/CoIOPT/A_HRC_40_74.pdf

BIBLIOGRAPHY

Human Rights Watch (n.d.) "United Nations General Assembly Resolution 194 (iii) of 11 December 1948." https://www.hrw.org/legacy/campaigns/israel/return/un194-rtr.htm

‗‗‗‗‗‗ (2024) "West Bank: Israel Responsible for Rising Settler Violence." https://www.hrw.org/news/2024/04/17/west-bank-israel-responsible-rising-settler-violence

‗‗‗‗‗‗ (2023) **"West Bank: New Entry Rules Further Isolate Palestinians."** https://www.hrw.org/news/2023/01/23/west-bank-new-entry-rules-further-isolate-palestinians

‗‗‗‗‗‗ (2019) "Born Without Civil Rights." https://www.hrw.org/report/2019/12/17/born-without-civil-rights/israels-use-draconian-military-orders-repress

‗‗‗‗‗‗ (2018) "Israel: Gaza Killings Unlawful, Calculated Officials Green-Light Shooting of Unarmed Demonstrators." https://www.hrw.org/news/2018/04/03/israel-gaza-killings-unlawful-calculated

‗‗‗‗‗‗ (2009) "White Flag Deaths: Killings of Palestinian Civilians During Operation Cast Lead." https://www.hrw.org/sites/default/files/reports/ioptwf0809webwcover_2.pdf

Hurst D and Butler J (2023) "Australia to officially resume use of term 'Occupied Palestinian Territories', reversing Coalition stance", *The Guardian*. https://www.theguardian.com/australia-news/2023/aug/08/australia-to-officially-resume-use-of-term-occupied-palestinian-territories-reversing-coalition-stance

Hutchinson J (2017). *'European War-Making and the Rise of Nation States', In Nationalism and War*, Oxford University Press, Oxford.

International Committee of the Red Cross (n.d.) "Article 8 – War Crimes."

https://ihl-databases.icrc.org/en/ihl-treaties/icc-statute-amendment-art8-2010/article-8?activeTab=undefined

_____ (n.d.) "Henry Dunant (1828-1910)."

https://www.icrc.org/en/doc/resources/documents/misc/57jnvq.htm

_____ (n.d.) "Rome Statute of the International Criminal Court, 17 July 1998."

https://ihl-databases.icrc.org/en/ihl-treaties/icc-statute-1998?activeTab=undefined

International Criminal Court (2011) "Rome Statute of the International Criminal Court."

https://www.icc-cpi.int/sites/default/files/RS-Eng.pdf

International Humanitarian Law Databases (n.d.) "Article 15 – Protection of civilian medical and religious personnel", *ICRC*.

https://ihl-databases.icrc.org/en/ihl-treaties/api-1977/article-15

_____(n.d.) "Article 33 – Individual responsibility, collective penalties, pillage, reprisals", *ICRC*.

https://ihl-databases.icrc.org/en/ihl-treaties/gciv-1949/article-33

_____(n.d.) "Article 50 – Regulations", *ICRC*.

https://ihl-databases.icrc.org/en/ihl-treaties/hague-conv-iv-1907/regulations-art-50

_____(n.d.) "Article 51 – Protection of the Civilian Population", *ICRC*.

https://ihl-databases.icrc.org/en/ihl-treaties/api-1977/article-51

_____(n.d.) "Article 77–Protection of children 1", *ICRC*.

https://ihl-databases.icrc.org/en/ihl-treaties/api-1977/article-77?activeTab=undefined

_____(n.d.) "Article 79 – Measures of protection for journalists 1", *ICRC*.

https://ihl-databases.icrc.org/en/ihl-treaties/api-1977/article-79?activeTab=undefined

BIBLIOGRAPHY

_____(n.d.) "Declaration (IV,3) concerning Expanding Bullets. The Hague, 29 July 1899", *ICRC*.
https://ihl-databases.icrc.org/en/ihl-treaties/hague-decl-iv-3-1899

_____ (n.d.) "Rule 1. The Principle of Distinction between Civilians and Combatants", *ICRC*.
https://ihl-databases.icrc.org/en/customary-ihl/v1/rule1

Isaac M (2023, December 24) "Isaac Sermon in the Liturgy of Lament: Christ in the Rubble" [video], YouTube, uploaded by *Munther Isaac*.
https://www.youtube.com/watch?v=aEGiANa0-oI&ab_channel=-MuntherIsaac

_____ (2023, October 22) "English translation of my sermon today to follow below." Facebook, *Munther Isaac*.
https://www.facebook.com/munther.isaac

_____ (2020) *The Other Side of The Wall*, InterVarsity Press, Downers Grove.

_____ (2015, February 10) "Munther Isaac. Palestinian Christian Response to Christian Zionism" [video], YouTube, uploaded by *Christ at the Checkpoint*.
https://www.youtube.com/watch?v=sD0FPD8-XoA&ab_channel=ChristatTheCheckpoint

ISGAP (n.d.) "Boaz Ganor."
https://isgap.org/fellow/boaz-ganor/

Israel Prime Minister's Office (2023) "PM Netanyahu asks Ministers to Rise for a Moment of Silence."
https://www.gov.il/en/pages/spoke-start151023

IVP (2023) "Colin Chapman."
https://www.ivpress.com/colin-chapman

Jamal U (2023) "What's Israel's Hannibal Directive? A former Israeli soldier tells all", *Al Jazeera*.

https://www.aljazeera.com/features/2023/11/3/whats-the-hannibal-directive-a-former-israeli-soldier-tells-all

Jaspan C (2024) "Antoinette Lattouf was sacked by ABC, Fair Work rules", *The Sydney Morning Herald.*
https://www.smh.com.au/business/companies/antoinette-lattouf-was-sacked-by-the-abc-fair-work-rules-20240603-p5jiqv.html

Jewish Virtual Library (n.d.) "Benjamin Netanyahu Administration: Speech at the Begin-Sadat Center at Bar-Ilan University (June 14, 2009)."
https://www.jewishvirtuallibrary.org/prime-minister-netanyahu-speech-at-the-begin-sadat-center-at-bar-ilan-university-june-2009

―――― (n.d.) "Likud Party: Original Party Platform (1977)."
https://www.jewishvirtuallibrary.org/original-party-platform-of-the-likud-party

―――― (n.d.) "Prevention of Infiltration (Offences and Jurisdiction) Law 1954 (5714)."
https://www.jewishvirtuallibrary.org/jsource/History/1954law.pdf

―――― (2023) "Vital Statistics: Latest Population Statistics for Israel (April 25, 2023)."
https://www.jewishvirtuallibrary.org/latest-population-statistics-for-israel#Christian

―――― (2021) "Vital Statistics: Total Casualties, Arab-Israeli Conflict."
https://www.jewishvirtuallibrary.org/total-casualties-arab-israeli-conflict

Johnson G (2023) "Sydney Opera House displays Israeli flag colours", *City Hub.*
https://cityhub.com.au/sydney-opera-house-to-display-israeli-flag-colours/

BIBLIOGRAPHY

Joseph D (n.d.) "When it comes to local politics, Jerusalem's Palestinians just can't win", *The National News*.
https://www.thenationalnews.com/opinion/comment/when-it-comes-to-local-politics-jerusalem-s-palestinians-just-can-t-win-1.779056

Jones O (2023) "Despite the truce, people in Gaza will keep dying – this horrifying death toll must never be forgotten", *The Guardian*.
https://www.theguardian.com/commentisfree/2023/nov/22/gaza-children-death-toll-israel-hamas

Joshua Project (2023) "Country: West Bank/Gaza."
https://joshuaproject.net/countries/we

Just Vision (2015) "Jenin Invasion."
https://justvision.org/glossary/jenin-invasion

J-Wire (2023) "Brisbane's Story Bridge to be lit blue and white."
https://www.jwire.com.au/brisbanes-story-bridge-to-be-lit-blue-and-white/

Kalic S N, Institute C S (2012) "Combating a Modern Hydra Al Qaeda and the Global War on Terrorism", *CreateSpace Independent Pub*.
https://apps.dtic.mil/sti/pdfs/ADA446134.pdf

Katz I (3:01 pm, October 14, 2023) "Indeed, Madam Congresswoman" [Tweet], @Israel_katz.
https://twitter.com/Israel_katz/status/1712876230762967222

Katz Y (2010) "Yadlin: Israel would be 'happy' if Hamas takes over Gaza", *The Jerusalem Post*.
https://www.jpost.com/defense/yadlin-israel-would-be-happy-if-hamas-takes-over-gaza

Keller-Lynn C (2023) "Amid war and urgent need to ID bodies, evidence of Hamas's October 7 rapes slips away", *The Times Of Israel*.
https://www.timesofisrael.com/amid-war-and-urgent-need-to-id-bodies-evidence of hamass-october-7-rapes-slips-away/

Khalek R (2014) "Why do media value Israeli children's lives more than those of Palestinian kids?" *The Electronic Intifada*.
https://electronicintifada.net/blogs/rania-khalek/why-do-media-value-israeli-childrens-lives-more-those-palestinian-kids

Khatib A, McKee M and Yusuf S (2024) "Counting the dead in Gaza: difficult but essential", *The Lancet*.
https://www.thelancet.com/journals/lancet/article/PIIS0140-6736(24)01169-3/fulltext

Khouri R G (2023) "Watching the watchdogs: Babies and truth die together in Israel-Palestine", *Al Jazeera*.
https://www.aljazeera.com/opinions/2023/10/13/watching-the-watchdogs-babies-and-truth-die-together-in-israel-palestine

Kindig J (2006) "Vietnam War: Student Activism", *University of Washington*.
https://depts.washington.edu/antiwar/vietnam_student.shtml

King Abdullah III (2024 February 13) "President Biden and His Majesty King Abdullah II of Jordan Deliver Remarks" [video], YouTube, uploaded by *The White House*.
https://www.youtube.com/watch?v=cGmkFDOibGI&ab_channel=TheWhiteHouse

Kirk M (2022) "American Evangelicals, the Gulf States, and Israel: A Cynical Covenant", *Arab Center* Washington DC.
https://arabcenterdc.org/resource/american-evangelicals-the-gulf-states-and-israel-a-cynical-covenant/

Knell Y (2023) "Palestinian fears grow amid rising Israeli settler attacks", *BBC News*.
https://arabcenterdc.org/resource/american-evangelicals-the-gulf-states-and-israel-a-cynical-covenant/

Kouddous S A (2023) "Israel's endgame is to push Palestinians into Egypt – and the West is cheering it on", *The Guardian*.

BIBLIOGRAPHY

https://www.theguardian.com/commentisfree/2023/oct/20/israel-palestinians-egypt-west-bombs-rafah-border-crossing

Krauss J (2022) "Many in Mideast see hypocrisy in Western embrace of Ukraine", *A News*.

https://apnews.com/article/russia-ukraine-islamic-state-group-jerusalem-migration-europe-1ce41cc04aed6afc415e6ed83f83c984

Kubovich Y, Samuels B, Hashmonai A, Tov M H and Reuters (2023) "IDF Ramps Up Strikes on Gaza and Prepares for Ground Invasion", *Haaretz*.

https://www.haaretz.com/israel-news/2023-10-11/ty-article/.premium/idf-ramps-up-strikes-on-gaza-prepares-for-ground-invasion/0000018b-1b4c-d2fc-a59f-db5d8aee0000

Laub Z and Robinson K (2023) "What is Hamas?" *Council on Foreign Relations*.

https://www.cfr.org/backgrounder/what-hamas

Lawler A (2010) "Who Wrote the Dead Sea Scrolls?" *Smithsonian Magazine*

https://www.smithsonianmag.com/history/who-wrote-the-dead-sea-scrolls-11781900/#:~:text=Among%20the%20texts%20are%20parts,version%20of%20the%20Ten%20Commandments.

Lazaro F de S (2029) "Water crisis may make Gaza Strip uninhabitable by 2020", *PBS*.

https://www.pbs.org/newshour/show/water-crisis-may-make-gaza-strip-uninhabitable-by-2020

Lazaroff T (2019) "Netanyahu: A Palestinian State won't be created", *The Jerusalem Post*.

https://www.jpost.com/arab-israeli-conflict/netanyahu-a-palestinian-state-wont-be-created-586017

_____ (2018) "IDF warns of larger military response to Gaza protest", *The Jerusalem Post*.

https://www.jpost.com/Israel-News/IDF-warns-of-larger-military-response-to-Gaza-protest-547595

Lee M (2024) "Journalist questions bombing of Gaza University", *Al Jazeera*.
https://www.aljazeera.com/program/newsfeed/2024/1/19/journalist-questions-bombing-of-gaza-university

Lewis A and Kidd J (2024) "Video analysis finds no evidence of 'gas the Jews' being chanted at Sydney Opera House protest, despite witness statements", *ABC*.
https://www.abc.net.au/news/2024-02-02/nsw-police-opera-house-protest-video-analysis/103418582

Lewis O (2014) "Palestinian driver rams Jerusalem station killing baby", *Reuters*.
https://www.reuters.com/article/mideast-violence-jerusalem-idINKCN0IB2PU20141022

Lowenstein A (2023) *The Palestine Laboratory*, Scribe Publications, Brunswick.

Lynk M (2018) "Gaza "Unliveable", UN Special Rapporteur for the Situation of Human Rights in the OPT Tells Third Committee" [press release excerpts], *UN*.
https://www.un.org/unispal/document/gaza-unliveable-un-special-rapporteur-for-the-situation-of-human-rights-in-the-opt-tells-third-committee-press-release-excerpts/

_____ (2016) "Proposed Israel law "gives green light to theft of Palestinian land"– UN expert", *Office of the High Commission of Human Rights*.
https://www.ohchr.org/en/2016/11/proposed-israel-law-gives-green-light-theft-palestinian-land-un-expert

Lyons J (2021) *Dateline Jerusalem: Journalism's Toughest Assignment*, Monash University Publishing, Clayton.

BIBLIOGRAPHY

_____ (2017) *Balcony Over Jerusalem*, Harper Collins Publishers, Sydney.

Lyons J, Cohen J and Le Clezio S (2014) "'Stone Cold Justice'" [video], Four Corners, uploaded by *ABC News*. https://www.abc.net.au/news/2014-02-10/stone-cold-justice-promo/5245064

MacLeod J (2021) "The struggle for Self-Determination in West Papua (1969-present)", *International Center on Non-Violent Conflict*. https://www.nonviolent-conflict.org/wp-content/uploads/2016/02/West-Papua-1.pdf

Madain Project (2023) "Cave of the Patriarchs." https://madainproject.com/cave_of_patriarchs

Marsi F (2024) "Gaza's mass graves: Is the truth being uncovered?" *Al Jazeera*. https://www.aljazeera.com/news/2024/5/11/gazas-mass-graves-is-the-truth-being-uncovered

Martin A (2019) "Gaza Fights for Freedom" [video], YouTube, uploaded by *Empire Files*. https://www.youtube.com/watch?v=HnZSaKYmP2s&t=2469s&ab_channel=EmpireFiles

Masalha N (2018) *Palestine A Four Thousand Year History*, Zed Books, London.

_____ (2007) *The Bible and Zionism Invented Traditions, Archaeology and Post-Colonialism in Palestine*, Zed Books, London.

Mashni N (2023, October 9) "The Project Nasser Mashni (Interview by Sarah Harris, Lisa Wilkinson and Waleed Aly for The Project)" [video], Vimeo, uploaded by *Australia Palestine Advocacy Network*. https://vimeo.com/873125605

Masoud B and Abu Mustafa I (2024) "Gaza doctor describes ordeal of detention", *Reuters*.

https://www.reuters.com/world/middle-east/gaza-doctor-describes-ordeal-detention-2024-02-04/

Masoud B and Williams D (2023) "Images from Gaza show dozens of detained Palestinian men stripped to their underwear", *The Sydney Morning Herald*.
https://www.smh.com.au/world/middle-east/catastrophic-hundreds-more-palestinians-killed-as-israel-pursues-hamas-in-south-gaza-20231208-p5eq0p.html

McGreal C (2022) "'US accused of hypocrisy for supporting sanctions against Russia but not Israel'", *The Guardian*.
https://www.theguardian.com/world/2022/mar/07/us-sanctions-against-russia-but-not-israel

McIlroy (2013) "Labor conference dodges Israel-Palestine fight", *Financial Review*.
https://www.afr.com/politics/federal/labor-conference-dodges-israel-palestine-fight-20230818-p5dxjw

McKernan B (2023) "A precious resource: How Israel uses water to control the West Bank", The Guardian (Italicise The Guardian).
https://www.theguardian.com/world/2023/may/17/how-israel-uses-water-to-control-west-bank-palestine

McKernan B and Taha S (2023) "Gaza civilians afraid to leave home after bombing of 'safe routes'", *The Guardian*.
https://www.theguardian.com/world/2023/oct/14/gaza-civilians-afraid-to-leave-home-after-bombing-of-safe-routes

Meagher J (2004) ""Orientalism in Nineteenth-Century Art". In Heilbrunn Timeline of Art History", *The Metropolitan Museum of Art*.
https://www.metmuseum.org/toah/hd/euor/hd_euor.htm

Mens Line Australia (n.d.) "Adjusting to Retirement."
https://mensline.org.au/mens-mental-health/adjusting-to-retirement/

BIBLIOGRAPHY

Middle East Eye (2.00 am February 9, 2024) "Dr Bilal Azzam, a Member", [Tweet], @MiddleEastEye.
https://twitter.com/MiddleEastEye/status/1755622518696595599?s=20

―――― (2023, December 26) "Female Israeli hostages played arm-wrestling with Hamas guard" [video], YouTube, uploaded by *Middle East Eye*.
https://www.youtube.com/watch?v=ZIMfc1y59mM&ab_channel=MiddleEastEye

Middle East Eye Staff (2017) "Hamas in 2017: The document in full."
https://www.middleeasteye.net/news/hamas-2017-document-full

Middle East Monitor (2024) "Israel's use of rape against Palestinian detainees from Gaza exposed."
https://www.middleeastmonitor.com/20240607-israels-use-of-rape-against-palestinian-detainees-from-gaza-exposed/

―――― (2023) "Israel settler: 'Israel forces killed hostages, not Hamas'."
https://www.middleeastmonitor.com/20231021-israel-settler-israel-forces-killed-hostages-not-hamas/

―――― (2023) "Israeli soldiers seal Palestinian well with concrete."
https://www.middleeastmonitor.com/20230727-israeli-soldiers-seal-palestinian-well-with-concrete/

Military Court Watch (2023) "Newsletter – June 2023 Detention figures."
https://www.militarycourtwatch.org/page.php?id=gvbnddwZdpa1779321A6q9rvacb70

Miller M (2023) "The United States is Deeply Troubled with Israeli Settlement Announcement", *U.S. Department of State*.
https://www.state.gov/the-united-states-is-deeply-troubled-with-israeli-settlement-announcement/

Ministry of Foreign Affairs and Expatriates (2024) "Mahmoud Abbas", *State of Palestine*. http://www.mofa.pna.ps/en-us/palestine/president

Mint (2023) "PM Netanyahu invokes 'Amalek' theory to justify Gaza killings. What is this Hebrew Bible nation?"
https://www.livemint.com/news/world/pm-netanyahu-invokes-amalek-theory-to-justify-gaza-killings-what-is-this-hebrew-bible-nation-11698555324918.html

Morgan M J (2004) "The Origins of the New Terrorism", *Parameters*, Vol 34:1, p.29-43.
https://press.armywarcollege.edu/cgi/viewcontent.cgi?article=2190&context=parameters

Mughaisib M Abu and Turtle, N (2021) "Born under attack to be buried under attack, a life without rest in Gaza", Médecins Sans Frontières.
https://msf.org.au/article/statements-opinion/gaza-born-under-attack-be-buried-under-attack-life-without-rest

Munayer S J (2012) "Theology of the Land", in Munayer S J and Loden L (eds), *The Land Cries Out*, Cascade Books, Oregon, USA.

Munayer S J and Loden L (2014) *Through My Eyes*, Crownhill, Milton Keynes.

Myeni T (2022) "South Africa calls for Israel to be declared an 'apartheid state'", *Al Jazeera*.
https://www.aljazeera.com/news/2022/7/26/south-africa-calls-for-israels-proscription-as-apartheid-state

National Army Museum (n.d.) "First China War."
https://www.nam.ac.uk/explore/opium-war-1839-1842

National Film and Sound Archive of Australia (n.d.) "Terrorism Strikes Sydney: Hilton Hotel Bombing."
https://www.nfsa.gov.au/collection/curated/terrorism-strikes-sydney-hilton-hotel-bombing

NAACP (2023) "Martin Luther King, Jr."

https://naacp.org/find-resources/history-explained/civil-rights-leaders/martin-luther-king-jr

ní Fhlathùin M (2008) "The British Empire in the Nineteenth Century", *Gale*. https://www.gale.com/intl/essays/maire-ni-fhlathuin-british-empire-nineteenth-century

Nimer M (2009) "Charting the Hamas Charter Changes", *Insight Turkey*, vol. 11, no. 4, pp. 115–30. http://www.jstor.org/stable/26331116

Norwegian Refugee Council (2023) "Palestine: Israeli settler attack forcibly transfer Jerusalem community." https://www.nrc.no/news/palestine-israeli-settler-attacks-forcibly-transfer-jerusalem-community/

_____ (2023) "West Bank: Entire Palestinian communities disappeared due to Israeli settler violence." https://www.nrc.no/news/2023/august/west-bank-entire-palestinian-communities-disappeared-due-to-israeli-settler-violence/

Office for the Coordination of Humanitarian Affairs (2024) "Hostilities in the Gaza Strip and Israel | Flash Update #86." https://www.ochaopt.org/content/hostilities-gaza-strip-and-israel-flash-update-86

_____ (2018) "Refugee needs in the Gaza Strip October 2018", *United Nations*. https://www.ochaopt.org/sites/default/files/gaza_thematic_6_0.pdf

_____ (2016) "Intensified restrictions on the entry of building materials Delay the completion of housing projects in Gaza", *United Nations*. https://www.ochaopt.org/content/intensified-restrictions-entry-building-materials-delay-completion-housing-projects-gaza

Office of Public Affairs (2022) "Pan Am Flight 103 Terrorist Suspect in Custody for 1988 Bombing over Lockerbie, Scotland", *U.S. Department of Justice.*
https://www.justice.gov/opa/pr/pan-am-flight-103-terrorist-suspect-custody-1988-bombing-over-lockerbie-scotland

Office of the European Union Representative (West Bank and Gaza Strip, UNRWA) (2023) "One Year Report on Demolitions and Seizures in the West Bank, including East Jerusalem."
https://www.eeas.europa.eu/sites/default/files/documents/2023/One Year Report on Demolitions and Seizures in the West Bank including East Jerusalem - 1 January %E2%80%93 31 December 2022.pdf

―――― (2023) "West Bank demolitions and displacement December 2022", *UN.*
https://www.ochaopt.org/content/west-bank-demolitions-and-displacement-december-2022

―――― (2021) "Most Palestinian plans to build in Area C not approved", *UN.*
https://www.ochaopt.org/content/most-palestinian-plans-build-area-c-not-approved

Ofir J (2023) "Israeli politician: 'The children of Gaza have brought this upon themselves'", *Mondoweiss.*
https://mondoweiss.net/2023/10/israeli-politician-the-children-of-gaza-have-brought-this-upon-themselves/

Omaar R (2023) "Israeli president Isaac Herzog says Gazans could have risen up to fight 'evil' Hamas", *ITV News.*
https://www.itv.com/news/2023-10-13/israeli-president-says-gazans-could-have-risen-up-to-fight-hamas

Organisation for the Prohibition of Chemical Weapons (n.d.) "Chemical Weapons Convention."

BIBLIOGRAPHY

https://www.opcw.org/sites/default/files/documents/CWC/CWC_en.pdf

Owda R (2023) "How Israeli Settlements Impede the Two-State Solution", *Carnegie Endowment for International Peace.*
https://carnegieendowment.org/sada/89215

Palestinian Central Bureau of Statistics (n.d.) "PCBS President: Despite tragic circumstances, Palestinians have multiplied seven times since the Nakba (Catastrophe) of 1948."
https://www.pcbs.gov.ps/Portals/_pcbs/PressRelease/nakba 60.pdf

Palestinian Central Bureau of Statistics (2023) "Presents the Main Findings of Labour Force Survey in 2022."
https://www.pcbs.gov.ps/post.aspx?lang=en&ItemID=4421

Palestine Chronicle Staff (2024) "The 'Lion of Gaza' Roars – Who is Hamza Abu Halima."
https://www.palestinechronicle.com/the-lion-of-gaza-roars-who-is-hamza-abu-halima/

Pandor N (2024 January 27) "ICJ Genocide Decision | Minister Pandor calls for ceasefire in Gaza" [video], YouTube, uploaded by *eNCA*.
https://www.youtube.com/watch?v=lcW4YU_84b8&ab_channel=eNCA

Pappé I (2024) *Lobbying for Zionism Both Sides of the Atlantic*, Oneworld Publications Ltd, London.

_____ (2011) *The Forgotten Palestinians* (Kindle edition), Yale University Press, New Haven.

_____ (2007) *The Ethnic Cleansing of Palestine* (Kindle edition), Oneworld Publications, Oxford.

Parliament of Australia (n.d.) "Definition of Terrorism."
https://www.aph.gov.au/Parliamentary_Business/Committees/Joint/Completed_Inquiries/pjcis/securityleg/report/chapter5#def

Parry T (2024) "Gaza conflict is creating a traumatised generation of child amputees, warn medics", *The Telegraph*.
https://www.telegraph.co.uk/global-health/terror-and-security/gaza-conflict-is-creating-a-generation-of-child-amputees/

Peace Now (2024) "The Government Declares 12,000 Dunams in the Jordan Valley as State Lands."
https://peacenow.org.il/en/state-land-declaration-12000-dunams

Peled M (2023, December 14) "Public forum with Miko Peled & Noura Mansour" [video], YouTube, uploaded by *Free Palestine Melb*.
https://www.youtube.com/watch?v=XIbqdl8iF-E&ab_channel=FreePalestineMelb

―――― (2016) *The General's Son Journey of an Israel in Palestine (second edition)*, Just World Books, Charlottesville, Virginia.

Penkower M N (2004) "The Kishinev Pogrom of 1903: A Turning Point in Jewish History", *Modern Judaism*, Oct. 2004, Vol. 24, No. 3, pp. 187-225, Published by: Oxford University Press.
https://www.jstor.org/stable/1396539

Perdue L G and Carter W (2015) *Israel and Empire A Postcolonial History of Israel and Early Judaism*. (Edited by Barker C A), T & T Clark, London.

Perry N J (2004) "The Numerous Federal Legal Definitions of Terrorism: The Problem of too Many Grails", *Journal of Legislation*, Vol. 30, Issue 2, pp. 249-274.
https://scholarship.law.nd.edu/jleg/vol30/iss2/3/

Pew Research Center (2022) "2. American Views of Israel."
https://www.pewresearch.org/global/2022/07/11/american-views-of-israel/

Phillips J and Simon-Davies J (2017) "Migration to Australia: a quick guide to the statistics", *Parliament of Australia*.

BIBLIOGRAPHY

https://www.aph.gov.au/About_Parliament/Parliamentary_Departments/Parliamentary_Library/pubs/rp/rp1617/Quick_Guides/MigrationStatistics

Pictet J S (1958) "The Geneva Conventions of 12 August 1949 Commentary", *ICRC*.
https://tile.loc.gov/storage-services/service/ll/llmlp/GC_1949-IV/GC_1949-IV.pdf

Pitkänen P (2016) "Settler Colonialism in Ancient Israel", from: *The Routledge Handbook of the History of Settler Colonialism,* Routledge.
https://www.academia.edu/31712835/Settler_Colonialism_in_Ancient_Israel

POICA (2023) "Israeli Settlements in the Occupied West Bank: from "outposts" to urban Blocks." http://poica.org/2023/05/israeli-settlements-in-the-occupied-west-bank-from-outposts-to-urban-blocks/

Pressman J (2006) "The Second Intifada: Background and Causes of the Israeli-Palestinian Conflict", *Journal of Conflict Studies, 23*(?)
https://journals.lib.unb.ca/index.php/JCS/article/view/220

PressTV (2023) "Israel's Ben-Gvir calls for assassination of 'thousands' of Palestinians."
https://www.presstv.ir/Detail/2023/06/24/705851/Palestine-Israel-Itamar-Ben-Gvir-West-Bank-settlement-construction-military-campaign-assassinate-Palestinians-Evyatar-outpost

Prior M (1997) The Bible and Colonialism: A moral Critique, Bloomsbury Publishing Plc, ProQuest Ebook Central.
https://ebookcentral.proquest.com/lib/slq/reader.action?docID=436833&ppg=16

Qumsiyeh M B (2004) *Sharing the Land of Canaan*, Pluto Press, London.

Ragless D (2018) "'One man's terrorist is another man's freedom fighter'. Discuss in Relation to the definitional problems" [unpublished paper], School of Humanities and Social Sciences, *Deakin University*.

Raheb M (2014) *Faith in the face of Empire The Bible Through Palestinian Eyes*, Obris Books, Maryknoll.

Rahman Y (2024) "This 11-month-old is the 1st confirmed case of in Gaza", *CBC*.
https://www.cbc.ca/news/world/polio-gaza-first-case-1.7306241

Reed W (2023) "Haaretz confirms Grayzone reporting it dismissed as 'conspiracy' showing Israel killed own festivalgoers", *The Grayzone*.
https://thegrayzone.com/2023/11/21/haaretz-grayzone-conspiracy-israeli-festivalgoers/

Refworld (1978) "Importance of the universal realization of the right of peoples to self-determination and of the speedy granting of independence to colonial countries and peoples for the effective guarantee and observance of human rights, A/RES/33/24", *UNHCR*.
https://www.refworld.org/docid/3b00f1a44c.html

Relief Web (n.d.) "Israeli Apartheid - The Legacy of the Ongoing Nakba at 75", *OCHA*.
https://reliefweb.int/report/occupied-palestinian-territory/israeli-apartheid-legacy-ongoing-nakba-75-enar

_____ (2023) "Fact Sheet: Movement and Access in the West Bank, August 2023." file:///Fact Sheet/ Movement and Access in the West Bank, August 2023

_____ (2023) "For Palestinians in the West Bank, 2023 was the deadliest year on record", *OCHA*.
https://reliefweb.int/report/occupied-palestinian-territory/palestinians-west-bank-2023-was-deadliest-year-record

BIBLIOGRAPHY

_____ (2023) "Parched: Israel's policy of water deprivation in the West Bank."
https://reliefweb.int/report/occupied-palestinian-territory/parched-israels-policy-water-deprivation-west-bank

_____ (2022) "Humanitarian Alert: Masafer Yatta School Demolition, 24 November 2022."
https://reliefweb.int/report/occupied-palestinian-territory/humanitarian-alert-masafer-yatta-school-demolition-24-november-2022

_____ (2009) "OPT: The Gaza blockade - Children and education fact Sheet."
https://reliefweb.int/report/occupied-palestinian-territory/opt-gaza-blockade-children-and-education-fact-sheet

_____ (2005) "Why is Israel pulling out settlers from Gaza, West Bank?"
https://reliefweb.int/report/israel/why-israel-pulling-out-settlers-gaza-west-bank

_____ (2002) "Israel's Apartheid Wall: we are here and they are there", OCHA.
https://reliefweb.int/report/israel/israels-apartheid-wall-we-are-here-and-they-are-there

Reskallah S (2021) "Food Insecurity in Palestine: A Future for Farmers", *Wilson Center*.
https://www.wilsoncenter.org/article/food-insecurity-palestine-future-farmers

Reuters (2023) "Explainer: What do we know about Israeli hostages in Gaza?"
https://www.reuters.com/world/middle-east/what-do-we-know-about-israeli-hostages-gaza-2023-11-22/

Reuters Staff (2008) "Israel warns Hezbollah war would invite destruction", *Reuters*.

https://www.reuters.com/article/uk-israel-lebanon-hezbollah-idUKTRE4923I020081003

Riley T (2012) "A History of The Geneva Conventions", *Moyers*.
https://billmoyers.com/content/a-history-of-the-geneva-conventions/

Robinson Kali (2023) "What to Know About the Arab Citizens of Israel", *Council on Foreign Relations*.
https://www.cfr.org/backgrounder/what-know-about-arab-citizens-israel

Rolef S H (n.d.) "'Basic Law: Israel - The Nation State of the Jewish People' (Unofficial translation)", *knesset.gov.il*.
https://main.knesset.gov.il/EN/activity/Documents/BasicLawsPDF/BasicLawNationState.pdf

Rosenzweig-Ziff D, Morse C E, Svrluga S, Cornejo D, Dormindo H and Ledur, J (2024) "Riot police and over 2,000 arrests: A look at 2 weeks of campus protests", *The Washington Post*.
https://www.washingtonpost.com/nation/interactive/2024/university-antiwar-campus-protests-arrests-data/

Saad L (2021) "Key trends in U.S views on Israel and the Palestinians", *Gallup*.
https://news.gallup.com/poll/350393/key-trends-views-israel-palestinians.aspx

Sagoo R (2024) "South Africa's genocide case against Israel: The International Court of Justice explained", *Chatham House*.
https://www.chathamhouse.org/2024/01/south-africas-genocide-case-against-israel-international-court-justice-explained

Said E W (1979) *Orientalism*. Kindle Edition, Random House, New York.

Sainsbury K (2006) "Port Arthur Massacre", *Centre for Tasmanian Historical Studies*.

BIBLIOGRAPHY

https://www.utas.edu.au/library/companion_to_tasmanian_history/P/Port A massacre.htm

Savyasachi B (2023) "Australia's Parliament House illuminated in blue in white to support Israel", *The Canberra Times*.
https://www.canberratimes.com.au/story/8380279/parliament-lights-up-in-blue-and-white-to-support-israel/

Schrader A (2024) "Nearly 9,000 Palestinians have been arrested in West Bank", *UPI*.

Scott-Bauman M (2021) *Palestinians and Israelis A short History of conflict* (Kindle edition), The History Press, Cheltenham.

Segal R (2023, November 21) "Gaza 'Textbook Case of Genocide' (interview by Owen Jones)" [video], YouTube, uploaded by *Owen Jones*.
https://www.youtube.com/watch?v=AUeEnjULHe0&ab_channel=OwenJones

Sengupta K (2014) "Israel-Gaza conflict: Myth of Hamas's human shield. Gazans deny being put in line of fire", *Belfast Telegraph*
https://www.belfasttelegraph.co.uk/news/world-news/israel-gaza-conflict-myth-of-hamass-human-shield-gazans-deny-being-put-in-line-of-fire/30448511.html

Shalash F (2023) "Displaced at Israeli gunpoint, Jenin residents return to find their homes in ruin", *Middle East Eye*.
https://www.middleeasteye.net/news/israel-jenin-displaced-gunpoint-residents-return-homes-ruins

_____ (2023) "Israeli settlers kill Palestinian in latest West Bank Rampage", *Middle East Eye*.
https://www.middleeasteye.net/news/israel-settlers-kill-palestinian-latest-west-bank-rampage

_____ (2023) "Night terror: The Israeli raids of Palestinian homes in the West Bank", *Middle East Eye*.

https://www.middleeasteye.net/news/israel-raids-palestinian-homes-west-bank

Shamir J (2023) "Hundreds of Israeli Academics and Public Figures: Judicial Coup and Occupation 'Directly Linked'", *Haaretz*.
https://www.haaretz.com/israel-news/2023-08-07/ty-article/.premium/israeli-and-palestinian-academics-judicial-coup-and-occupation-directly-linked/00000189-cf40-d821-afdd-df-64709b0000?lts=1693515265414

Shapira A (2018) "Israel's Politics of Citizenship", *Israel Studies Review*, 33(3), 99–120.
https://www.jstor.org/stable/48563807?seq=5

Sharaka (n.d.) "What are the Abraham Accords?"
https://www.sharakango.com/resources/what-are-the-abraham-accords

Sharp J M (2023) "U.S. Foreign Aid to Israel", *Congressional Research Service*.
https://sgp.fas.org/crs/mideast/RL33222.pdf

Shehada M (11:19 pm December 3 2023) "Important! Haaretz definitely debunks" [Tweet], @muhammadshehad2.
https://twitter.com/muhammadshehad2/status/1731302039378882594

Sherwood H (2023) "Israel-Hamas war: what has happened and what has caused the conflict?" *The Guardian*.
https://www.theguardian.com/world/2023/oct/08/israel-hamas-gaza-palestinian-territories

―――― (2012) "Gilad Shalit: the real Prisoner of War", *The Guardian*.
https://www.theguardian.com/world/2012/may/09/gilad-shalit-real-prisoner-of-war

BIBLIOGRAPHY

Shezaf H (2020) "Israel Rejects Over 98 Percent of Palestinian Building Permit Requests in West Bank's Area C", *Haaretz*.
https://www.haaretz.com/israel-news/2020-01-21/ty-article/.premium/israel-rejects-98-of-palestinian-building-permit-requests-in-west-banks-area-c/0000017f-f7ce-d044-adff-f7ff0b250000

―――― (2022) 'Israel Begins Demolition in Contentious West Bank Village Following Court Ruling", *Haaretz*.
https://www.haaretz.com/israel-news/2022-05-11/ty-article/.premium/israel-begins-demolition-in-west-bank-village-following-court-ruling/00000180-d630-d452-a1fa-d7ff4b810001

Shoaibi H (2011) "Childbirth at checkpoints in the Occupied Palestinian Territory", *The Lancet (abstracts)*.
https://www.thelancet.com/pb/assets/raw/Lancet/abstracts/palestine/palestine2011-4.pdf

Silberberg N (n.d.) "Star of David: The Mystical Significance", *Chabad.org*.
https://www.chabad.org/library/article_cdo/aid/788679/jewish/Star-of-David-The-Mystical-Significance.htm

Silver L and Fagan M (2022) "2. American views of Israel", *Pew Research Center*.
https://www.pewresearch.org/global/2022/07/11/american-views-of-israel/

Sinmaz E (2024) "UNRWA staff accused by Israel sacked without evidence, chief admits", *The Guardian*.
https://www.theguardian.com/world/2024/feb/09/head-of-unwra-says-he-followed-reverse-due-process-in-sacking-accused-gaza-staff

Sizer S (2007) *Zion's Christian Soldiers*, Inter-Varsity Press, Downers Grove, Illinois.

―――― (2004) *Christian Zionism*, Inter-Varsity Press, Nottingham, England.

Sky News (2023) "Israel-Hamas war: 'We will fight and we will win', says Benjamin Netanyahu" [video], YouTube, uploaded by *Sky News*. https://www.youtube.com/watch?v=P5LmB6uup3o&ab_channel=SkyNews

Smith C D (2010) *Palestine and the Arab-Israeli Conflict A History with Documents 10th Edition*, Bedford, Boston.

Sommer A K (2023) "The Druze Community in Israel, Explained", *Haaretz*. https://www.haaretz.com/israel-news/2023-06-11/ty-article/.premium/the-druze-community-in-israel-explained/00000188-8c42-d3c4-afec-9ed397020000

Sorrells K (2013) "Intercultural communication: globalization and Social justice", *Sage*, Thousand Oaks, California. https://library.deakin.edu.au/record=b2962438

Sovereign Imperial & Royal House of Ghassan (n.d.) "History", *Royal Ghassan*. https://www.royalghassan.org/history.html

Stephan M J Chenoweth, Erica (2008) "'Why Civil Resistance Works: The Strategic Logic of Nonviolent Conflict", *International Security*, Summer, 2008, Vol. 33, No. 1 pp.7-44 Published by: The MIT Press. https://www.jstor.org/stable/40207100

Stock E (1972) "The Reconstitution of the Jewish Agency: A Political Analysis", *The American Jewish Yearbook* Vol 73, pp.178-193, American Jewish Committee. https://www.jstor.org/stable/23603460

Stone D (2023) "Catch-22: The cost of rejecting local democracy for Palestinians in East Jerusalem", *The Jewish Independent*. https://plus61j.net.au/featured/catch-22-the-cost-of-rejecting-local-democracy-for-palestinians-in-east-jerusalem/

BIBLIOGRAPHY

Strickland P O (2014) "Wave of oppression targets Palestinians in Israel", *The Electronic Intifada*.
https://electronicintifada.net/content/wave-oppression-targets-palestinians-israel/14049

Suárez T (2017) *State of Terror*, Olive Branch Press, Massachusetts.

Survey Research Unit (2023) "Public Opinion Poll No (88)", *Palestinian Center for Policy and Survey Research*.
https://www.pcpsr.org/sites/default/files/Poll 88 English full text June 2023.pdf

Tamini A and Takruri D (2022) *They Called Me a Lioness*, Kindle, Oneworld, New York.

Tamimi B (2018) "Empire Files: Abby Martin Meets Ahed Tamimi—Message From A Freedom Fighter" [video], YouTube, uploaded by *Empire Files*.
https://www.youtube.com/watch?v=yV1HwG1_phs&ab_channel=TeleSUREnglish

Tanis F (2022) "Palestinians grow frustrated with militants in Gaza, and a rift could be forming", *NPR*.
https://www.npr.org/2022/08/26/1119220569/palestinians-gaza-hamas-islamic-jihad-israel

Tapper J and Appleton K (2023) "Israel investigates sexual violence committed by Hamas as part of October 7 horror", *CNN*.
https://edition.cnn.com/2023/11/17/world/israel-investigates-sexual-violence-hamas/index.html

Tekuma M (2014) "How Israel Helped Spawn Hamas", *Transcend Media Service*.
https://www.transcend.org/tms/2014/07/how-israel-helped-to-spawn-hamas/

The Cradle (2023) "Video confirms tank struck home with Israeli captives on 7 Oct."
https://thecradle.co/articles-id/15975

The Economist (2014) "Why Hamas fire those rockets."
https://www.economist.com/middle-east-and-africa/2014/07/19/why-hamas-fires-those-rockets

The Hill (2024) "NYT pulls Hamas rape story from podcast over internal turmoil over shoddy reporting: Max Blumenthal" [video].
https://thehill.com/video/nyt-pulls-hamas-rape-story-from-podcast-over-internal-turmoil-over-shoddy-reporting-max-blumenthal/9385492/

Theocracy Watch (2004) "The Rise of the Religious Right in the Republican Party." http://theocracywatch.org/middle_east2.htm#Jerry

The Presidency (2024) "South Africa makes urgent request to International Court of Justice on Rafah offensive", *Republic of South Africa.*
https://www.thepresidency.gov.za/south-africa-makes-urgent-request-international-court-justice-rafah-offensive

The Times of Israel Staff (2023) "Visiting Evyatar, Ben Gvir tells settlers to 'head for the hilltops,' expand outposts", *The Times of Israel.*
https://www.timesofisrael.com/visiting-evyatar-ben-gvir-tells-settlers-to-head-for-the-hilltops-expand-outposts/

The White House (n.d.) "The Constitution: The First Amendment."
https://www.whitehouse.gov/about-the-white-house/our-government/the-constitution/

Totman S (25 July 2018) "Zionism and the Push for a Jewish Homeland" [lecture], Arab Israeli Conflict AIE364, *Deakin University.*

_____ (3 March 2017) "Introduction to Orientalism" [lecture], Historical Foundations of the Middle East AIE153, *Deakin University.*

Trading Economics, (2023) "Israel – Military Expenditure (% Of GDP)."

BIBLIOGRAPHY

https://tradingeconomics.com/israel/military-expenditure-percent-of-gdp-wb-data.html

Translation in (2023) "Israel-Hamas war: 'We will fight and we will win', says Benjamin Netanyahu", *Sky News*. https://news.sky.com/video/israel-hamas-war-we-will-fight-and-we-will-win-says-benjamin-netanyahu-12995212

Ullah A (2023) "Gaza-Israel: How the world reacted to the surprise assault", *Middle East Eye*. https://www.middleeasteye.net/news/gaza-israel-how-world-reacted UNICEF (2023) "Situation Analysis of Children's Rights and Wellbeing in the State of Palestine." https://www.unicef.org/sop/media/2471/file/Situation Analysis of Children%27s Rights and Wellbeing in the UNICEF State of Palestine.pdf

United Nations (n.d.) "International Convention on the Suppression and Punishment of the Crime of Apartheid." https://www.un.org/en/genocideprevention/documents/atrocity-crimes/Doc.10_International Convention on the Suppression and Punishment of the Crime of Apartheid.pdf

_____ (n.d.) "Genocide." https://www.un.org/en/genocideprevention/genocide.shtml

_____ (2023) "South Africa institutes proceedings against Israel and requests the International Court of Justice to indicate provisional measures – ICJ Press Release." https://www.un.org/unispal/document/icj-southafrica-israel-genocide-29dec2023/

_____ (2023) "Gaza is 'running out of time' UN experts warn, demanding A ceasefire to prevent genocide."

https://www.un.org/unispal/document/gaza-is-running-out-of-time-un-experts-warn-demanding-a-ceasefire-to-prevent-genocide/#:~:text=%E2%80%9CWe%20remain%20convinced%20that%20the,of%20action%2C%E2%80%9D%20they%20said.

_____ (2022) "Israel's occupation of Palestinian Territory is 'apartheid': UN rights expert."
https://news.un.org/en/story/2022/03/1114702

_____ (2009) "Restricting space: The planning regime applied by Israel In Area C of the West Bank."
https://www.un.org/unispal/document/auto-insert-201838/

_____ (1974) "United Nations Human Rights/self-determination – GA Resolution."
https://www.un.org/unispal/document/auto-insert-177633/

_____ (1949) "IV Geneva Convention Relative to the protection of Civilian Persons in time of war of 12 august 1949."
https://www.un.org/en/genocideprevention/documents/atrocity-crimes/Doc.33_GC-IV-EN.pdf

United Nations Commission on Human Rights (2005) "Human Rights Resolution2005/7: Israeli Practices Affecting the Human Rights of the Palestinian People in the Occupied Palestinian Territory, Including East Jerusalem, 14 April 05, E/CN.4/RES/2005/7", *RefWeb*.
https://www.refworld.org/docid/45377c820.html

United Nations Country Team in Palestinian (2017) "Gaza Ten Years Later", *UNSCO*.
https://unsco.unmissions.org/gaza-ten-years-later-report-july-2017

United Nations General Assembly (2010) "Resolution adopted by the General Assembly on 28 July 2010 64/292. The human right to water and sanitation."

BIBLIOGRAPHY

https://documents-dds-ny.un.org/doc/UNDOC/GEN/N09/479/35/PDF/N0947935.pdf?OpenElement

_____ (1974) "Importance of the universal realization of the Right of peoples to self-determination and of the speedy granting of independence to colonial countries and peoples for the effective guarantee and observance of Human rights _RES_3246(XXIX)."
https://digitallibrary.un.org/record/190185?ln=en&v=pdf

United Nations Human Rights (2024) "Gaza: UN experts condemn killing and silencing of journalists."
https://www.ohchr.org/en/press-releases/2024/02/gaza-un-experts-condemn-killing-and-silencing-journalists

United Nations News (2023) "UN General Assembly adopts Gaza resolution calling for immediate and sustained 'humanitarian truce'."
https://news.un.org/en/story/2023/10/1142847

United Nations Office for the Coordination of Humanitarian Affairs (n.d.) "Gaza crossings: movement of people and goods."
https://www.ochaopt.org/data/crossings

United Nations Peacemaker (n.d.) "Israeli-Palestinian Interim Agreement on the West Bank and The Gaza Strip."
https://peacemaker.un.org/sites/peacemaker.un.org/files/ILPS_950928_InterimAgreementWestBankGazaStrip%28OsloII%29.pdf

United Nations Relief and Works Agency (UNRWA) (n/d.) "2014 Gaza Conflict."
https://www.unrwa.org/2014-gaza-conflict

United States Department of State (n.d.) "Foreign Terrorist Organisations."
https://www.state.gov/foreign-terrorist-organizations/

United States National Security Council (1952) "NSC-68: Excerpts", *Digital History.*

https://www.digitalhistory.uh.edu/disp_textbook.cfm?smtID=3&psid=3630

Varanasi L (2023) "How the mighty watermelon became a symbol of pro-Palestinian resistance on social media", *Business Insider*.
https://www.businessinsider.com/why-watermelon-symbol-of-palestinian-resistance-2023-11

Volkmann C S (2023) "Current Israeli Plan to Double the Settler Population in the Occupied Syrian Golan by 2027 is Unprecedented, and that 700,000 Israeli Settlers Are Living Illegally in the Occupied West Bank", *United Nations Office at Geneva*.
https://www.ungeneva.org/en/news-media/meeting-summary/2023/03/afternoon-human-rights-council-hears-current-israeli-plan-double

WAFA (2024) "Over 9,000 Palestinians detained in West Bank since October 7, 2023 by Israel - Prisoners' institutions."
https://english.wafa.ps/Pages/Details/144707

Waldman A (2014) "The Shame of Shuhada Street", *The Atlantic*. file:///C:/Users/deenaragless/Library/Containers/com.microsoft.Word/Data/Library/Preferences/AutoRecovery/Waldman, Ayelet, The Shame of Shuhada Street

Weber T P (2004) *On the road to Armageddon*, Baker Academic, Grand Rapids.

West M (2024) "Australia keen to resume Palestine aid 'soon': minister", *Michael West Media*.
https://michaelwest.com.au/australia-keen-to-resume-palestine-aid-soon-minister/

Wezeman P D, Kuimova A and Wezeman S T (2022) "Trends in International Arms Transfers, 2021", *SIPRI*.

BIBLIOGRAPHY

https://www.sipri.org/sites/default/files/2022-03/fs_2203_at_2021.pdf

Winstanley A (2023) "The evidence Israel killed its own citizens on 7 October", *The Electronic Intifada*. https://electronicintifada.net/content/evidence-israel-killed-its-own-citizens-7-october/41156

World Fact Book (2024) "The Gaza Strip: Religion", *CIA.gov*. https://www.cia.gov/the-world-factbook/countries/gaza-strip/

World Health Organisation (2023) "Lethal combination of hunger and disease to lead to more deaths in Gaza." https://www.who.int/news/item/21-12-2023-lethal-combination-of-hunger-and-disease-to-lead-to-more-deaths-in-gaza

Worldometer (2023) "State of Palestine Population." https://www.worldometers.info/world-population/state-of-palestine-population/

World Population Review (2022) "Palestine Religion, Economy and Politics." https://worldpopulationreview.com/countries/palestine-population

Xpath.global (2022) "How to live the expat life in Israel." https://xpath.global/how-to-live-the-expat-life-in-israel/

Younger Jnr. K L (1998) "The Deportations of the Israelites", *Journal of Biblical Literature*, Vol. 117, No. 2, pp. 201-227. https://www.jstor.org/stable/3266980?read-now=1#page_scan_tab_contents

Zhang S (2024) "80 Percent of Global Famine Is Currently in Gaza, UN Expert Warns", *Truthout*. https://truthout.org/articles/80-percent-of-global-famine-is-currently-in-gaza-un-expert-warns/

Zitun Y and Bergman R (2024) "The first hours of the Black Sabbath", *Ynet*.
https://w.ynet.co.il/yediot/7-days/time-of-darkness

Ziv O (2024) "Israel razes entire Bedouin village to expand a highway", *+972 Magazine*.
https://www.972mag.com/israel-razes-bedouin-village-wadi-al-khalil/

NOTES

Introduction

1. M Fisher. "Everything you need to know about the 2014 Ukraine crisis."
2. Chris McGreal. "US accused of hypocrisy for supporting sanctions against Russia but not Israel"; J Krauss. "Many in Mideast see hypocrisy in Western embrace of Ukraine."
3. Jonathan Cook. "Social media giants allow hate speech against Russia but silence Israel's critics."
4. Mens Line Australia. "Adjusting to Retirement."
5. Professor Mazin Qumsiyeh is highly regarded worldwide as a scientist and activist. He is well-read about many religions and is a Christian.
6. Nur Masalha. Palestine A Four Thousand Year History, 2.
7. Masalha, Palestine 5.

Chapter 1

8. Asha Khatib, Martin McKee, Salim Yusuf. "Counting the dead in Gaza: difficult but essential."
9. According to their Mission Statement ADANAC Christian Youth Camps "exists to create opportunities for all people to personally encounter the living God through camping, conferencing, facilities and programs" https://cyc.org.au/mission-statement/, accessed 10 July 2022.
10. Dana Joseph. When it comes to local politics, Jerusalem's Palestinians just can't win.
11. Deborah Stone. "Catch-22: The cost of rejecting local democracy for Palestinians in East Jerusalem; Joseph, Dana. When it comes to local politics, Jerusalem's Palestinians just can't win."
12. al-Warra. "Palestinians say Israel is using power cuts to apply pressure in the West Bank."
13. I A Hamdy. Although the Druze are Arab, they are "perceived as 'non-Arab Arabs', who, though sharing the language and culture of the latter, have nevertheless preserved

a distinct identity molded by their close religion, geographic isolation, and centuries of Muslim and Christian persecution", 409-410.
14. Ilan Pappe. The Forgotten Palestinians, 62.
15. Allison Kaplan Sommer. "The Druze Community in Israel, Explained."
16. Andrew Lawler. "Who Wrote the Dead Sea Scrolls?"
17. B'tselem. "Restrictions on Movement."
18. John Lyons. Balcony Over Jerusalem, 191-192.
19. Ayelet Waldman. "The Shame of Shuhada Street."
20. Waldman.
21. Waldman.
22. Madain Project. "Cave of the Patriarchs."
23. Madain Project.
24. Miko Peled. The General's Son, 27-28.
25. Peled. General's, 133.
26. Peled. General's, 134.
27. Zionism, in its current form, is a secular political movement where Jews rejecting the notion of assimilation in Europe wanted land in Palestine. Charles D Smith. Palestine and the Arab-Israeli Conflict, 26.
28. Naftali Silberberg. "Star of David: The Mystical Significance."
29. Sovereign Imperial & Royal House of Ghassan. "History."
30. Munther Isaac is the Academic Dean at Bethlehem Bible College and Christ at the Checkpoint Conference Director. He has a doctorate from Oxford Centre for Mission Studies, lectures globally and is an author of numerous articles and books. See https://bethbc.edu/Faculty/munther-isaac/
31. Munther Isaac. "Munther Isaac: Palestinian Christian Response to Christian Zionism", 00:4:55.

Chapter 2

32. Genesis 2:15-17.
33. Stephen Sizer is the founder and director of Peacemaker Trust, a registered charity dedicated to peacemaking, especially where minorities are persecuted, where justice is denied, human rights are suppressed or reconciliation is needed. He is also an ordained minister in the Church of England. See https://stephensizer.com/about/ accessed 07 April 2023.
34. According to Euan Cameron, the Reformation was a movement that divided European Christianity into Catholic and Protestant traditions. It began with some clergy and scholars protesting against their superiors who seemed to threaten the prestige and privilege of priesthood and papacy, 1-2; Stephen Sizer. Christian Zionism, 27.
35. Genesis 12:1-5, 7a.
36. Genesis 15:18, 17:8
37. Sizer. Zion's Christian Soldiers, 23.

NOTES

38 Genesis 11:31.
39 Genesis 21:5.
40 Genesis 24:1, 35.
41 Carol Bakhos. "What's in a name? The implications of 'Abrahamic' for Jewish, Christian, and Muslim relations", 8.
42 Bakhos, 4.
43 Gary M Burge. Whose Land? Whose Promise? 75.
44 Anyone who is not a Jew.
45 Genesis 15:18.
46 Genesis 26:2-6.
47 Genesis 28:12-14.
48 Genesis 28:15-21.
49 Psalm 24:1.
50 Leviticus 25:23b.
51 Leviticus 25:23a.
52 Leviticus 25:13-15.
53 Genesis 17:8.
54 Exodus 29:45a.
55 R H Alexander, "Ezekiel,", 908.
56 Burge, 78-80; Awad, Alex. A Palestinian Theology of the Land, 202-203.
57 Leviticus 18:28, 20:22.
58 Leo G Perdue and Warren Carter. Israel and Empire A Postcolonial History of Israel and Early Judaism, 39.
59 K Lawson Younger. Jnr. "The Deportations of the Israelites", 216.
60 Amos 5:1-2.
61 Amos 5:3.
62 Amos 9:11-12.
63 1 Chronicles 17:1, 10-14
64 R H Alexander. "Ezekiel", 9-10.
65 Jeremiah 32:7, 14-15.
66 Matthew 24:1-2.
67 2 Kings 5:1-17.
68 Josephus Flavius. The Works of Josephus, 737.
69 Mazin B Qumsiyeh. Sharing the Land of Canaan, 12.
70 Amos 9:14-15.
71 Amos 9:11-12.
72 Acts 15:15-18.

Chapter 3

73 Edward Said. Orientalism, 4.
74 Jennifer Meagher. "Orientalism in Nineteenth-Century Art."

75. Said, 108.
76. Said, 2.
77. K Sorrells. "Intercultural communication: globalization and social Justice", 3.
78. Sorrells, 4.
79. Sorrells, 18.
80. Sorrells, 58.
81. Sally Totman. "Introduction to Orientalism."
82. Totman. Orientalism.
83. ní Fhlathùin, Máire The British Empire in the Nineteenth Century.
84. ní Fhlathùin.
85. National Army Museum. "First China War."
86. Pekka Pitkänen. "Settler Colonialism in Ancient Israel from: The Routledge Handbook of the History of Settler Colonialism", 25-36.
87. Michael Prior. "The Bible and Colonialism: A moral Critique", 39.
88. Qumsiyeh, 12.
89. Ernest Stock. "The Reconstitution of the Jewish Agency: A Political Analysis", 178.
90. Palestinian Central Bureau of Statistics. "PCBS President: Despite tragic circumstances, Palestinians have multiplied seven times since the Nakba (Catastrophe) of 1948."
91. Sharif Abdel Kouddous. "Israel's endgame is to push Palestinians into Egypt – and the west is cheering it on."
92. Relief Web. "Israeli Apartheid - The Legacy of the Ongoing Nakba at 75."
93. Palestinian Central Bureau of Statistics. PCBS President: Despite tragic circumstances, Palestinians have multiplied seven times since the Nakba (Catastrophe) of 1948."
94. Peled, 11.
95. Nathan Citino, Ana Martín Gil, and Kelsey P. Norman. "Generations of Palestinian Refugees Face Protracted Displacement and Dispossession."
96. Leena Dallasheh. "Persevering through Colonial Transition: Nazareth's Palestinian Residents after 1948", 10.
97. Dallasheh. Persevering through Colonial Transition 10.
98. Orly Halpern. "Deadly Pattern: 20 journalists died by Israeli military fire in 22 years. No one has been held accountable."

Chapter 4

99. Masalha, Palestine, 2, 59.
100. Masalha. Palestine, 55.
101. Masalha. Palestine, 59.
102. Masalha. Palestine, 81.
103. John Hutchinson. "European War-Making and the Rise of Nation States", 2.
104. Masalha. Palestine, 6.
105. Qumsiyeh, 11.

NOTES

[106] Central Bureau of Statistics. "The Muslim Population in Israel 2022"; Jewish Virtual Library. "Vital Statistics: Latest Population Statistics for Israel (April 25, 2023)."
[107] Joshua Project. "Country: West Bank/Gaza."
[108] Jewish Virtual Library. "Benjamin Netanyahu Administration: Speech at the Begin-Sadat Center at Bar-Ilan University (June 14, 2009)."
[109] Mint. "PM Netanyahu invokes 'Amalek' theory to justify Gaza killings. What is this Hebrew Bible nation?"
[110] Jewish Virtual Library. "Likud Party: Original Party Platform (1977)."
[111] The World Fact Book. "The Gaza Strip: Religion."
[112] Peter R Mansoor. "In the wake of the shocking invasion of southern Israel by Hamas militants on October 7, Prime Minister Benjamin Netanyahu vowed to destroy Hamas."
[113] Peter R Mansoor. "In the wake of the shocking invasion of southern Israel by Hamas militants on October 7, Prime Minister Benjamin Netanyahu vowed to destroy Hamas."
[114] Leviticus 19:33-34.
[115] Matthew 7:12.
[116] Salim J Munayer & Lisa Loden. Through My Eyes, 124.

Chapter 5

[117] Yonat Shimron. "Poll: White evangelical support for Israel higher than any other Christian group."
[118] Laura Silver and Moira Fagan. "2. American views of Israel."
[119] John Hagee. "Who owns the land of Israel?"
[120] Mimi Kirk. "American Evangelicals, the Gulf States, and Israel: A Cynical Covenant."
[121] Sizer. Zion's, 23.
[122] Sizer. Zion's, 23.
[123] Salim Munayer. 'Theology of the Land', 236.
[124] Munayer, 236.
[125] Timothy P. Weber. "...eschatology includes what happens after death, how the world will end, the inevitability of divine judgement, and the ultimate destination of humanity in either heaven or hell". On the road to Armageddon, 9; Mimi Kirk. "American Evangelicals, the Gulf States, and Israel: A Cynical Covenant."
[126] Sizer. Christian, 21.
[127] Theocracy Watch. "The Rise of the Religious Right in the Republican Party."
[128] Grace Halsell. Prophecy and Politics: Militant Evangelists on the Road to Nuclear War,. 89.
[129] Naim Ateek. A Concluding Theological Postscript, 218.
[130] Sharaka. The Abraham Accords is a series of peace agreements brokered by the United States between Israel and several Arab countries, which is seen as an essential step

towards peace between Israel and the Arab world; Kirk, Mimi. American Evangelicals, the Gulf States, and Israel: A Cynical Covenant.
[131] Munther Isaac. The Other Side of The Wall, 96.
[132] Pew Research Center. "2. American Views of Israel."
[133] Pew Research Center. "2. American Views of Israel.
[134] Australia Palestine Advocacy Network. "Poll: Government out of touch with Australians on Palestine."
[135] Australia Palestine Advocacy Network.
[136] Australia Palestine Advocacy Network.
[137] Australia Palestine Advocacy Network.
[138] Lydia Saad. "Key trends in U.S views on Israel and the Palestinians."
[139] Saad. Key trends.
[140] Saad. Key trends.
[141] Lydia Saad. "Americans still pro-Israel, though Palestinians gain."
[142] Sizer. Christian, 27.
[143] Romans 11:25
[144] Sizer. Christian, 27.
[145] Ilan Pappe. Lobbying for Zionism Both Sides of the Atlantic, 1-2.
[146] Sizer. Christian, 28.
[147] Sizer. Christian, 30-32.
[148] Sizer. Christian, 32-33.
[149] Pappe. Lobbying, 3-4.
[150] Sizer. Christian, 33-34.
[151] Smith, 28-29.
[152] Smith, 30.
[153] Sally Totman. "Zionism and the Push for a Jewish Homeland", 00:19:07-00:26:45.
[154] Totman," Zionism", 00:32:37-00:32:47.
[155] Theodore Herzl. The Complete Diaries of Theodore Herzl, 88, 90.
[156] Smith, 33.
[157] Nur Masalha. The Bible & Zionism, 24.
[158] Masalha. The Bible, 28.
[159] Uri Davis. "Apartheid Israel: Possibilities for the Struggle Within", 200.
[160] Smith, 33.
[161] Smith, 33-197.
[162] Smith, 196.
[163] Al Jajeera. "'Accusing Israel of apartheid is not anti-Semitic': Holocaust historian; Jonathan Shamir. Hundreds of Israeli Academics and Public Figures: Judicial Coup and Occupation 'Directly Linked'."
Amira Howeidy. "Jewish personalities accuse Israel of apartheid"; Canadians for Justice and Peace in the Middle East. "Who is talking about Israeli Apartheid?"

NOTES

Chapter 6

164 Neve Gordon. "Boycott Israel."
165 Gordon.
166 B'tselem. "A regime of Jewish supremacy from the Jordan River to the Mediterranean Sea: This is apartheid."
167 United Nations. "International Convention on the Suppression and Punishment of the Crime of Apartheid", 2.
168 United Nations. "International Convention", 2.
169 Nasreen Haddad Haj-Yahya, Muhammed Khalaily, Arik Rudnitzky, Ben Fargeon. "Statistical Report on Arab Society in Israel: 2021."
170 Kali Robinson. "What to Know About the Arab Citizens of Israel."
171 Nasreen Haddad Haj-Yahya, Muhammed Khalaily, Arik Rudnitzky, Ben Fargeon.
172 Marshall. Zionism.
173 Assaf Shapira. "Israel's Politics of Citizenship." Israel Studies Review, 103.
174 Shapira, 103.
175 Xpath.global. "How to live the expat life in Israel."
176 The Knesset is Israel's parliament which passes laws, supervise government work, choose the President, and deliberate over state issues. See https://www.gov.il/en/departments/knesset/govil-landing-page, accessed 30 August 2023; Susan Hattis Rolef. "'Basic Law: Israel - The Nation State of the Jewish People (Unofficial translation)'."
177 Rolef.
178 Rolef.
179 Rolef.
180 Rolef.
181 Diana B Greenwald. "Military Rule in the West Bank"; Human Rights Watch. "Born Without Civil Rights."
182 Alia Aghajanian, Arden Fin, Gianluca Mele & Nadir Mohammed. "The intersection of economic conditions, trauma and mental health in the West Bank and Gaza."
183 Mohammed al-Kassim. "Palestinians furious over Netanyahu claims that Israel must 'crush' statehood ambitions."
184 Peace Now. "The Government Declares 12,000 Dunams in the Jordan Valley as State Lands."
185 Peace Now.
186 International Committee of the Red Cross. "Henry Dunant (1828-1910)."
187 Theresa Riley. "A History of The Geneva Conventions."
188 Alan Baker. "Addressing the Components of the Delegitimization of Israel", 34.
189 Baker, 34.
190 United Nations. "IV Geneva Convention Relative to the protection of civilian persons in time of war of 12 August 1949", 185.
191 Jean S Pictet, "The Geneva Conventions of 12 August 1949 Commentary", 283.

[192] An Israeli settlement outpost usually takes the form of a new building or a number of caravans/structures (mobile homes) with limited area and separated from the urban area of a mother settlement. The settlement outpost is linked to a mother settlement by a dirt road, and it is constructed with the aim of expanding an existing settlement in the future, or as a ground for the establishment of a new settlement in the area. See POICA Israeli Settlements in the Occupied West Bank: from "outposts" to urban blocks, accessed 19 August 2023; Lynk, Michael. Proposed Israel law "gives green light to theft of Palestinian land" – UN expert.

[193] Allyson Horn, Haidarr Jones and Orly Halpern. "Israel is rapidly expanding Jewish settlements in the West Bank. This Australian man is among them."

[194] Alan Baker. "Addressing the Components of the Delegitimization of Israel", 35.

[195] International Committee of the Red Cross. "Rome Statute of the International Criminal Court, 17 July 1998."

[196] International Committee of the Red Cross. "Article 8 – War Crimes."

[197] B'Tselem. "This Is Ours – And This, Too: Israel's Settlement Policy in the West Bank."

[198] ABC News. "Australian among expanding Jewish settlements in West Bank", 1 minute 48 seconds.

[199] Matthew Miller. "The United States is Deeply Troubled with Israeli Settlement Announcement."

[200] ABC News. Australian, 00:1:53; Miller.

[201] ABC News. "Government to harden stance against Israel's 'illegal settlements in occupied' West Bank."

[202] Daniel Hurst and Joel Butler. "Australia to officially resume use of term 'Occupied Palestinian Territories', reversing Coalition stance."

[203] McIlroy. "Labor conference dodges Israel-Palestine fight."

[204] Oslo II seeks to implement the Oslo I Agreement of 13 September 1993. It defines the security, electoral, public administration and economic arrangements during the interim period of five years from the date of the Agreement on the Gaza Strip and the Jericho Area of 4 May 1994 until permanent settlement in accordance with Security Council Resolution 242 and 338. It also calls for Israeli-Palestinian cooperation and the release of Palestinian detainees. See https://peacemaker.un.org/israelopt-osloII95.

[205] United Nations Peacemaker. "Israeli-Palestinian Interim Agreement on the West Bank and the Gaza Strip", 31.

[206] Al Jazeera. "What are areas A, B, and C of the occupied West Bank?"

[207] Office for the Coordination of Human Services. "Most Palestinian plans to build in Area C not approved."

[208] United Nations. "Restricting space: The planning regime applied by Israel in Area C of the West Bank."

[209] Hagar Shezaf. "Israel Rejects Over 98 Percent of Palestinian Building Permit Requests in West Bank's Area C."

[210] United Nations Office for the Coordination of Humanitarian Affairs. "West Bank demolitions and displacement December 2022"; Office of the European Union

NOTES

Representative (West Bank and Gaza Strip, UNRWA). "One Year Report on Demolitions and Seizures in the West Bank, including East Jerusalem. Reporting Period: 1 January – 31 December 2022."

[211] United Nations Office for the Coordination of Humanitarian Affairs. "West Bank demolitions and displacement December 2022."

[212] OCHA. "Hostilities in the Gaza Strip and Israel | Flash Update #86."

[213] Hagar Shezaf. Israel Begins Demolition in Contentious West Bank Village Following Court Ruling.

[214] Relief Web. Humanitarian Alert: Masafer Yatta School Demolition, 24 November 2022

[215] Office for the Coordination of Humanitarian Affairs. "50 years of Occupation: Occupied Palestinian Territory Humanitarian Facts and Figures, 3."

[216] CWRC is a Palestinian governmental commission… activating international resolutions regarding the Annexation & Expansion Wall, including the decision of the International Court of Justice in Hague which was adopted in 2004, providing legal protection for Palestinian citizens. See https://www.cwrc.ps/page-917-en.html; CWRC. "CWRC: 4073 occupation violations in the first half of 2023."

[217] International Humanitarian Law Databases. "Article 50 - Regulations."

[218] International Humanitarian Law Databases. "Article 33 – Individual responsibility, collective penalties, pillage, reprisals."

[219] B'Tselem. "Home demolition as collective punishment."

[220] The Green Line, also known as "1967 border." Refers to the 1949 Armistice Line following the 1948 War, a line that demarcated boundaries between Jordan, Israel, Lebanon, Syria and Egypt. Since the 1967 War, the Green Line has denoted, according to most international opinion and United Nations resolutions, the boundary between territory recognized as part of the legitimate, sovereign State of Israel and the Occupied Palestinian Territories. See https://justvision.org/glossary/green-line, accessed 21 August 2023; Relief Web. "Israel's Apartheid Wall: we are here and they are there."

[221] J Pressman. The Second Intifada was an uprising of the Palestinian people due to the increasing Israeli occupation during the Oslo years. Also, the Palestinian expectations for greater political freedom and economic improvement, led to popular discontent, bringing on Palestinian protests, with militants becoming involved which resulted in increased confrontation from both sides and resulting in high Palestinian casualties. See "The Second Intifada: Background and Causes of the Israeli-Palestinian Conflict."; Oded Balility. "AP PHOTOS: Israel's separation barrier 20 years on."

[222] B'Tselem. The Separation Barrier; Balility.

[223] B'Tselem. "The Separation Barrier."

[224] Noura Erakat. Justice for Some, 211.

[225] B'Tselem. "The Separation Barrier."

[226] Anna Baltzer. Witness in Palestine, 24.

[227] Balzer, 25.

[228] Balzer, 22-24.

229 B'Tselem. "The Separation Barrier."
230 Relief Web. "Fact Sheet: Movement and Access in the West Bank, August 2023."
231 Halla Shoaibi. "Childbirth at checkpoints in the occupied Palestinian territory."
232 UN Commission on Human Rights "Human Rights Resolution 2005/7: Israeli Practices Affecting the Human Rights of the Palestinian People in the Occupied Palestinian Territory, Including East Jerusalem."
233 International Criminal Court. "Rome Statute of the International Criminal Court", 3.
234 Anthony Lowenstein. The Palestine Laboratory, 60.
235 Lowenstein, 60.
236 B'tselem. "Restrictions on Movement."
237 Michael Scott-Baumann. "Palestinians and Israelis", 141; Norman G. Finkelstein. Gaza An Inquest into its Martyrdom, 6.
238 Michael Scott-Baumann. Palestinians and Israelis, 156.
239 B'tselem. "Restrictions on Movement."
240 Susanna Reskallah. "Food Insecurity in Palestine: A Future for Farmers."
241 Human Rights Watch. "West Bank: New Entry Rules Further Isolate Palestinians."
242 Human Rights Watch. "West Bank: New.
243 Cloé Benoist. "Fear of the dark: The crushing impact of Israeli night raids on Palestinians."
244 Benoist.
245 Fayha Shalash. "Night terror: The Israeli raids of Palestinian homes in the West Bank."
246 Shalash.
247 Michal Fruchtman. "Who Will Protect the Thousands of Palestinian Children Israel Detains?"
248 Detentions without a court order or explanation; handcuffing and blindfolding; a ban on parents, relatives or lawyers from accompanying the children; and beatings and cursing and more, all of which cause the children to suffer physical pain and emotional stress. They experience harsh loneliness, intense fear, disorientation, humiliation, helplessness and often a sense that their lives are in danger. These are traumatic experiences that are etched into memory and affect personality, risking mental illness to the children… These experiences can gravely and irreversibly damage the children's development, and their ability to adjust in later life and live with a basic sense of security". See https://www.haaretz.com/israel-news/2023-05-28/ty-article/.; Michal Fruchtman.
249 Al Jajeera Staff. "Palestinian children traumatised by Israeli home invasions."
250 Addameer. "Administrative Detention in the Occupied Palestinian Territory", 7.
251 B'Tselem. "Administrative Detention."
252 Julia Frankel. Israel holds over 1,200 detainees without charge. That's the most in 3 decades, a rights group says.
253 Military Court Watch. "Newsletter – June 2023."
254 WAFA. "Over 9,000 Palestinians detained in West Bank since October 7, 2023 by Israel - Prisoners' institutions."

NOTES

255 Al Jazeera. "Jenin updates: Israel hits Gaza after 12 killed in Jenin raid."; Fayha Shalash. "Displaced at Israeli gunpoint, Jenin residents return to find their homes in ruins."; Al Jazeera. "Physicians for Human Rights say Israeli forces attacked Jenin hospitals."
256 Just Vision. "Jenin Invasion."
257 Belén Fernández. "Israel wants to turn Jenin into another Gaza, siege by siege."
258 Jeff Halper. An Israeli in Palestine, 278-279.
259 Bethan McKernan. "A precious resource: How Israel uses water to control the West Bank."
260 Middle East Monitor. "Israeli soldiers seal Palestinian well with concrete."
261 Relief Web. "Parched: Israel's policy of water deprivation in the West Bank."
262 Relief Web. Parched.
263 CIA World Factbook. "Gaza Strip: Population; CIA World Factbook. Gaza Strip: Median Age."
264 Palestinian Central Bureau of Statistics. "Presents the Main Findings of Labour Force Survey in 2022."
265 Office for the Coordination of Humanitarian Affairs. "Refugee needs in the Gaza Strip October 2018."
266 Isaac. The Other, 150.
267 Moshav Tekuma. "How Israel Helped Spawn Hamas."
268 Mehdi Hasan and Dina Sayedahmed. "Blowback: How Israel Went From Helping Create Hamas to Bombing It."
269 Ami Ayalon. "Self-defence or genocide? Asking Israel's powerful voices about Gaza", 00:29:57-00:30:32.
270 Ehud Barak. "Self-defence or genocide? Asking Israel's powerful voices about Gaza", 00:30:45-00:31:02.
271 Isaac. The Other, 150.
272 Miko Peled. "Public forum with Miko Peled & Noura Mansour", 01:52:31-01:52:56.
273 Daub Abdullah. "Engaging the World: The Making of Hamas's Foreign Policy", 1.
274 Lamisse Hamouda. The Shape of Dust, 186.
275 Miko Peled. Injustice The Story of the Holy Land Foundation Five, 58.
276 Miko Peled. Injustice, 59.
277 Miko Peled. Injustice, 59.
278 Miko Peled. Injustice, 59.
279 Tareq Baconi. "On the Origins, Goals and Future of Hamas", 00:1:05.
280 Miko Peled. Injustice, 59.
281 Tareq Baconi. Hamas Contained: The Rise and pacification of Palestinian Resistance, 26.
282 Amira Hass. "Broken Bones and Broken Hopes."; Baconi. Future of Hamas, 25.
283 Baconi. Hamas Contained, 26.
284 Mohamed Nimer. "Charting the Hamas Charter Changes", 122.
285 Middle East Eye Staff. "Hamas in 2017: The document in full."
286 Baconi. Hamas Contained, 11-24.

287 Ministry of Foreign Affairs and Expatriates. "Mahmoud Abbas."
288 Zena Al Tahhan. "Hamas and Fatah: How are the two groups different?"; Ahed Tamini and Dena Takruri. They Called Me a Lioness, 95.
289 Karen Andrews. "Hamas listed as terrorist organisation."
290 United States Department of State. "Foreign Terrorist Organisations."
291 Zachary Laub and Kali Robinson. "What is Hamas?"
292 Laub and Robinson.
293 Adnan Abu Amer. "Hamas' Inability to Capitalize on the War in Gaza."; Khaled Abu Toameh. "Why is Hamas popular in Jerusalem? - analysis."
294 Fatma Tanis. "Palestinians grow frustrated with militants in Gaza, and a rift could be forming."
295 Adnan Abu Amer. "Postponed Palestinian Elections: Causes and Repercussions."
296 Survey Research Unit. "Public Opinion Poll No (88)", 6.
297 Office for the Coordination of Humanitarian Affairs. "Intensified restrictions on the entry of building materials delay the completion of housing projects in Gaza."
298 Kevin M Cahill. "Gaza Destruction and Hope", 5.
299 United Nations Country Team in Palestine. "Gaza Ten Years Later", 14.
300 Human Rights Watch. "United Nations General Assembly Resolution 194 (iii) of 11 December 1948."
301 Ilan Pappé. The Ethnic Cleansing of Palestine, Loc 753.
302 Jewish Virtual Library. "Prevention of Infiltration (Offences and Jurisdiction) Law 1954 (5714)", 1.
303 Abby Martin. "Gaza Fights for Freedom", 00:17:31-00:17:52.
304 Martin, 00:19:42.
305 Martin, 00:20:00-00:20:54.
306 Lakshmi Varanasi. "How the mighty watermelon became a symbol of pro-Palestinian resistance on social media."
307 Yaakov Katz. "Yadlin: Israel would be 'happy' if Hamas takes over Gaza."
308 Daniel Estrin, Abu Bakr Bashir. "Here's What Tourists Might See If They Were Allowed To Visit Gaza."
309 Reuters Staff. "Israel warns Hezbollah war would invite destruction."
310 Naom Chomsky and Ilan Pappe. Gaza in Crisis, 188.
311 ReliefWeb. "Why is Israel pulling out settlers from Gaza, West Bank?"
312 Smith, 499.
313 Smith, 500.
314 Casebook. "Indiscriminate Attacks."
315 International Humanitarian Law Databases. "Rule 1. The Principle of Distinction between Civilians and Combatants."
316 Amnesty International. "Israel/Gaza: Operation 'Cast Lead' - 22 Days of Death and Destruction."; The Euro-Med Human Rights Monitor. "Suffocation and Isolation: 15 Years of Israeli Blockade on Gaza", 8-9.
317 ReliefWeb. "OPT: The Gaza blockade - Children and education fact sheet."

NOTES

318 Human Rights Watch. "White Flag Deaths: Killings of Palestinian Civilians during Operation Cast Lead", 11-12.
319 Al Jazeera. "Timeline: Israel's attacks on Gaza since 2005."
320 The Euro-Med Human Rights Monitor. "Suffocation: 15 Years, 9."
321 The Euro-Med Human Rights Monitor. "Suffocation: 15 Years, 9."
322 Finkelstein, 212-213.
323 Finkelstein, 213.
324 Finkelstein, 213.
325 Max Blumenthal. The 51 Day War, 26.
326 Al Jazeera. Timeline.
327 Al Jazeera. Timeline.
328 The Euro-Med Human Rights Monitor. "Suffocation: 17 Years of Israeli Blockade on Gaza."
329 Mohammed Abu Mughaisib and Natalie Turtle. "Born under attack to be buried under attack, a life without rest in Gaza."
330 Al Jazeera. Timeline.
331 France24. "Israel social security data reveals true picture of Oct 7 deaths."
332 Linal Alsaafin and Usaid Siddiqui. "Israel's war on Gaza updates: 'No homes, no hope' in Rafah – UN chief. Ahmed Asmar. Gaza death toll from Israeli attacks since Oct. 7 surges to 36,284."
333 Ofer Aderet. "Israeli Prime Minister After Six-Day War: 'We'll Deprive Gaza of Water, and the Arabs Will Leave'."
334 Fred de Sam Lazaro. "Water crisis may make Gaza Strip uninhabitable by 2020."
335 General Assembly. "64/292. The human right to water and sanitation.
336 Michael Lynk. "Gaza "Unliveable", UN Special Rapporteur for the Situation of Human Rights in the OPT Tells Third Committee."

Chapter 7

337 National Film and Sound Archive of Australia. "Terrorism Strikes Sydney: Hilton Hotel Bombing."; Ben Doherty, Bridie Jabour, Brigid Delaney, Calla Wahlquist, Helen Davidson, Michael Safi, Oliver Milman and Paul Farrell. "Sydney siege: how a day and night of terror unfolded at the Lindt café."
338 Kate Sainsbury. "Port Arthur Massacre."
339 United Nations Relief and Works Agency. "2014 Gaza Conflict."
340 Associated Press in Jerusalem. "Israeli-Palestinian violence in 2014-timeline."
341 Ori Lewis. "Palestinian driver rams Jerusalem station killing baby."
342 Rania Khalek. "Why do media value Israeli children's lives more than those of Palestinian kids?"
343 Patrick O Strickland. "Wave of oppression targets Palestinians in Israel."
344 Boaz Ganor, "Defining Terrorism: Is One Man's Terrorist Another Man's Freedom Fighter?", 129.

[345] ABC News. "Train Passenger hurt by thrown rock."
[346] John Lyons, Janine Cohen, Sylvie Le Clezio. "Stone Cold Justice", 00:22:43.
[347] Nicholas J Perry. "The numerous federal legal definitions of terrorism: The problem of too many grails", 253; D Ragless. "'One man's terrorist is another man's freedom fighter'. Discuss in relation to the definitional problems", 5-6.
[348] Federal Bureau of Investigation. "(b). What We Investigate."
[349] Parliament of Australia. "Definition of Terrorism."
[350] Al Jazeera. "#illridewithyou goes viral after Sydney siege."
[351] S N Kalic, Institute C S. "Combating a Modern Hydra Al Qaeda and the Global War on Terrorism", 34; Matthew J Morgan. "The Origins of the New Terrorism", 29.
[352] Federal Bureau of Investigation. "(a). Pan Am 103 Bombing."
[353] Office of Public Affairs. "Pan Am Flight 103 Terrorist Suspect in Custody for 1988 Bombing over Lockerbie, Scotland."
[354] Laub and Robinson.
[355] Halper, 256.
[356] UN General Assembly. "Importance of the universal realization of the right of people to self-determination and of the speedy granting of independence to colonial countries and peoples for the effective guarantee and observance of human rights, A/RES/33/24."
[357] United Nations. "Human Rights/self-determination - GA Resolution."
[358] United Nations. Human Rights.
[359] Middle East Eye Staff. "Hamas in 2017: The document in full."
[360] Prof. Boaz Ganor is the founder and executive director of the International Institute for Counter-terrorism (ICT) and the Ronald S Lauder Chair for counter-terrorism at Reichman University, Herzliya, Israel. See https://isgap.org/fellow/boaz-ganor/, accessed 19 August 2022; Ganor, 126.
[361] Ganor, 128.
[362] International Criminal Court. "Rome Statute, 4-8."
[363] United Nations Office for the Coordination of Humanitarian Affairs. "Gaza crossings: movement of people and goods."
[364] BBC News. "David Cameron describes blockaded Gaza as a 'prison'."
[365] Nasser Mashni. "The Project Nasser Mashni", 00:03:48.
[366] The Economist. "Why Hamas fire those rockets."
[367] Francesca Albanese. "Address to the National Press Club of Australia", 00:27:39.
[368] Patrick Gathara. "The fallacy of the colonial 'right to self-defence'."
[369] International Humanitarian Law Databases. "Article 51 – Protection of the Civilian Population."
[370] Human Rights Watch. "White Flag Deaths: Killings of Palestinian Civilians during Operation Cast Lead, 3."
[371] Amnesty International. "Israel/Gaza conflict: Questions and Answers."
[372] Kim Sengupta. "Israel-Gaza conflict: Myth of Hamas's human shield. Gazans deny being put in line of fire."

NOTES

373 Mitri Raheb. Faith in the Face of Empire, 120.
374 Census. "76th India Independence Day (1947): August 15, 2023."
375 NAACP. "Martin Luther King, Jr."
376 Maria J Stephan, Erica Chenoweth. "Why Civil Resistance Works: The Strategic Logic of Nonviolent Conflict", 25.
377 Stephan, Chenoweth, 26.
378 Stephan, Chenoweth, 27.
379 Stephan, Chenoweth, 27-29.
380 Jason MacLeod. "The struggle for Self-Determination in West Papua (1969-present)", 2.
381 Bassem Tamimi. "Abby Martin Meets Ahed Tamimi—Message From A Freedom Fighter", 00:14:19-00:15:40.
382 Peled. Public forum, 01:15:50-01:17:13.
383 Tovah Lazaroff. "IDF warns of larger military response to Gaza protest."
384 Nidal al-Mughrabi. "Israeli forces kill three Gaza border protesters, wound 600: medics."
385 Human Rights Council. "Report of the independent international commission of inquiry on the protests in the Occupied Palestinian Territory", 4.
386 Martin, 00:26:05.
387 Human Rights Council, 4.
388 Martin, 00:26:26; Human Rights Council, 4.
389 Human Rights Watch. "Israel: Gaza Killings Unlawful, Calculated."
390 Human Rights Council, 6.
391 Human Rights Council, 16.
392 Human Rights Council, 8.
393 Human Rights Council, 11.
394 International Community of the Red Cross. 'Article 77 – Protection of children 1."
395 Human Rights Council, 12.
396 Human Rights Council, 13.
397 Department of Economic and Social Affairs. "Article 11 – Situations of risk and humanitarian emergencies."
398 Martin, 00:49:46.
399 International Humanitarian Law Databases. "Article 79 – Measures of protection for journalists 1."
400 International Humanitarian Law Databases. "Declaration (IV,3) concerning Expanding Bullets. The Hague, 29 July 1899."
401 Martin, 00:54:15-00:54:41.
402 Organisation for the Prohibition of Chemical Weapons. "Chemical Weapons Convention", 1.
403 Human Rights Council, 14.
404 International Human Law Databases. "Article 15 - Protection of civilian medical and religious personnel", 1-2.

405 Human Rights Council, 14.
406 Human Rights Council, 19.
407 Human Rights Watch. "Israel: Gaza Killings Unlawful, Calculated."
408 Human Rights Council, 20.
409 Tamar Hermann and Ephraim Yarr. "The Majority of the Israeli Public Believes Moving the US Embassy to Jerusalem is in Israel's Best Interests."
410 Peled. General's, 235-236.
411 United Nations. "Israel's occupation of Palestinian Territory is 'apartheid': UN rights expert."; Thabi Myeni. "South Africa calls for Israel to be declared an 'apartheid state'."; Nour Haydar. "Greens say Israel is 'practising crime of apartheid' and call for boycotts of far-right figures."; B'tselem. "A regime of Jewish supremacy".
412 Thomas Suárez. State of Terror, 268.
413 Suárez, 309.
414 Suárez, 307.
415 Suárez, 309.
416 Suárez, 269.
417 Finkelstein, 6.
418 Finkelstein, 6.
419 Jewish Virtual Library. "Vital Statistics: Total Casualties. Arab-Israeli Conflict."
420 Al Jazeera. "PA health minister seeks probe into deadly Israeli raid on Gaza hospital."
421 Trading Economics. "Israel – Military Expenditure (% Of GDP)."; Government Press Office. "Ministry of Defense Spokesperson's Statement: Israel Sets New Record in Defense Exports: Over $12.5 Billion in 2022."
422 Emanuel Fabian. "Israeli arms sales break record for 3rd year in row, reaching $13 billion in 2023."
423 Loewenstein, 77.
424 Loewenstein, 77.
425 Keren Assaf. "The Israeli arms companies that will profit from the latest assault on Gaza."
426 Emmanuel Fabian. "Israeli arms sales hit new record of $11.3 billion in 2021 — with 7% to Gulf."
427 Pieter D Wezeman, Alexandra Kuimova and Siemon T Wezeman. "Trends in International Arms Transfers, 2021", 2.
428 Matt Kennard Grantee. "The Cruel Experiments of Israel's Arms Industry."
429 Matt Kennard Grantee.
430 Ajaz Ashraf. "How US, Israel Birthed the Suicide Car Bomber."
431 John Lyons. Dateline Jerusalem: Journalism's Toughest Assignment, 7.
432 Lyons. Dateline, 7.
433 Christian Salazar Volkmann. Current Israeli Plan to Double the Settler Population in the Occupied Syrian Golan by 2027 is Unprecedented, and that 700,000 Israeli Settlers Are Living Illegally in the Occupied West Bank.
434 Reham Owda. "How Israeli Settlements Impede the Two-State Solution."

NOTES

435 Yolande Knell. "Palestinian fears grow amid rising Israeli settler attacks."
436 OCHA. "Hostilities."
437 Norwegian Refugee Council. "Palestine: Israeli settler attacks forcibly transfer Jerusalem community."
438 Norwegian Refugee Council. "West Bank: Entire Palestinian communities disappeared due to Israeli settler violence."
439 Times of Israel Staff. "Visiting Evyatar, Ben Gvir tells settlers to 'head for the hilltops,' expand outposts."
440 PressTV. "Israel's Ben-Gvir calls for assassination of 'thousands' of Palestinians."
441 B'Tselem. "A wave of settlers' riots across the West Bank."

Chapter 8

442 Mat Hardy. "The United States and the Middle East", 00:9:41-00:58:09.
443 Although both the United States and the Soviet Union joined together to defeat Germany in World War II, afterwards, they began a struggle which lasted for decades, ending 26 December 1991, to gain world supremacy. See https://www.jfklibrary.org/learn/about-jfk/jfk-in-history/the-cold-war, accessed 23 September 2023.
444 U.S National Security Council. "NSC-68: Excerpts", 00:16:15.
445 Energy Information Administration. "How much petroleum does the United States import and export?"
446 Sally Totman. "The United States and the Middle East", 00:41:36.
447 Jeremy M Sharp. "U.S Foreign Aid to Israel."
448 Worldometer. "State of Palestine Population."
449 Scott Burchill. "Lecture 8: The English School", 7.

Chapter 9

450 Al Jazeera. "Why the Palestinian group Hamas launched an attack on Israel? All to know."
451 Human Rights Council. "Detailed findings on attacks carried out on and after 7 October 2023 in Israel", 6; France24. "Israel social security data reveals true picture of Oct 7 deaths."
452 Osama Hamden. "Why did Hamas attack Israel on October 7?", 00:00:33-00:00:39, 00:01:02-00:01:13; Max Blumenthal. "Mass Rape By Hamas on Oct 7th? NYT Coverage Questioned By Max Blumenthal: Rising Debates", 00:10:31-00:10:41.
453 Hamas. "Our Narrative… Operation Al-Aqsa Flood", 7
454 Harriet Sherwood. "Gilad Shalit: the real Prisoner of War."
455 Max Blumenthal. Mass Rape, 00:10:16-00:10:30; Reuters. "Explainer: What do we know about Israeli hostages in Gaza?"
456 Hamden, 00:00:43-00:00:45.

457 Harriet Sherwood. "Israel-Hamas war: what has happened and what has caused the conflict?"
458 Sherwood. Israel-Hamas.
459 Hamden, 00:00:45-00:00:59.
460 Relief Web. "For Palestinians in the West Bank, 2023 was the deadliest year on record."
461 Ahmed Asmar. "Over 48,000 Israeli settlers stormed Al-Aqsa Mosque in 2023."
462 Hamden. 00:01:02-00:01:11.
463 Munther Isaac. "Munther Isaac Sermon in the Liturgy of Lament: Christ in the Rubble", 00:05:36-00:05:57.
464 Jonathan Cook. "The West's hypocrisy towards Gaza's breakout is stomach-turning."
465 Jonathan Cook. The West's.
466 Areeb Ullah. "Gaza-Israel: How the world reacted to the surprise assault."
467 Nasser Mashni. "Interview with Nasser Mashni", 00:03:00.
468 Mashni, 00:05:40.
469 Euro-Med Monitor. "Israel commits widespread war crimes in Gaza, humanitarian catastrophe is imminent."
470 Issam Adwin. "Unprecedented Israeli bombardment lays waste to upscale Rimal, the beating heart of Gaza City."
471 Al Jazeera. "Q&A: Former UN official Craig Mokhiber on Gaza, Israel and genocide."
472 United Nations. "Gaza is 'running out of time' UN experts warn, demanding a cease-fire to prevent genocide."
473 Francesca Albanese. "Address to the National Press Club of Australia", 00:12:38.
474 United Nations. "Genocide."
475 Raz Segal. Gaza. "Textbook Case of Genocide", 00:03:49.
476 Segal, 00:04:08.
477 Segal, 00:04:41.
478 Segal, 00:05:01-00:05:21.
479 Rageh Omaar. "Israeli president Isaac Herzog says Gazans could have risen up to fight 'evil' Hamas."
480 UNICEF. "Situation Analysis of Children's Rights and Wellbeing in the State of Palestine", 5.
481 Raz Segal, 00:05:54-00:06:11.
482 Sky News. "Israel-Hamas war: 'We will fight and we will win', says Benjamin Netanyahu", 00:1:50.
483 Emanuel Fabian. "Defense minister announces 'complete siege' of Gaza: No power, food or fuel."
484 Bloomberg. "Israeli Defence Minister Warns Hamas 'Will Regret' Deadly Attacks."
485 Israel Katz. "Indeed, Madam Congresswoman."
486 Fabian. 'complete siege' of Gaza: No power, food or fuel.
487 Al Jazeera. "Is 'total' Gaza blockade a collective punishment against Palestinians?"
488 Yaniv Kubovich, Ben Samuels, Adi Hashmonai, Michael Hauser Tov, Reuters. "IDF Ramps Up Strikes on Gaza and Prepares for Ground Invasion."

NOTES

489 Bethan McKernan and Sufian Taha. "Gaza civilians afraid to leave home after bombing of 'safe routes'."
490 Forensic Architecture. "Israeli Disinformation: Al-Ahli Hospital."
491 Emma Graham-Harrison. "'Destruction chased them': funeral held for those killed in Gaza church airstrike."
492 Munther Isaac. "English translation of my sermon today to follow below."
493 United Nations News. "UN General Assembly adopts Gaza resolution calling for immediate and sustained 'humanitarian truce'."
494 Owen Jones. "Despite the truce, people in Gaza will keep dying – this horrifying death toll must never be forgotten."
495 Matt Lee. "Journalist questions bombing of Gaza university."
496 Euro-Med Human Rights Monitor. "Euro-Med: 100,000 Palestinians killed, wounded, missing in Gaza."
497 Euro-Med Monitor. "Israeli Strike on Refaat al-Areer Apparently Deliberate."
498 United Nations Human Rights. "Gaza: UN experts condemn killing and silencing of journalists."
499 World Health Organisation. "Lethal combination of hunger and disease to lead to more deaths in Gaza."
500 World Health Organisation. Lethal.
501 Yasmine Rahman. "This 11-month-old is the 1st confirmed case of polio in Gaza."
502 Al Jazeera. "'Ticking time bomb': Poliovirus found in Gaza sewage."
503 Sharon Zhang. "80 Percent of Global Famine Is Currently in Gaza, UN Expert Warns."
504 Zhang.
505 Bassam Masoud and Dan Williams. "Images from Gaza show dozens of detained Palestinian men stripped to their underwear."; Peter Beaumont. "Footage shows IDF parading scores of Palestinian men around in underwear."
506 Al Jazeera Staff. "Palestinians detained by Israel in Gaza blindfolded, stripped to underwear."
507 Palestine Chronicle Staff. "The 'Lion of Gaza' Roars – Who is Hamza Abu Halima?"
508 Bassam Masoud and Ibraheem Abu Mustafa. "Gaza doctor describes ordeal of detention."
509 Middle East Eye. "Dr Bilal Azzam, a member."
510 Federica Marsi. "Gaza's mass graves: Is the truth being uncovered?"
511 Middle East Monitor. "Israel's use of rape against Palestinian detainees from Gaza exposed."
512 Fayha Shalash. "Israeli settlers kill Palestinian in latest West Bank rampage."
513 Al Jazeera. "Israeli minister dismisses US 'terror' label after deadly settler attack."
514 Rami G Khouri. "Watching the watchdogs: Babies and truth die together in Israel-Palestine."
515 Max Blumenthal and Alexander Rubinstein. "Source of dubious 'beheaded babies' claim is Israeli settler leader who incited riots to 'wipe out' Palestinian village."

516 Blumenthal and Rubinstein.
517 Blumenthal and Rubinstein.
518 Turgut Alp Boyraz. "Israeli army says it does not have 'confirmation' about allegations that 'Hamas beheaded babies'."; Jonathan Cook. "Why is the media ignoring evidence of Israel's own actions on 7 October?"; Muhammad Shehada. "Important! Haaretz definitely debunks."
519 Ahmed Asmar. "Released Israeli woman says she was treated well in Hamas captivity."
520 Middle East Eye. "Female Israeli hostages played arm-wrestling with Hamas guard", 00:01:58.
521 Jake Tapper and Kirsten Appleton. "Israel investigates sexual violence committed by Hamas as part of October 7 horror.'
522 Carrie Keller-Lynn. "Amid war and urgent need to ID bodies, evidence of Hamas's October 7 rapes slips away."
523 Max Blumenthal and Aaron Maté. "Screams without proof: questions for NYT about shoddy 'Hamas mass rape' report."
524 Silaiman Ahmed. "Breaking: Gal Abduah's sister denies rape claims in NYT article and says NYT manipulated the family."
525 The Hill. "NYT pulls Hamas rape story from podcast over internal turmoil over shoddy reporting: Max Blumenthal."
526 Owen Jones. "I Watched The Hamas Massacre Film. Here Are My Thoughts", 00:5:06-00:5:49.
527 France24. "UN seeks Israel access for Hamas sexual violence investigation.'
528 AFP Agence France Presse. "Over 1,400 Killed In Hamas Attacks On Israel: PM Office."
529 France24. "Israel social security."
530 Max Blumenthal. "October 7 testimonies reveal Israel's military 'shelling' Israeli citizens with tanks, missiles."
531 Asa Winstanley. "The evidence Israel killed its own citizens on 7 October."
532 Winstanley.
533 Yoav Zitun and Ronen Bergman. "The first hours of the Black Sabbath, (English version)", 8:32.
534 Wyatt Reed. "Haaretz confirms Grayzone reporting it dismissed as 'conspiracy' showing Israel killed own festivalgoers."
535 Urooba Jamal. "What's Israel's Hannibal Directive? A former Israeli soldier tells all."
536 "Video confirms tank struck home with Israeli captives on 7 Oct."; Anadolu staff. "Israel allegedly enforces 'Hannibal Protocol' on Oct. 7, killing festival-goers to prevent their captivity."
537 Middle East Monitor. "Israel settler: 'Israel forces killed hostages, not Hamas'."
538 The Cradle.
539 CBN News. Hamas Supporters Shout 'Gas' and 'F the Jews' in Sydney", 00:00:18.
540 Alexander Lewis and Jessica Kidd. "Video analysis finds no evidence of 'gas the Jews' being chanted at Sydney Opera House protest, despite witness statements", 00:00:6.

NOTES

541 Arab News. 'Australia's ABC staff raise concerns over alleged Israeli bias in Gaza reporting."
542 Calum Jaspan. "Antoinette Lattouf was sacked by ABC, Fair Work rules.'
543 Janet Phillips, Joanne Simon-Davies. "Migration to Australia: a quick guide to the statistics."
544 Paul Erickson. "ALP National Party Platform', 217.
545 Grace Johnson. "Sydney Opera House displays Israeli flag colours."; Bageshri Savyasachi. "Australia's Parliament House illuminated in blue in white to support Israel."; J-Wire. "Brisbane's Story Bridge to be lit blue and white."
546 David Aidone, Sara Tomevska. "Senate condemns 'from the river to the sea' chant after Labor MP broke ranks."
547 Natassia Chrysanthos. "Wong steps up calls for 'humanitarian pause' to hostilities in Gaza."
548 Jessie Kindig. "Vietnam War: Student Activism."
549 Omar Barghouti, Tanaquil Jones and Barbara Ransby. "Let us remember the last time students occupied Columbia University."
550 Then New Arab Staff. "Global action for Gaza: Which universities worldwide have joined US students in pro-Palestine protests?"
551 The White House. "The Constitution: The First Amendment."
552 Dan Rosenzweig-Ziff, Clara Ence Morse, Susan Svrluga, Drea Cornejo, Hannah Dormido and Júlia Ledur. "Riot police and over 2,000 arrests: A look at 2 weeks of campus protests."
553 Caitlin Cassidy. "Monash University: police investigate alleged attack on pro-Palestine camp."
554 Human Rights Watch. "West Bank: Israel Responsible for Rising Settler Violence."
555 Zena Al Tahhan. "Israel doubles number of Palestinian prisoners to 10,000 in two weeks."
556 Defence For Children International. "Israeli forces kill six Palestinian children in the occupied West Bank."
557 King Abdullah III. "President Biden and His Majesty King Abdullah II of Jordan Deliver Remarks", 00:10:00-00:11:20.
558 Hugo Bachega. "Deadly West Bank settler attacks on Palestinians follow Israeli boy's killing."
559 Adam Schrader. "Nearly 9,000 Palestinians have been arrested in West Bank."
560 B'Tselem. "Under cover of Gaza war, settlers working to fulfil state goal of Judaizing Area C."
561 Oren Ziv. "Israel razes entire Bedouin village to expand a highway."
562 ABC News. "Israel-Gaza updates: US government imposes sanctions on Israeli settlers accused of West Bank violence."
563 United Nations. "South Africa institutes proceedings against Israel and requests the International Court of Justice to indicate provisional measures – ICJ Press Release."

564 Rashmin Sagoo. "South Africa's genocide case against Israel: The International Court of Justice explained."
565 Sagoo.
566 Naledi Pandor. "ICJ Genocide Decision | Minister Pandor calls for ceasefire in Gaza", 00:00:40-00:00:50 seconds.
567 Noura Erakat." Quick thoughts on the ICJ decision this morning."
568 Erakat. Quick.
569 The Presidency. "South Africa makes urgent request to International Court of Justice on Rafah offensive.'
570 Jonathan Ofir. "Israeli politician: 'The children of Gaza have brought this upon themselves'."
571 Monty Noam Penkower. "The Kishinev Pogrom of 1903: A Turning Point in Jewish History, 187."
572 Emine Sinmaz. "UNRWA staff accused by Israel sacked without evidence, chief admits."
573 Michael West. "Australia keen to resume Palestine aid 'soon': minister."
574 Asha Khatib, Martin McKee, Salim Yusuf. "Counting the dead in Gaza: difficult but essential."
575 Susan Abulhawa. "Math proves that Israel's stated goals are an epic lie."
576 Jonathan Cook. 'Israel's long-held plan to drive Gaza's people into Sinai is now within reach."
577 Mersiha Gadzo. "Israel's war on Gaza live: Wave of attacks as Israel told to end occupation."; Peter Beaumont. "Why ICJ ruling against Israel's settlement policies will be hard to ignore."
578 C Chapman. Whose Promised Land? 181-182.
579 Tovah Lazaroff. "Netanyahu: A Palestinian State won't be Created."
580 Mohammed Al-Kassim. "Palestinians furious over Netanyahu claims that Israel must 'crush' statehood ambitions."
581 Everett Henry. "Modern Age History, Timeline & Facts\ What is the Modern Era?"

Chapter 10

582 Tom Parry. "Gaza conflict is creating a traumatised generation of child amputees, warn medics."
583 Chapman, 188, 190.
584 Psalm 82:3-4.

www.ingramcontent.com/pod-product-compliance
Lightning Source LLC
Chambersburg PA
CBHW031943080426
42735CB00007B/244